Opposing Hate Speech

Opposing Hate Speech

Anthony Cortese

Foreword by Richard Delgado

Westport, Connecticut
London

Library of Congress Cataloging-in-Publication Data

Cortese, Anthony Joseph Paul.
  Opposing hate speech / Anthony Cortese ; foreword by Richard Delgado.
    p. cm.
  Includes bibliographical references and index.
  ISBN 0–275–98427–3 (alk. paper)
    1. Oral communication—Social aspects. 2. Hate speech. 3. Racism. 4. Freedom
of speech. I. Title.
  P95.54.C67 2006
  302.2'242—dc22   2005019176

British Library Cataloguing in Publication Data is available.

Library of Congress Catalog Card Number: 2005019176
ISBN: 0–275–98427–3

First published in 2006

Praeger Publishers, 88 Post Road West, Westport, CT 06881
An imprint of Greenwood Publishing Group, Inc.
www.praeger.com

Printed in the United States of America

The paper used in this book complies with the
Permanent Paper Standard issued by the National
Information Standards Organization (Z39.48–1984).

10 9 8 7 6 5 4 3 2 1

*To the victims of hate speech and violence—
past, present, and future.*

Contents

Foreword: Several Things We Know about Hate Speech . . . and Several Misconceptions

This fine book synthesizes and brings into bold relief a number of truths about hate speech. It also dispels a number of misconceptions, including the old adage that hate speech is essentially harmless or a mere annoyance—that in the words of the old refrain, "sticks and stones may break my bones, but words will never hurt me."

Anthony Cortese reviews evidence that hate speech harms both individual victims and society at large. The harms to individuals include damage to psyches (especially those of children), such as depression, internalized anger, and diminished self-concept. They include, too, physical harms, such as high blood pressure, rapid breathing, and inability to sleep, as well as diminished pecuniary and social prospects as the victim withdraws from settings where he or she has experienced discrimination and becomes defensive and wary.

But some of the most serious harms are societal. Cortese describes in chilling detail how societies have used hate speech to stereotype a group as stupid, dangerous, or impure—and later deployed that stereotype to justify atrocities such as slavery, Indian removal, or genocide. United States law currently deems speech regulable only if it presents an imminent danger. But Cortese shows that hate speech is most dangerous when it is slow-building and concerted. The occasional fistfight that breaks out from an incident of "fighting words" is much less dangerous than a campaign of vilification, such as the one that led to the Rwanda massacre or the extermination of Native Americans under the banner "the only good Indian is a dead one."

Cortese also stands out above other writers by adding an elegant developmental model that divides hate speech into degrees of severity corresponding to stages of personality development. Insofar as these steps correspond to social stages as well, they enable us to gauge how seriously mired in hate a culture or institution has become and what corrective measures may be in order.

This book also outlines some of the legal dimensions of the hate speech controversy in terms a lay reader can understand. Most Americans know that our Constitution protects freedom of speech, deeming it one of the most precious rights. But Cortese reminds us that freedom of speech is not absolute but subject to a host of exceptions—words of threat, libel, defamation; disrespectful words uttered to a judge or other authority figure; commercial or military secrets; and plagiarism, copyright, false advertising, obscenity, and pornography, just to name a few. Each of these exceptions captures some important countervailing social interest, and was, at one time, new. The issue, then, is whether society's interest in protecting outsider groups from vituperation is comparable in degree to that of a consumer in receiving truthful information about a loaf of bread, or of a judge in being addressed as "Your Honor" instead of "Mr. Smith." For Cortese, as for most of us, it is.

Cortese also points out that hate speech infringes on constitutional values lying on the other side of the equation. Does not the victim of hate speech enjoy a constitutional right under the Fourteenth Amendment not to be marginalized, reviled, and cast into disrepute merely on account of who he is? Hate speech, then, requires delicate interest balancing: In our society we value the right to say what we want. But we also value equality and want our public and private law to reflect the premium we place on the equal worth of each citizen. When hate speech endangers this value, it requires sober consideration, not a flip, pat response.

One also hears that the best cure to bad speech is more speech. According to this view, the remedy for hate speech is not prohibition, but talking back to the aggressor. Responding in kind, it is said, may educate the bigot, who may have been unaware that his view was not widely shared. It may also empower the victim, who takes forceful action instead of withdrawing into a shell or running to the authorities every time he suffers a wounded feeling.

While talking back may sometimes be useful, it will generally not work for the most severe forms of hate speech. How can one counter an expression like "Nigger, get off this campus, you don't belong here—go back to Africa" by a snappy comeback, a patient rejoinder, or by explaining to the hurler of hate speech that one is, in fact, just as worthy as he and entitled to seek an education on that campus? Hate speech is rarely an invitation to a dialog; it is more like a slap in the face. It is true that our society values free expression as a means of correcting error and arriving at consensus on important decisions. But hate speech silences the victim, so that the amount of speech that results is less, not more, than it would be if hate speech were ruled out of bounds. Consider, as well, how a great deal of hate speech is delivered anonymously, by means of an unsigned letter, e-mail, or graffiti scrawled on a campus dorm or bulletin board. In such circumstances, talking back to the offender is impossible.

At other times, it will prove downright dangerous. Often, hate speech will be delivered in a many-on-one setting, such as when a group of drunken fraternity boys berate a lonely Black or gay undergraduate walking home at night from the campus library. Then, responding in kind can be an invitation to disaster. In fact, many incidents of hate crime have begun in exactly such fashion. The victim spoke back—and paid with his life.

Other times, one hears that hate speech is a useful corrective that serves as a type of pressure valve. The hate speaker "gets it out of his system." Instead of bottling up rage, we ought to let it find a harmless outlet in mere words. Repressing anger just means that it is likely to boil over later in a more dangerous form, such as physical violence. Free speech, then, is not only constitutionally preferred; it is the safest course for minorities to follow.

The problem with the pressure-valve argument is that it simply does not comport with what we know about human behavior. Tanks, pressure valves, and other inanimate objects may be safer after they have released steam, but human beings are not. Social science research shows that a speaker who utters hate speech is more, not less, likely to do something violent later. Furthermore, bystanders who see him getting away with it may be more likely to join in. Speech is the prime means by which society constructs a stigma-picture—a category of deserving victims who merit their fate, whether that fate is to suffer more hate speech, exclusion from a social circle, a racist joke, a hate crime, or in extreme cases group violence such as that which broke out in Rwanda.

One also hears that hate speech is "the price we pay" for living in a free society. The law does not cure every wounded ear or slighted pride; victims should toughen up and learn to reply in kind or ignore the insult and go on about their business. This argument overlooks the fact that the price hate speech exacts falls on one group only. The "we" in "the price we pay" in reality means "they." Hate speech visits gays, foreigners, women, people of color, and only rarely middle-class Whites. One searches the English language in vain for terms of contempt for Caucasians. What is the counterpart for a term like "nigger," "spic," "kike," "fag," or "wop"? "Honkey" is certainly unflattering, but carries a grudging tone of respect. The same is true for "cracker." And "trailer trash," although often encompassing Whites, does not single them out for the color of their skin, but for their lifestyle and inability to rise.

An additional argument is that hate speech serves as a bellwether. Better to have it out in the open than underground where one never knows from whence it will strike. It is true, the racist who is known is less dangerous than the one who is not. But what this argument ignores is a third alternative: The racist who is deterred by firm rules and social expectations is safer than either of the others. Since measures against hate speech seem likely to exert at least some deterrence, the bellwether argument would seem to deserve little weight.

A further argument stems from the psychology of speakers. It is said that placing restraints on speech will deter speakers from addressing controversial topics, such as affirmative action or immigration policy. Not knowing where the line falls separating hate speech from the protected kind, speakers will shy away from any topic that could lead to a charge of racism. This "chilling effect" argument holds particular appeal in the area of the First Amendment, because our society is said to rely on free speech and dialog to define itself, reach consensus, and deliberate on vital matters of social policy.

But it should be easily possible to draw up hate speech guidelines that are readily understandable and that do not threaten legitimate speech or inquiry. Other Western societies that restrain hate speech, Holocaust denial, and similar forms of opprobrious language have not suffered a decline in civic discourse or free inquiry. Indeed, nations such as Canada, Great Britain, and Germany, which sharply rein in hate speech, boast a press and a spirit of political debate exceeding that which one finds here. We should be able to follow their example without suffering the decline some profess to fear.

A final argument holds that measures to combat hate speech are unnecessary because hate speech is declining, or at least not increasing. Any apparent upsurge may be due to more socially sensitive or better reporting. The truth is that no one knows for certain how much hate speech takes place. Cortese gives figures suggesting that the amount is considerable; other authorities believe it visits Black undergraduates more often at universities that have a majority of White students. FBI statistics on hate crime show a steady increase. But whether hate speech is increasing, decreasing, or remaining constant, the ideal amount of it is still zero. As with murder, theft, or any other kind of crime, our inability to ascertain precisely how often it occurs is almost beside the point. It is reprehensible, and we owe it to ourselves to counter it with effective measures.

As has been seen, hate speech serves little social purpose. It silences and marginalizes the victim, depriving the community of his voice and contribution. If the purpose of our system of First Amendment protection is to encourage speech and dialog, hate speech is one of the few forms of that activity that reduce the vitality of the marketplace of ideas. It tells the victim nothing he has not heard before. It silences him and encourages others to think he is less worthy than they. Authors like Cortese perform a vital service by showing how hate speech works its pernicious effects, how it carries special dangers for children, and how it can anesthetize a society with consequences that can range from simple injustice to outright atrocity.

We need more books like this. Written with the attention to detail and disciplined judgment of the trained social scientist, as well as a commitment to human flourishing, this book is a triumph.

—Richard Delgado, University Distinguished Professor of
Law and Derrick Bell Fellow, University of Pittsburgh

Preface

Whoever you hate will end up in your family.
            —Chris Rock, actor/comedian

Freedom of speech does not mean freedom to terrorize or incite hatred. Is burning a cross in the front yard of a Black family that has recently moved into a previously all-White neighborhood an expression of free speech protected by the First Amendment? Is angrily shouting "nigger" repeatedly at a Black high school football referee simply exercising the democratic ideal of freedom of expression? Is a White, heterosexual, "Christian" male, who makes homophobic comments in his Literature and Cultural Diversity class merely exercising his constitutional rights? Were protestors led by the Reverend Fred Phelps at the funeral of Matthew Shepard, carrying signs with the words "Matthew burns in hell" and "AIDS cures faggots," just exercising the democratic principle of free speech?

Hate speech denigrates people on the basis of their race or ethnic origin, religion, gender, age, physical condition, disability, sexual orientation, and so forth (Sedler, 1992). Hate speech says much more about the messenger than the target. Hateful words spoken with the blessing of absolute legal protection (based on the supremacy of the First Amendment) have muted minority messages and have resulted in micro-aggressions and other forms of unequal treatment.

The primary goal of *Opposing Hate Speech* is to provide a stimulating rebuttal and rigorous strategy for productive opposition to speech that incites hatred or violence. There have been calls for the legal restriction of hate speech by critical race theorists. The legal hurdles for establishing proof of emotional damage are staggering (see Chapter 1). But we are overly eager to sue. The number of attorneys and court cases in the United States is overwhelming compared to other countries. Litigation is probably not the most time-efficient and cost-effective way of opposing hate speech. Still, it is an invaluable weapon as part of a wide-ranging arsenal of strategies for eradicating hate speech.

Some institutions of higher learning have established rules prohibiting hateful speech in an effort to curb tensions between different racial or ethnic groups. Yet the establishment of speech codes on college and university campuses is problematic. Despite their best intentions to eradicate hate speech, legal restrictions and campus speech codes may be a Trojan horse (e.g., see the Crystall case, Chapter 5) that ends up being used against those trying to end hate speech; but speech codes on college and university campuses may provide excellent pedagogical arenas for changing bigoted attitudes in people.

To really eliminate hate speech, we must nip it in the bud. Prevention is more effective and less costly than treatment. If hate speech is learned behavior (and it clearly is learned and not innate), we can unlearn it or—better yet—never learn it at all. Given psychological evidence that the personality is basically formed as early as age five, sociological and psychological theory and research emphasizing the long-lasting effects of values and attitudes learned through early socialization, and the aggressive and continuous media blitz of images, concepts, and messages on individuals, it seems evident that an inoculation against the bigoted virus of hate speech should begin at an early age. Moral education can eliminate or—better yet—prevent hate speech.

This book attempts to provide a rational basis for rejecting hate speech by focusing on equal treatment and equal protection under the law. I emphasize hate speech based on religion, race, ethnicity, gender, and sexual orientation. Although hate speech is often spewed from the mouths of individuals against specific targets, the focus of this book is on media sources of hate speech against generalized targets (categories of people based on religion, race, ethnicity, gender, or sexual orientation). I focus on the Internet, specifically hate Web sites; film, television, and radio, specifically racist, misogynist, or homophobic talk radio; and print media such as newspapers and magazines. I also discuss social movements, pride marches, and demonstrations, those that fight for minority rights and those that oppose them, and look at the many different examples of publicly expressed hate speech and their consequences. Although various mass media (film, television, the Internet, radio, print) are connected to particular types of hate speech (racist, misogynist, ethnocentric, religious, or homophobic), special effort is made to evaluate a particular form of hate speech from the specific type of media that are especially prevalent and damaging to a particular category of people. Consequently, for racist and ethnocentric speech, I also address the upsurge of White supremacist Web sites and KKK marches in Black neighborhoods, and racism in advertising.

For religious intolerance, we focus on conservative talk radio and the Internet. This includes hate speech directed at members of non-Christian faiths (especially Jews and Muslims) on the Internet by "Christian" hate groups as well as hate speech by Muslim extremists directed at all non-Muslim "infidels." Pornographic film is a driving force of hateful speech and misogynist ideologies against women. For images of sexual orientation, television is a key socializing force setting the standard for acceptable behavior and appearance.

As mentioned above, attention is focused on prevention as well as treatment. Accordingly, the book ends with a practical guide to what you can do to oppose and eliminate hate speech at the individual level. Silence is acceptance. Speak loudly against hate. Talk back.

1

Free Expression versus Equal Protection: What Harm Is Hate Speech?

Tolerance of hate speech is not borne by the community at large. Rather it is a psychic tax imposed on those least able to afford it.
—Mari Matsuda, 1993: 18

Hell is just other people.

—Jean-Paul Sartre, *No Exit*

On the campus of a private university in the southwest, a first-year Latino student receives an anonymous late-night phone call in his dormitory room. The brief but cruel message was spoken angrily: "Go home—spic! You don't belong here." African American law students discover anonymous fliers, crammed inside their lockers, accusing them of severely lowering the school's ratings and reputation. Nameless vandals spray-paint Nazi swastikas and other hateful graffiti on the walls of a Jewish student center.

Hate speech puts people down based on their race or ethnic origin, religion, gender, age, physical condition, disability, or sexual orientation. Absolutist interpretations of the First Amendment maintain that such hate messages, fliers, and graffiti are simply examples of individuals exercising their constitutional right of free speech. After all, it is much easier to permit speech with which we agree than speech we consider abhorrent.

Notice, though, that in each case, the receiver of the hate message is not able to respond directly to the sender of the message. With anonymous hate speech, the victim cannot verbally defend himself or herself. The sender of the message is not only hateful but also spineless. Besides, verbally countering hate aggressors is not always the best option. In fact, many hate crimes began just like this: The victim replies—and is then physically assaulted or murdered.

Hate speech is seldom an invitation to politely chat. It is more like a breathtaking punch to the stomach, a quick stiff jab to the nose, or a forcible slap in the face. Hate speech pummels, ambushes, cuts, insults, and silences. Consequently, it is not surprising that campuses where highly publicized incidents of hate speech have taken place show a decline in minority enrollment as students of color choose to attend schools where the environment is healthier (Delgado, 2004b).

Hate speech has reached near-epidemic proportions on American college campuses. Twenty-five percent of all students are subject to ethnoviolence (threats or overt violence on the grounds of race, gender, ethnicity, religion, or sexual orientation); one-third of the victims are attacked more than once (Schmitt, 2000). In response, some universities have enacted regulations prohibiting speech that assaults ethnic minorities and other historically subordinated groups. Individuals have been punished when their conduct interferes with the educational opportunities of others. Such policies have prompted a heated and wide-reaching debate over their efficacy.

In spite of the fear such restrictions sometimes draw out, they are merely trying to enforce equal treatment and equal protection under the law—rights guaranteed by the Fourteenth Amendment. Limits on the most offensive forms of speech are sensible. Federal courts have extended "hostile environment" case law to schools that tolerate a climate of hate for women and students of color (Delgado, 2004a).

Some federal courts have rightly confirmed that overly broad hate-speech codes are unconstitutional. Academic freedom sometimes includes the discussion of controversial subjects such as gay marriage, evolution, or affirmative action. Colleges and universities are known for the intellectual exploration of controversial views. College and university speech codes should not be written in a manner so broad it could be interpreted as academic censorship.

However, this is not hate speech. Moreover, institutions of higher education can legally adopt measures to restrict behavior that interferes with learning or otherwise creates or maintains a hostile environment for students because of their membership in a particular ethnic or social category. When they do, courts typically rule in their favor. Recent Supreme Court rulings striking down laws that ban sodomy, upholding affirmative action, and supporting punishment for cross-burning demonstrate that the court is dismantling institutional discrimination. As society becomes more racially, ethnically, and culturally diverse, social accommodation is needed to prevent exploitation and discrimination. Reasonable rules aimed at accommodating cultural diversity and regulating the conduct of bullies and bigots are to be applauded—not feared (Delgado, 2004a).

In short, college campuses, long known as bastions for dissent and forums for free speech, are appearing more and more like legal battlegrounds. The central issue is the intersection of free speech—First Amendment rights—and freedom from discrimination, as protected by the Fourteenth

Amendment. A series of lawsuits targeted at abolishing all restrictions on speech has flooded the courts. The legal challenge represents the sharply rising discomfort among absolutist civil libertarians, who believe that the range of restrictions of campus speech creates a precarious chilling effect.

This introductory chapter takes a brief look at the development of "hate" as a topic of sociological research often tied to prejudice, discrimination, stereotypes, and violence. A four-stage developmental model for classifying the severity of hate speech is offered based on critical race, cultural transmission, and group-identification theories. The chapter also provides a sociohistorical framework for restricting free speech, highlighting relevant Supreme Court decisions such as the recent ban on cross-burnings that are meant to terrorize, and focuses on First Amendment issues. The United States is compared to some European nations on free speech and protection from discrimination. Critical race theory is used to support a formal, legal-structural response to hate speech.

A NEW SPIN ON "HATE"

Until approximately 20 years ago, "hate" referred to any intense disliking or hostility, whatever its object. Consequently, an individual may be said to "hate" his or her chemistry class, the taste of liver, the music of Yoko Ono, or even himself or herself. Hate, in this generic sense could be directed at virtually anything—a person, a group, an idea, some other abstraction, or an inanimate object (Levin and Paulsen, 1999).

Since the mid-1980s, "hate" began to be used in a much more restricted sense to characterize an individual's negative beliefs and especially feelings about the members of some other category of people based on their ethnicity, race, gender, sexual orientation, religion, age, or physical or mental disability (Jacobs and Potter, 1998; Jennes and Broad, 1997; Lawrence, 1999; Levin, 1992–1993; Levin and McDevitt, 1993). As contained in the concept "hate speech," this more limited use overlaps with prejudice, bigotry, racism, misogyny, homophobia, ageism, bias, and xenophobia.

Hate is a result of both culture (cultural transmission) and self-interest (group identification) as discussed in the next two sections.

CULTURAL TRANSMISSION THEORY

Children learn hate speech and prejudice in virtually the same way they learn, for example, to speak Spanish, dress in hip-hop style, or eat with chopsticks. Society's mainstream culture, or a subculture, transmits the building blocks of hate speech to children as much at home as throughout the community. For example, the media also transmit stereotypes (Ehrlich, 1973: 32). Ethnic minorities are stereotypically portrayed or conform to mainstream standards of beauty in advertising (Cortese, 2004). Minority characters in films, textbooks, television, and short stories have historically been typecast (Berelson and Salter, 1946; Elson, 1964).

Stereotypes and social distance play a major role in the development of hate speech and prejudice, because they are based on shared beliefs that the members of one group have about members of other groups within or across societies. Children are apt to learn, both through instruction and by accident, that members of various groups are thought to possess a cluster of distinctive traits. These clusters of presumed group characteristics are called stereotypes (McLemore and Romo, 2005).

Stereotypes are common, overgeneralized beliefs about the traits of members of different racial, ethnic, or religious groups, gender or sexual orientation. Stereotypes of out-groups set in stark contrast with positively spun characteristics of reference groups. Thus, there are also stereotypes resulting from favorable images that in-groups ordinarily take pleasure in about themselves. Derogatory stereotypes are evidence of prejudiced attitudes about members of various groups.

Social distance refers to the grades and degrees of understanding, acceptance, and intimacy that usually characterize personal and social relations, especially between ethnic or racial groups. The more inauspicious the stereotypes about a group, the greater social distance between that group and the one that holds the stereotypical attitude. Bogardus (1933) developed the primary research methodology for studying social distance. He asked people to pick various types of social contacts they would be willing to allow with members of different ethnic and racial groups. The types of social contacts represent various points running from a high willingness to permit social contact (e.g., "Would allow their daughter to marry an African American") to, at the other extreme, a low willingness to allow social contact (e.g., "Would exclude Muslims from the United States").

Cultural transmission is used to pass hate on to each succeeding generation. In this context, hate is normal or conventional, expected, and in many cases (e.g., competition for scarce resources) quite rational. Respect for social diversity can be so costly in a psychological or economic sense that it may actually require rebellious or deviant behavior (Levin, 2002).

GROUP-IDENTIFICATION THEORY

Group membership is a very powerful factor that shapes an individual's self-identity. A basic fact concerning human groups is that as their members are drawn together by a common interest and come to see themselves as an in-group, outsiders are likely to be described in terms that are disparaging and derogatory, reflecting negative stereotypes (Sumner, [1906] 1960: 27). In the United States, for example, expressions like "nigger," "spic," "chink," "gringo," "dago," "mick," "kike," "honkey," "limey," and so on have been applied to out-groups as terms of great contempt.

Ethnocentrism is a prevalent tendency to consider one's own group as superior to all others. Children normally learn very early to make a distinction between the group to which they belong and all others. Of course, they typically bond strongly to, as well as have a preference for, their own group and its culture, including hate speech and racial and ethnic stereotypes. Hate speech from others in their culture becomes their own. A group's ideology and enemies also become those of the individual within that group.

To grow up as a member of a given group is automatically to place that group at the center of things and to adopt its evaluations as the best. Hate speech, prejudice, discrimination, and hostility toward members of other groups and preferential treatment for those in the same group are expected outcomes of this "natural" ethnocentrism. Discrimination against outgroup members may happen even among groups whose members have been chosen randomly (Stephan, 1985: 613).

This phenomenon is a potent source of hate speech and prejudice against those who are different from us in various ways. Loyalty to one's ethnic group is sometimes accompanied by an admiration for some specific presumed traits of the members of other groups (Williams, 1964: 22). Even in the midst of war, hated enemies may be granted a reluctant respect for their skill or daring (McLemore and Romo, 2005). The fact that an enemy group is respected in some particular manner does not mean it is generally liked by members of other groups.

Human infants at first look at the world only from their own perspective, according to social self-theory (Mead, 1934). Children learn to communicate symbolically with family members—primarily through language but also through facial expression, body posture, and gestures (Goffman, 1976). Through communication, young children become aware of themselves as distinct individuals who are members of particular groups. An individual's developing self-concept consists of his or her personal identity and also of a variety of social identities that correspond to the groups of which the person is a member (Deaux et al., 1995).

Thus, as individuals endeavor to establish and retain their self-esteem, they derive power and self-importance both from their own achievements and through being associated with groups having relatively high prestige. In this way, a person's sense of confidence may be elevated either by accepting an exaggerated view of the value and importance of his or her group or by downgrading the value and importance of other groups. Pride in one's groups may become excessive and give rise to hate speech and prejudice.

The sense of self-worth of children who grow up as members of an ethnic minority group that occupies a position of low status in social stratification is precarious. When one group is resentful toward another group, members of the targeted group usually react by becoming prouder and more determined to maintain their social identities. However, domination of one group by another may set into motion an often vicious circle, called a self-fulfilling prophecy (Merton, 1957: 423).

If a young Latina child, for example, learns that teachers and other students do not expect her to perform well in school, she may become apprehensive, impairing efforts and resulting in poor academic attainment. This fallout may then be perceived as "proof" that the preliminary low expectations were justified. In this manner, such a process may become a cruel descending spiral. If children are victims of hate speech at school, it may affect their confidence to perform well in class and on exams. If they lower their expectations, they are likely to perform even less well.

CRITICAL RACE THEORY

Critical race theory is a "radical legal movement that aims to transform the relationship among race, law, and power" (Delgado, 2004b: 230). The present examination builds on this significant relationship by including the concept of distributive justice in this analysis. Distributive justice is "the equitable sharing of social and economic resources . . . among the various segments of our population" (Cortese, 2003: viii, 170). More specifically, this implies "sharing material and/or human resources without regard to ethnicity, gender, social class, religion or other subcultural differences" (Cortese, 2003: 162–163). The key to addressing the problem of hate speech is political pressure. Such pressure should be based on principles of equal treatment and distributive justice.

The critical race theory movement emerged in the late 1970s in response to the retrenchment of previous gains through the civil rights movement. Central to critical race theory is recognition that the vested interests of the economically, politically, and socially dominant classes play a key role in ethnic, racial, gender, and class stratification as well as in the dynamic ebb and flow of civil rights. Accordingly, racism is much more institutional, vis-à-vis individual or small group. Racism and sexism are not primarily "isolated instances of conscious bigoted decision-making or prejudiced practice, but . . . larger, systemic, structural, and cultural. . . . [They are] deeply psychologically and socially ingrained" (Matsuda et al., 1993: 5).

Critical race theory contains the following elements (Delgado and Stefancic, 2001; Matsuda et al., 1993):

1. Racism is endemic to everyday life. Traditional interests and values are vessels of racial subordination. Racial stratification has both materialist and symbolic functions. Races are categories that society invents, manipulates, or retires when convenient for hegemonic groups. Shared physical traits that distinguish categories of people from one another pale next to

that which they have in common and have nothing to do with distinctly human, high-order traits, such as personality, intelligence, and moral judgment and behavior.

2. Dominant legal claims of neutrality, objectivity, color blindness, and meritocracy are self-delusional and seriously flawed.

3. Racism has contributed to all contemporary markings of group advantage and disadvantage along ethnic and racial lines. This includes but is not limited to differences in education, employment, housing, health and health care, incarceration, political representation, and military service. Such current inequalities and institutional racism can be directly linked to earlier periods in which the intent, consequences, and cultural meanings of these practices were to dominate and subordinate. Consequently, contemporary law and social custom must be analyzed from this historical context.

4. Experiential knowledge of people is crucial to analyses of contemporary political practice toward the elimination of racism. Critical reflection on the lived experience of racism is vital to such investigation.

5. Analysis should be interdisciplinary and eclectic, borrowing from sociology, ethnic studies, gender studies, criminology, social psychology, political science, psychology, and critical legal theory.

6. The objective of eliminating ethnic and racial oppression is part of a larger project targeted at ending all forms of oppression, especially those related to social class, gender, religion, and sexual orientation.

Critical race theory provides a pragmatic response to victims of hate speech who are daily silenced, intimidated, and subjected to severe psychological and physical trauma by racist perpetrators who employ pejorative words (e.g., nigger, spic, gook) and symbols (burning crosses, swastikas) as part of a complex and integrated arsenal of weapons of oppression, domination, and subordination.

A STAGE-DEVELOPMENTAL MODEL OF HATE-SPEECH SEVERITY

Some hate speech is more reprehensible than others; not all discriminatory statements are equally serious. There is quite a difference between an offensive remark and an incitement to commit murder. There is also a fundamental distinction between intentional and unintentional discrimination.

Developed from cultural transmission, group-identification, and critical race theories, a four-stage developmental model of hate speech severity is proposed to classify discriminatory statements. They form a sequence from least severe to most severe. The model is developmental, presupposing a logical flow from the least to most severe, often culminating in a violent hate crime, but an individual may fixate at any stage in the scale.

Strategies for intervention are also presented at each stage.

Stage 1: Unintentional Discrimination (Offending Minorities, But Not on Purpose)

Just below the surface of ordinary everyday social behavior, countless murders of the mind and spirit occur on a daily basis. These events are sometimes referred to as micro-transgressions. They are stunning, small encounters with racism, sexism, or homophobia by members of the majority race or group. For example, a White woman walks up to a Black woman whom she has never met and, without permission, takes the liberty of grabbing the Black woman's long braids with her hands while complementing her on her hair. Another example is an affluent Southern woman who does not understand why Black folks resent being called "colored."

Education is the major intervention. This involves speaking out when one hears hate speech in order to teach the offender that what s/he said was stereotypical, discriminatory, or hateful, and why.

Stage 2: Conscious Discrimination (Intentionally Denigrating Minorities)

Education again is the major intervention. Second, speech codes prohibiting hate speech could be enacted within institutions. Third, the tort of intentional infliction of emotional distress makes litigation possible. Under what conditions is hate speech perceived as harmful? Proving one's case is extremely difficult. To receive compensation from this cause of action, the plaintiff must meet four basic criteria:

1. Intent
2. Extreme and outrageous behavior
3. Causation
4. Severe emotional distress

It is clear that Stage 2 reasoning satisfies the requirement of intent. However, there is a lot of hate speech that does not cause severe emotional distress. There is also plenty of hateful talk that does not constitute extreme and outrageous behavior. In conclusion, perhaps civil restitution depends on the severity of Stage 3 hate speech.

Stage 3: Inciting Discriminatory Hatred (Generating Feelings of Hatred for Minorities)

This form of hate speech is more severe than that of Stage 2. Education is not likely to change the attitude of an established bigot. This type of hate speech falls within the purview of speech codes. However, hate speech is often spoken out in public, for example, on the streets, and thus is typically beyond the scope of any institution's speech code. The severity of Stage 3 hate speech makes it perhaps less difficult to litigate than Stage 2.

Stage 4: Inciting Discriminatory Violence (Encouraging Violence Against Minorities)

Stages 2–4 meet the definition of hate speech.

This type of hate speech clearly incites imminent criminal behavior, expression that the judiciary has never protected. However, "imminent" is the key criterion.

Throughout the book, this model will be used to analyze and evaluate the severity of numerous examples of hate speech. There are linguistic analyses of media scripts (including investigative journalism, quotes, press conferences, news programs) and policy statements.

A SOCIOHISTORICAL FRAMEWORK FOR RESTRICTING HATE SPEECH

Throughout American history, significant repercussions of the First Amendment have gone virtually unscrutinized, resulting in unshakable faith in self-righteous principles whose everyday-life consequences are never examined or confronted. The present analysis suggests a rethinking of some of these issues that have been silenced in ways harmful to many—especially those who have been oppressed, brutalized, manipulated, dominated, segregated, and disadvantaged—in our society.

In 1954, in *Brown v. Board of Education*, the U.S. Supreme Court ruled the racial segregation of public schools to be unconstitutional. Underlying the decision was a keen detection of the deleterious effects of compulsory segregation on the psyches of its victims. In essence, the case focused on the severe nature of the injury caused by the defamatory symbolism of segregation (i.e., hate speech).

Hate speech is comprised of words that are used to terrorize, humiliate, degrade, ambush, lacerate, pummel, assault, and injure. It is important to draw on the minority experience of injury from hate speech to develop a First Amendment interpretation that recognizes and responds to such injuries (e.g., Supreme Court Justice Clarence Thomas, Jr.'s discussion on cross-burnings, below). Why is it that death threats, child pornography, fraud, defamation, and invasion of privacy are exempt from free-speech/expression guarantees while debilitating ethnic and racist verbal assaults are not? The answer: a history of xenophobia, ethnocentrism, and racism.

Supreme Court Rules on Cross-Burning to Intimidate

Until recently, absolutist views on the sacredness of the First Amendment have dominated legislation, court decisions, and popular opinion. Now, however, cracks are beginning to appear. On April 8, 2003, the U.S. Supreme Court, in *Virginia v. Black*, invalidated a Virginia law prohibiting cross-burning undertaken with "intent to intimidate a person or group of persons." This decision is important because the Court announced itself willing to uphold a law that was limited to prohibiting cross-burning as a "true threat," that is, with the intent "to communicate a serious expression of an intent to commit an act of unlawful violence to a particular individual or group of individuals." The problem with the Virginia law was that it was not so limited because it permitted a jury to find the requisite intent from the mere fact of cross-burning. In essence, the Court was protecting minorities from racial intimidation at the expense of symbolic—albeit hurtful—expression.

The Court ruled that states can punish Ku Klux Klansmen and others who set crosses afire, finding that a burning cross is an instrument of racial terror so threatening that it overshadows free-speech concerns (*New York Times*, 2003). The Court voted 6–3 to uphold a 50-year-old Virginia law making it a crime to burn a cross as an act of intimidation. Dissents were based on free-speech grounds.

Justice Sandra Day O'Connor, writing for the majority, said the protections afforded by the First Amendment "are not absolute" and do not necessarily shield cross burners. Justice Clarence Thomas, the Court's only Black member and a law-and-order conservative who frequently departs from conventional civil rights beliefs, wrote separately, "those who hate cannot terrorize and intimidate to make their point." Cross-burning combines speech with physical threat. Implicit in the speech is a threat of physical harm.

The burning cross historically has been an aggressive display of racial hatred by the Ku Klux Klan and other White supremacists. The Klan was formed in 1866. It used mysterious language and incantations in its secret rituals and initiations, fought against reconstruction, and attempted to maintain the subordinate status of former Black slaves. It used cross-burnings and gloomy warnings delivered during the night by people in costumes consisting of white robes and hoods. If these threats did not produce the necessary intimidation, the Klan resorted to whippings, arson (house burning), and even brutal and sadistic killings.

The Klan was at its strongest in the 1920s and 1930s, with massive demonstrations in the nation's capital and millions of members, both men and women. Klan meetings would have hooded figures, hate mongers spewing White racial superiority, and the obligatory large burning cross. The *Virginia* case evoked a mostly bygone era in the South, when "nightriders" set crosses ablaze as a symbol of intimidation to terrorize Blacks and civil rights sympathizers. Justice Clarence Thomas grew up in then-segregated Georgia. During arguments in the case, he broke his customary silence and spoke of cross-burning as a symbol of a century of violence and terror at the hands of the Klan and other White supremacy groups.

The 2003 Supreme Court decision reversed the 1992 Supreme Court decision on a cross-burning on the lawn of a Black family in St. Paul, Minnesota (*R.A.V. v. St. Paul*, 1992). The Court used a mechanical perspective in declaring an ordinance that prohibited hate speech unconstitutional because it singled out racial motivation for harsh treatment. Subsequent to that ruling, a Black Texas family won a large settlement against five men who trespassed on their property while wearing pillowcases over their heads and carrying a large wooden cross wrapped in sheets. One night, the family awakened to discover a huge smoldering cross in their yard. Within a year, family members filed suit alleging violation of their civil rights, conspiracy to violate those rights, and various common law torts such as slander, nuisance, and intentional infliction of emotional distress (Delgado, 2004b). After a week-long trial a jury with two African American members awarded compensatory damages for the family's claims (Upmeyer, 2003).

A Florida statute prohibits behavior that can be considered a threat of violence. An illicit cross-burning by trespassers on someone else's private property comprises a direct threat to one's privacy and security. In particular, a cross-burning has been historically and forever connected to sudden and precipitous violence—lynchings, shootings, whippings, mutilations, and house-burnings. The link between a burning cross in the front yard of a Black family and impending violence is obvious and direct. A greater, more terrorizing sign of danger is hard to picture.

A cross-burning does not necessarily constitute "fighting words." A "fighting word" must be delivered face-to-face. Thus, burning a cross on another's property might qualify, depending on the context. But a burning cross at a Ku Klux Klan rally with only true believers present—not directed at an individual or a discernible group of individuals—surely would not. The Court in *Virginia v. Black* concluded that "true threat" was the best category for assessing cross-burnings for a reason.

A burning cross raised by intruders on someone else's private property inflicts emotional harm on victims in the form of fear and intimidation and also tends to incite an immediate breach of the peace where the intruder or victim might be apt to erupt in violence. What is central in the eyes of the Supreme Court is not the idea expressed, but rather *how* the idea is expressed—the mode of communication. Once again, it is tough to imagine a case more prevalent for potential for reflexive violence and breaking the peace.

The Paladin Case

On April 20, 1998, the U.S. Supreme Court refused to hear an appeal regarding a lawsuit accusing Paladin Publishers of aiding the hired killings of a Maryland woman, her 8-year-old disabled son, and the boy's nurse, in 1993. The crime was committed after the killer read the book *Hit Man: A Technical Manual for Independent Contractors*. The manual offers detailed advice on how to carry out a professional killing, get away with it, and how to hide a body. The book's author, a single mother, used the *nom de plume* Rex Feral—Latin for "King of Beasts."

Paladin originally won the case. A federal judge threw out the lawsuit citing a 1969 Supreme Court ruling that said speech advocating an illegal act is legally protected unless it is "directed to inciting or producing imminent lawless action." Courts generally have not allowed lawsuits against authors or moviemakers over "copycat crimes" committed by people who imitate what they see. But the Fourth U.S. Circuit Court of Appeals reinstated the lawsuit against Paladin, saying the case was unique. "*Hit Man* is, pure and simple, a step-by-step murder manual, a training book for assassins" and therefore has no free-press protection, the appeals court judge, whose father had been murdered, ruled in November 1997. Paladin agreed in September 2000 to stop selling the book, in a settlement of the Maryland lawsuit.

More recently, on February 2, 2002, Paladin settled a similar lawsuit filed by a woman who fought off a hired killer who used the book as a guide. The lawsuit, the first to be filed after the Maryland lawsuit, triggered national concern that free-speech rights might erode as more people blame publishers and movie producers for crimes inspired by their work. The lawsuit boiled down to whether the publisher conspired or aided and abetted in the crime. This kind of activity is not generally recognized as being protected by the First Amendment. The case began in 1998 while the woman and her husband were getting a divorce. The husband hired a hit man to murder his wife in exchange for $100,000 from her life insurance policy. Both men were sentenced in 1999 to 17½ years in prison.

In court, the hired killer testified that the husband recruited him to kill his wife. The hired killer then purchased the book. The lawsuit outlined two dozen points of advice from the book that the would-be killer closely followed in planning the murder. The advice covered such points as disposing of evidence, creating a disguise, selecting weapons, and avoiding conviction if caught.

Not all rulings, however, have opposed regulations or restrictions on the First Amendment. In 1997, the Ohio State Supreme Court ruled in favor of a member of the Ku Klux Klan who had advocated the murder of minority group members. The court decided that the defendant's speech did not pose an *immediate* physical threat to the lives of people of color.

HATE SPEECH IN THE NEW MILLENNIUM

Hate speech is an institutionalized social phenomenon that has gained considerable momentum in the new millennium. The terrorist attacks on September 11, 2001, have given rise to a sharp increase in hate speech and hate crimes against Muslims and Arabs—or those who are perceived to be Muslims or Arabs.

The continuous uprising of the Palestinian people against Israel on the West Bank and in the Gaza Strip has been characterized by an increasingly lethal cycle of suicide bombings followed by severe retaliation by the Israeli military. This retaliation has been widely condemned. In the United States and throughout the world, there have been demonstrations against Israel in solidarity with the Palestinian cause. Many demonstrators carry signs that target all Jews. They oppose Israel and anyone who supports Israel. Anti-Semitic slogans are shouted and chalked or painted on the streets and public walls.

The Internet has become an extremely important vehicle of free speech, even for people living in countries where such freedom does not exist. On the Net, opinions are promulgated, discussions carried on, activities announced, and communication established. Every form of censorship or restriction forms a threat to freedom on the Internet. Neo-Nazis and skinheads spread their cyberhate as well. Ku Klux Klan and Aryan Nation demonstrations and propaganda openly incite people to violence.

The number of "hate" Web sites is skyrocketing, providing opportunities for loners to receive encouragement, affirmation, and a sense of belonging otherwise unachievable. On many of these sites violence is encouraged, the existence of the Holocaust is denied, and the ideology of National Socialism is glorified. Although legal in the United States, sites like these are forbidden or subject to criminal prosecution in a number of European countries.

Hate speech against gays and lesbians is also surging. It provides support and justification for hate crimes against gays, most notably, the 1998 torture murder of Matthew Shepard in Laramie, Wyoming. Such hate speech emanates not only from racist skinheads and other violent outcasts, but from mainstream society as well. It comes from the lyrics of Eminem's rap music as well as some of the homophobic and misogynist "gangsta" rap artists. It comes also from the religious right. For example, at Matthew Shepard's funeral, Fred Phelps, a minister of a Baptist church in Kansas, held a cruel demonstration. He and his followers (almost exclusively relatives by blood or marriage) shouted epithets and carried signs with the words "Matthew burns in hell" and "AIDS cures faggots."

Hate speech against immigrants is also on the rise. The 1990s saw a record number of immigrants in the United States (U.S. Census Bureau, 2001). The majority of these immigrants come from Central America, Asia, and Mexico, and, to a lesser extent, South America and Africa. Thus, most of them are people of color. This trend in immigration has been referred to as the "Browning of America" (McLemore and Romo, 2005). Hate speech against recent immigrants is increasing for three reasons: (1) their record-setting numbers; (2) their race and ethnicity (they do not look like the Euro-American majority); and (3) perceived or actual competition for scarce resources (decent, affordable housing, stable employment, social welfare, and slots in quality schools).

Not only in the United States, but also in other first-world countries, most notably Western European nations such as Germany, the Netherlands, Belgium, Great Britain, and France, there have been large increases of immigrants of color from third-world countries. A surge of hate speech and an explosion of nativistic and anti-immigration movements in the host countries, including the United States, have rapidly followed this large influx.

In short, hate speech (or support for hate speech) originates not only in the ranting and raving of bigoted extremists on the fringes of society, but in the implied approval of ordinary, even decent, folks in mainstream society. Although most people would not commit a hate crime, they nevertheless contribute to the production of hate speech and prejudice by sympathizing with it and those who do perpetuate hate crimes. Moreover, there are those who are otherwise well-mannered that are passive spectators to bigoted hate speech because they benefit either economically or psychologically from existing social arrangements. Although these people do not carry the virus of bigotry or chauvinism within them, they nonetheless are without the courage to confront those who spread hate speech and propagate hate crimes.

Although many people believe that bigotry, prejudice, and discrimination are declining, hate speech is thriving and continues to adversely impact access to opportunities, to terrorize and to serve as a symbol of violence threatening the safety of millions of Americans and others throughout the world. Is there a limit to freedom of expression in a democracy, and if so, where should the line be drawn?

FREE SPEECH AND EQUAL PROTECTION ISSUES: AN INTERNATIONAL PERSPECTIVE

In the United States and other Western democracies, free speech and freedom from discrimination are regarded as fundamental rights that most citizens take for granted. But what happens when these two rights clash? Which right carries the trump card? There is no place in a democratic society for book-burning or censorship. Freedom of expression is the ultimate good—the foundation of any democratic society. It should be possible to freely and publicly express a vast range of ideas, opinions, and concepts.

Just as essential is the right not to be discriminated against. Certainly, in a democratic society all people are guaranteed equal treatment and protection under the law. Discrimination—treating various categories of people unequally *and unfairly*—is clearly contrary to the democratic principle of equality. Any democratic government is therefore expected to use legislation and other means to protect its citizens from discrimination.

A democratic government will use many means, including legislation, to guarantee its citizens free speech. But freedom of expression does not mean that anyone can get away with saying or shouting anything one wants to in public. The United States has regulations and laws that set limits on freedom of expression. For example, certain forms of slander are regarded as punishable offenses, as are the spreading of particular lies and the incitement to murder or to commit violence. Legal innovation is a means to prohibit hate speech and providing protection from discrimination.

The United States takes a distinct approach to the conflict between free speech and equal treatment compared to the democratic societies in Western Europe (Boyle, 2001). In the United States, there is genuine reluctance to set limits on freedom of speech. In fact, according to the First Amendment of the American Constitution, lawmakers may not pass any legislation that unnecessarily limits freedom of speech.

In Western Europe, there is a greater tendency to place limits on freedom of expression if the right to protect against discrimination is at issue. The Constitution of the Netherlands, for example, begins with a ban on discrimination: All residents of the country must be treated equally under equivalent circumstances. Other countries of Western Europe are also more inclined to limit the freedom of speech than the United States. For example, in many Western European countries, public denial of the Holocaust is a punishable offense. In the United States it is not.

Most other countries provide regulations against hate speech. The theory is that there must be a balance between individual rights and collective welfare. Universal human rights and freedom, accordingly, include a shared, as well as individual, component. Moreover, a citizen's right to promote hate speech must be assessed along with the general good of society.

Moreover, some Western European nations regulate hate speech in hopes of curbing ethnoviolence and intergroup hostilities. Still others ban hate speech because it flies in the face of equal treatment and human dignity, principles on which the countries are based.

Europe is densely populated and has exhibited a recurring pattern of ethnic hatred and conflict—even genocide. Consequently, European concern with hate speech—especially organized hate groups with a mastery of mass media—is certainly understandable. Virtually every European nation punishes hate speech and propaganda (Delgado, 2004b). Germany, for example, bans the organization of neo-Nazi groups as well as neo-Nazi Web sites in cyberspace. The European Commonwealth has also been fleshing out court procedures to access and rule on hate speech and ethnoviolence.

There is an established pattern of banning speech that is discriminatory, hateful, or threatening violence. These concepts are central to the hate-speech severity model presented above. Many of these national policies resulted from U.N. conventions and agreements and were intended to provide support at the local level. The United Nations ratified the Universal Declaration of Human Rights after World War II; the Declaration guarantees free speech as a basic human right (Article 19). A second human rights manifesto also pledged freedom of expression along those same lines. The International Covenant on Civil and Political Rights (Article 19) guarantees that all citizens shall have the right to hold and express opinions without interference.

As posited throughout this monograph, however, there are limits to free speech. The exercise of the rights of free speech and opinion carry with them special duties and responsibilities. Member nations in the Covenant had the prerogative to elaborate on these special duties and responsibilities through laws and social policies. Such accountability includes protection of national security, public health or social or moral order, and respect for the rights and reputation of others. The Covenant also supports prohibition of any hate speech based on ethnic, racial, religious, or national background that constitutes provocation to discriminate or to engage in hostile or violent action. Warfare propaganda is also banned.

A third manifesto on human rights is the International Convention on the Elimination of All Forms of Racial Discrimination. It requires member nations to prohibit hate speech or other modes of distributing racial or ethnic supremacy propaganda. It also prohibits inciting ethnic or race discrimination, hatred, and violence. The Council of Europe follows this pattern of prohibiting dangerous hate speech. The European convention on the Protection of Human Rights and Fundamental Freedoms legitimates free speech (Article 9) but cautions that it may be tempered by any restrictions necessary for a democratic society (Article 10). That is, there are penalties, conditions, and restrictions prescribed by law to protect citizens from discrimination and to promote collective good. The common ground between all these declarations: When hate speech infringes on the rights of others it should be banned. There is also the protection against defaming the reputation of others; this translates into respect for the dignity of all citizens. Armed with effective hate-speech laws, the European Court of Human Rights and parallel councils have established that various forms of hate speech, including Holocaust denial, Nazi propaganda, and racist flyers or pamphlets, go beyond the bounds of permissible expression (McGonagle, 2001).

Beyond Western Europe, other countries that share a history of ethnic conflict have passed similar laws. For example, many countries in the Caribbean have passed the major European human rights treaties clarifying that freedom of expression does not extend to hate speech (Modeste, 2001). In the Pacific region, New Zealand bans publishing or broadcasting hate speech that is likely to incite racial tensions or hostility or cause contempt for ethnic minorities. In Asia, India has enacted hate-speech laws; likewise, the South African Constitution guarantees free speech but specifically bans hate speech. New Zealand has also passed laws against inciting racial tensions.

In the Americas, Canadian federal and provincial laws criminalize hate speech and hate crime. In the well-known 1990 Canadian Supreme Court decision, *Regina v. Keegstra* (Boyle, 2001), a teacher used racist and anti-Semitic hate speech, resulting in charges being filed against him under the national hate-speech law. Attorneys for the defendant claimed that the conviction violated the teacher's right to free speech as guaranteed in the Canadian Charter—a document not unlike the U.S. Constitution.

The Supreme Court preserved the conviction in its opinion, arguing that Canada's national values also guarantee social welfare and a multicultural environment. The Court ruled that the guarantee of free speech must be recognized within a broader range of social values, including ethnic and cultural diversity. Canada's hate-speech law, which prohibits any statement that is likely to expose a person or group of persons to hatred or contempt based on ethnicity, race, place of origin, religion, sex, or sexual orientation, is one of the global community's most harsh regulations; it is not required that the prosecuting attorney(s) demonstrate proof of malicious intent or actual harm to obtain a conviction (Pearlstein, 1999).

Hate-speech laws are effective in discouraging racist incitement and abuse. Moreover, such laws have not led to the loss of free-speech rights. Hate-speech laws facilitate monitoring offenses, collecting statistics, writing and disseminating status reports, and organizing the efforts of various countries. Hate laws also provide the basis for the occasional prosecution of notorious hate-mongers, which presumably has some deterrent (Kubler, 1998; Modeste, 2001). Ostensibly, even a sporadic conviction functions as a general deterrent for those inclined to incite discrimination, hatred, or violence. The climate of public opinion in these countries is not any less open than that in the United States.

Words That Wound

We should recognize the grave injuries inflicted by racist hate speech and the potential tensions between legal solutions to those injuries and the First Amendment. Sociology, psychology, and political theory can be used to explain the nature of such harm. Values central to the First Amendment itself are subverted by hate speech. Racism is the cause of this selective disregard. The inhibition to restrict hate speech is based on unconscious racism. The ACLU has issued a position paper that reflects sensitivity to the damage that hate speech does to both its victims and to the political discourse that the First Amendment is intended to protect (ACLU, 1994).

Often, victims of hate are unable to articulate what they feel. They may internalize the injury, rendering them silent in the face of continuing injury. The origins are often masked in the language of shared values and objective legal principles. If ideology is deconstructed and the harm generated from hate speech is identified and defined, degraded victims find their voices. They discover their subordination is shared, thus enabling collective empowerment.

The thread of subordination weaves through analyses of hate speech, legal history, affirmative action, desegregation, religious freedom, civil rights, and reparations. Not surprisingly, there has been a vigorous backlash to affirmative action. In academia, this backlash has been apparently polite, using code words such as merit, rigor, standards, qualifications, and excellence. Those who favor regulating hate speech have been labeled intolerant, silencing, McCarthyists, and censors. The language of the debate provides a multilayered blanket of multiple meanings.

Traditional interpretation of the First Amendment arms conscious and unconscious racists—both members of the Ku Klux Klan and political liberals—with the right to be racist. Accordingly, racism is merely another idea that deserves to be protected by the Constitution. The First Amendment is misused to nullify the only substantive meaning of the equal protection clause of the Fourteenth Amendment, that the Constitution requires the dismantling of racist ideology.

CONCLUSION

Some believe that hate-speech regulations constitute a serious danger to First Amendment liberties. Others believe that these regulations are needed to protect the rights of those who have been and continue to be denied access to equal opportunity. This argument has deeply divided civil libertarians, driving a wedge between the membership of the American Civil Liberties Union (ACLU) and other similar organizations.

Those who support regulating hate speech are the minority both numerically and sociologically. They have been called "First Amendment revisionists" and "thought police." In essence, this movement is part of a larger struggle against dehumanization and oppression, borne out of passion and hope.

Freedom and equality are the two major principles supported by the Constitution. Freedom connotes freedom from "degradation, humiliation, battering, starvation, homelessness, hopelessness and other forms of violence to the person that deny one's full humanity" (Matsuda et al., 1993: 15). The danger of White supremacist groups such as the White Aryan Resistance (WAR), the Ku Klux Klan, and the neo-Nazi skinheads surpasses their violent hate crimes. Their mere existence and the active distribution of racist propaganda result in the nullification of personal security and liberty for targeted victims in their everyday life. Consequently, formal criminal and administrative censure—public vis-à-vis private prosecution—is an appropriate reply to hate speech (Matsuda, 1993).

This push for a formal, legal-structural response to hate speech flies in the face of a long-standing and healthy mistrust of government authority. Hate speech opposes our tradition of tolerance that is precious and valuable, yet fragile. The basic purpose for the legal restriction of hate speech is to reinforce our commitment to tolerance as a value.

2

Race, Ethnicity, and Hate Speech

Take that bone out of your nose and call me back.
—Rush Limbaugh, to an African American caller to
his radio program

It's our contention that . . . the usage of the racial slur was not racially motivated. He probably would have used some other word had the official been white.
—Dan Hawkley, attorney for Lonny Rae, sentenced
to seven days in detention for shouting "nigger" at an
African American football official

A White man was sentenced to seven days in jail for repeatedly shouting "nigger" at a Black man. Outside the stadium entrance, Rae shouted, "Tell that nigger to get out here, 'cuz I'm a gonna kick his fuckin' ass." Receiving no response to Lonny's verbal challenge, the Raes contacted the police and demanded they charge Manley with assault and battery. The Adams County Prosecutor, Myron Dan Gabbert, originally charged Lonny Rae under Idaho's felony "hate crime" statute, which carries a maximum penalty of five years in the state penitentiary. Although the jury refused to convict Mr. Rae of the felony, it did find him liable for assault in having hurled the epithet.

The October 2000 confrontation happened in the small town of Council in southern Idaho at a high school football game. Notus High School had defeated Council High School in a game that sent Notus to the playoffs and ended Council's season. During the game, Council fans became upset at the referees because they thought there were too many penalties called.

Rae's wife, Kimberly, was covering the game as a freelance reporter and photographer for the *Adams County Record*. After the game, she tried to take a photograph of one of the referees. Kenneth Manley, a Black man from Boise, Idaho, objected to his picture being taken and attempted to take her camera. The neck strap prevented him from securing the camera and caused a minor burn on her neck. Rae's lawyer, Dan Hawkley, said his client was simply coming to the defense of his wife, who was just doing her job.

Idaho District Court Judge Stephen Drescher sternly remarked from the bench that Mr. Rae "deserved some retribution" for his conduct and that it was important that "sports officials be protected from unruly by-standers." Lonny Rae's trial attorney, Edgar J. Steele, of Sandpoint, Idaho, had urged the judge to set aside the conviction or, at most, impose no jail time. "This is an important First Amendment case," said Steele. "Send Mr. Rae to jail and the citizens of America will be afraid to say anything to one another, for fear of being locked up." Judge Drescher was unmoved by Steele's plea.

Mr. Rae was handcuffed and about to be led away to his cell, when Steele persuaded the judge to defer the sentence while he appealed the case to the Idaho Supreme Court. Steele vowed a battle "all the way to the U.S. Supreme Court, if necessary." Steele also noted, "this case is far too important for all of us to allow this ruling to go unchallenged."

"I'm innocent. They bashed my name and my wife's name—they nearly destroyed our lives. We were a toy to them. What they did was wrong. The criminal was let go because he was Black and they were afraid of him. They overlooked the law," Rae said.

The Idaho Athletic Association, which had assigned the referees to the game, subsequently placed Council High School on a year's probation due to the officials having suffered "fan abuse." The local school board barred both the Raes from the school grounds for a year, although their two daughters were then enrolled. The Adams County Record published an article in which school officials blamed the Raes for causing the school to be put on probation.

Within days, Lonny Rae was charged with a misdemeanor under Idaho's "hate-crime" law, known as the "Malicious Harassment" statute. Media from the surrounding area converged on the town to cover the hate crime.

One day before the trial was to begin, the Raes learned that the indictment against him was elevated to a full felony, punishable by up to five years in prison. In addition, prosecution of the case was transferred from the city to the Adams County prosecutor.

The goal of the defense was to overturn the "hate crime" law. Steele said:

> This is another clear case of local government run amuck, just as with so many other recent Idaho cases that have achieved national profiles. Lonny Rae is being sacrificed on the altar of political correctness so that Idaho can

be seen as the so-called Human Rights State and to counter recent negative publicity garnered from the McGuckin, Aryan Nations and Ruby Ridge affairs.

These hate crime statutes generally have been deemed not to violate the First Amendment's guarantee of free speech. However, some actual criminal act in conjunction with the hate speech is required before one can be charged. We haven't yet reached the point of criminalizing mere speech or thought. . . . The "Adams County thought police" have applied Idaho's little-used Malicious Harassment statute in such a way as to achieve that very result in Lonny Rae's case. Thus, while the statute may be constitutional, its usage by the Adams County thought police is clearly unconstitutional and an affront to all who value the right to speak their mind without fear of government interference (Steele, 2001).

" 'Hate words' according to the Idaho legislature," Rae indicated, "are nigger, spook, gook, dike, fag, chink, spic—there's not one of them in there relating to White people. There ain't 'cracker' or 'honky.' So I say to myself, this is a law for minorities only, and that violates equal protection."

"My very best friend was a Black kid. He lived with me and my mom growing up. He got stabbed by other Blacks for associating with Whites," Rae continued. "This ordeal has almost made me racist. To be honest. I still have a hard time explaining to my kids why our lives were torn apart because this Black guy attacked their mother (they saw the injuries) and nothing happens to him. My kids are being taught that Blacks can get away with anything."

After a two-day trial, the jury acquitted Rae of the "hate crime." The jurors found him guilty of assault, however. Idaho District Court Judge Stephen Drescher had included the charges of assault and disturbing the peace in his jury instructions as "lesser-included offenses."

"The way I see it, what the judge did was illegal," remarked Rae. "How far are we going to bend the law until it's broken?"

"The legal system is irretrievably and irredeemably broken. And you'll never use it to fix itself either," concluded Steele.

Rae's statements may be considered Stage 4 (Inciting Discriminatory Violence) in the model of hate speech severity (see Chapter 1), since he was personally threatening violence against Manley. Moreover, his remarks may have encouraged other violence to Blacks.

In a postscript to the story, Kimberly Rae, who was covering the football game as a photographer for the *Adams County Record*, was terminated by the newspaper. Lonnie Rae's construction business quickly failed. Finally, referee Kenneth Manley soon moved away from Boise, Idaho.

This chapter examines race, ethnicity, and hate speech. There is special emphasis on hate speech as self-expression and possible limits to freedom of speech on the Internet. Hate speech and other discriminatory statements on the Internet Web sites of Stormfront.org, Knights of the Ku Klux Klan, White Aryan Resistance, and National Alliance are examined. We start with a brief examination of the Internet, its cultural impact, and First Amendment issues.

THE INTERNET IMPACTS SOCIETY

Political and legal boundaries mean little in cyberspace, making regulation of the Internet difficult and almost by default protecting "free speech."

—James Magee, 2002: 283

During the infancy of the United States, communication depended on word of mouth, handwritten letters, a basic printing press, and a primitive postal system that used horse riders, carriages, and ships. The notion of free speech was based on these mediums. The country's founders could not have anticipated the technological inventions and innovations during the next two centuries that broadened and reconstructed the methods and character of communication, forcing us to reexamine the issue of free speech. Such technological innovations as the telegraph, steam engine, telephone, celluloid film, radio, television, videotape, fiber-optic cable, computers, satellites, microchips, and wireless transmissions via pulses of laser light have revolutionized communication throughout the world. These changes have resulted in a restructuring of the constitutional principle of free speech and the more wide-ranging commitment to free expression that has developed as a crucial characteristic of American political culture.

Technology affects the speed and value of communication and the numbers of message senders and receivers (the viewers or listeners). Hundreds of millions of people use the Internet, talk on cell phones, and view CNN on television throughout the world. Communication that once took days, weeks, or months to permeate the social and political systems now is virtually instantaneous to a global audience. There is no more poignant example than the live media coverage of the second jetliner smashing and exploding into the south tower of the World Trade Center on the morning of September 11, 2001. Vivid and dramatic photos and reports from New York, and later from the Pentagon, confirmed to a horrified global community that the United States was under attack by terrorists.

Television and radio continue to be the dominant mass communications media. Yet the most vibrant advances relating to freedom of speech have come from computer technology and the microchip guiding the Internet. No communications network has developed so quickly in the last 20-plus years or touched so much of the earth's population than this new mode. The Internet evolved from a 1969 military program, ARPANET, created to allow computers operated by the military, defense contractors, and research universities to communicate with one another. The number of "host" computers used to store and transmit information on the budding Internet in 1981 was approximately 300; at the new millennium, that number had risen to approximately 10 million (Magee, 2002).

The growth of the microchip and its phenomenal productivity rates in such a short time have catapulted the Internet as an instrument of worldwide communication, changing the face of business, economics, culture politics, and law. By mid-2001, 60 percent of households in the United States were connected to the Internet, with people spending an average of 16 hours per month online (Magee, 2002). At the time of this writing, in 2005, American Internet users number more than 215 million.

The Internet provides great quantities of information, in multisensory forms and in ways that require participation and reaction, but not necessarily detachment, reason, and reflection. Neither space nor time is relevant to the usual fare of continuous and instantaneous stimulation. The availability of gigantic quantities of information, unsorted, remote and without perspective, and often anonymous, can affect the meaning and importance of information itself. With no effective controls on the accuracy or value of information, what should be believed?

Shared experience molds both culture and individual nature. What we see and hear, to a large extent, shapes what we know and believe. There appears to be no effective way to patrol the Internet, offering little control over what can be experienced (i.e., seen and heard). Consequently, the symbolic meaning dominates the particular information displayed. Technology can allow the user a modicum of control over exposure to content; for example, the V-chip acts as a filter in computer chips that screens out certain kinds of material, providing a means to monitor indecency on the Internet or television.

In December 2000, Congress passed legislation called the Children's Internet Protection Act (CIPA), which cuts off federal funds to libraries and schools that do not use filtering software, such as Cyber Patrol, even if they employ other methods to protect children from sexually explicit materials. Opponents say the filters, which are not always effective, block legitimate materials from children and confine adult library users to Internet information appropriate for minors.

Political advocacy in the United States has manifested itself in many ways, and the Internet has added an unparalleled new feature. The U.S. Congress in 2000 received 80 million e-mail messages (Magee, 2002). Although some undoubtedly were "spam" messages sent in bulk format, there is little doubt that Americans are increasingly equipped to make their complaints and support known to members of Congress. Congressional offices typically reply to messages sent from political constituents. This new "cyber-advocacy" furthers citizen participation and democratic self-government. The Internet can furnish the means to extend grassroots political action to wider national and international venues.

The vast scope of the Internet has even required a new vocabulary to convey and understand its dimensions. Cyberspace is an "integrated network of Web sites and computers enabling rapid transmission of messages and data" (Delgado, 2004b: 230). It has emerged as a common way to access a place without physical dimensions—where ordinary telephone conversations "happen," where voice mail and e-mail messages are stored and sent back and forth, and where computer-generated graphics are transmitted and transformed, all in the form of interactions, among countless users, and between users and the computer itself (Tribe, 1991).

The World Wide Web is obviously the best-known category of the Internet. The "Web" permits users to find and retrieve information housed in remote computers all over the world, information stored in a computer file that can be read online. The reduction of time and space is one outstanding characteristic of the information age. The Internet can also produce live digitized voices and images to facilitate instantaneous worldwide conferencing, providing a virtual presence anywhere on earth.

Cyberspace is dissimilar from any other medium, with wide-ranging impact on everything from social relationships to how law and government function. In the United States, the judiciary has been called upon to update constitutional principles that were created when no one could have foreseen the complex world of cyberspace—where virtual reality resists even the traditional jurisdiction of law and regulations. The consequences and astonishing speed of the information revolution have driven Congress and judges to keep up with every significant technological innovation. The Internet has tested established law with an array of peculiar problems, including many free-speech and privacy issues.

By confining fighting words to "face-to-face" confrontations, the judiciary exempts hate speech on the Internet because online speech is never actually face-to-face. Expression often emanates from outside the jurisdiction of the United States, but is still widely received by Americans. What is prohibited in other countries may be protected in the United States. For example, a French court ruled that because online displays of Nazi memorabilia messages are illegal in France, Yahoo, Inc., a Delaware-based firm, must also limit such displays in the United States (Magee, 2002). Through the Internet, these forbidden symbols and messages are accessible to computer-equipped French citizens who surf the world of cyberspace. However, on November 7, 2001, a California court ruled that a French court's order restricting Internet speech is unenforceable in the United States. The U.S. District Court (NDCal) issued its order granting motion for summary judgment in support of Yahoo in *Yahoo v. LICRA*. The case, which concerned a French court order limiting speech on Yahoo servers located in the United States, involves constitutional and procedural issues raised by Internet speech. The District Court threw out the French defendants' procedural arguments that the U.S. District court should not address the merits of the motion for summary judgment, and then ruled that the decision by the French court is rendered unenforceable in the United States by the First Amendment.

Privacy and security have been revamped as government—and private entities—attempt to eavesdrop, for both illegitimate and legitimate reasons, such as the U.S. government's war against terrorism and drug trafficking. In response to the terrorist attacks of September 11, the USA Patriot (Uniting and Strengthening America by Providing Appropriate Tools Required to Intercept and Obstruct Terrorism) Act sped through Congress and was signed into law on October 25, 2001, by President George W. Bush. This legislation permits the United States or any state attorney general, without the usual authorization needed from a judge, to install Carnivore, the controversial e-mail "wire-tapping" system, to fight suspected terrorists.

WHITE SUPREMACIST WEB SITES

> *Proclaiming a message of hope and deliverance for White Christian America!*
> —kkk.com (Knights of the Ku Klux Klan Web site, home page, 2003)

The Internet has been and will continue to be a significant mouthpiece for free expression and speech, especially for societies where there are no such liberties. On the Internet, messages are launched, goings-on and events of common interest are publicized, attitudes are disseminated, and conversations are transmitted. Any type of restriction becomes a potential danger to free speech on the Net.

White supremacists and skinheads spread cyberhate on the Net. In April 1995, Don Black unveiled what is generally believed to be the first significant "hate site" on the World Wide Web, representing a departure for right-wing extremism online (Levin, 2003). After Black began Stormfront.org, other extremists rapidly followed with hate sites of their own. The number of hate Web sites is skyrocketing. The Southern Poverty Law Center's Intelligence Project found 762 active hate groups in the United States in 2004 (Southern Poverty Law Center, 2005), including 162 sites for various branches of the Ku Klux Klan, 158 for neo-Nazi organizations, 48 for racist skinhead organizations, 28 for the Christian Identity movement, 108 for black separatist organizations, 97 for neo-Confederacy organizations, and 161 containing other material.

In 2002, the Council of Europe adopted a measure that would criminalize Internet hate speech, including hyperlinks to pages that contain offensive content. The provision, passed by the council's decision-making body (the Committee of Ministers), brought up-to-date the European Convention on Cybercrime. Specifically, the amendment bans any written material, any image, or any other representation of ideas or theories that advocates, promotes, or incites hatred, discrimination, or violence against any individual or group of individuals, based on race, religion, national or ethnic origin. It also indirectly alludes to the Holocaust, outlawing sites that deny, minimize, approve, or justify crimes against humanity, particularly those that occurred during World War II.

The mandate to investigate and prosecute hate speech is important because of the Internet's emergence as the primary international communications network. The Internet provides individuals with contemporary and powerful means to support racism, homophobia, religious intolerance, and xenophobia and enables them to easily and widely disseminate expressions containing such hateful ideas. With most Internet investigation, international cooperation is vital.

Many European countries have existing laws banning Internet racism, which is generally protected as free speech in the United States; 2,500 of 4,000 racist sites were created in the United States. Will these laws help to eliminate hate speech in Europe or merely push hate groups to set up virtual shop in the United States? In 2001, a U.S. judge ruled that Yahoo did not have to block French citizens' access to online sales of Nazi memorabilia, which are illegal in that country. The judge determined that U.S. Web sites are only subject to American law.

This is a culture war. Spain, for example, has decided to censor U.S.-based Web sites for their content. Spanish judges have the authorization to shut down Spanish sites and block access to U.S. Web sites that do not conform to national law. With European laws banning hate speech and prosecuting its messengers, more communication between law enforcement in Europe and the United States about Web site sponsors is likely.

European countries may now be more likely to adopt the Internet hate-speech amendment of the European Council in their governing bodies. Consequently, these countries will also be able to block American Web sites in spite of free speech being guaranteed by our First Amendment.

The separation of free speech from unprotected "fighting words" makes it complicated for the American government to regulate free expression. The federal government could reprimand online speech that clearly incites imminent criminal behavior, expression that the judiciary has never protected.

HAS RACISM DECLINED?

> They're just different. It's kind of bad to say, but I mean they do have
> an odor that's different from white people unless they cover it up with
> a deodorant or cologne or something of that nature. You know, their

*hair is different. It's just that I don't seek interest in these people and
don't think I'm prejudiced because of that.*
                                        —White man discussing Blacks

The quote above most closely fits into Stage 1 (Unintentional Discrimination) since the speaker does not seem to be aware that his comments are offensive. American society continues to be profoundly troubled by racism, much of it unconscious. Long before slavery became the mainstay of the plantation society of the antebellum South, White attitudes of racial superiority left their stamp on the developing culture of colonial America (Higginbotham, 1978). In contemporary society, many citizens experience discriminatory attitudes and practices, which affect our economy; our educational, cultural, and political institutions; and the daily interactions of individuals. The notion that skin color signifies racial or ethnic inferiority and a justification or an excuse for the denial of opportunity and equal treatment is strongly embedded in the psyches of both majority and minority group members.

Racism is thriving in America, affecting residential patterns, educational achievement, health, and quality of life. Racist attitudes are prevalent in the new millennium. The majority of Whites believe Blacks and Latinos are likely to prefer welfare to hard work and tend to be lazier, louder, more pushy and prone to violence, less intelligent, and less patriotic than Whites (Lawrence and Matsuda, 2000). Focus group participants criticize and ridicule Blacks, and frankly express feelings of disgust toward them. While a few challenge the racist stereotypes uttered by others, most concede to group consensus.

One notable case where racist hate speech led to sanctions is Bob Grant. In 1996, Disney/ABC fired Bob Grant for publicly stating his regret that Ron Brown, an African American, then the secretary of commerce during President Clinton's administration, might be the only survivor in a deadly plane crash (he was not). Nevertheless, Grant had a new job within two weeks when another station picked up his program. Moreover, he was not terminated in 1995 for expressing his opinion that the police should have used machine guns to mow down demonstrators at a gay pride rally (see Chapter 5).

The fact that the majority of Whites also believe that minorities have too much power gives the Ku Klux Klan and other neo-Nazi organizations a rather large pool of potential applicants with a shared ideology. Tom Metzger, Director of White Aryan Resistance (WAR) won the Democratic primary in 1980 in the largest congressional district in the United States (openly as a Klansman) and gathered 75,000 votes for U.S. Senator in 1982. Especially disturbing is that young people under age 30 are especially likely to have racist attitudes and feelings (Lawrence and Matsuda, 2000).

The 1990s also saw a significant rise in the number of hate crimes motivated by racial prejudice. Racist hate groups such as the Ku Klux Klan have had an alarming increase in membership. Racial hatred has remained constant or increased in recent years. Blacks and Latinos continue to be discriminated against when seeking housing and applying for mortgages. Residential segregation is still prevalent. The poor are disproportionately Black and Latino, especially single mothers with young children. One-third of America's Blacks live in urban ghettos; Latinos are similarly isolated (Lawrence and Matsuda, 2000).

Fifty years after the Supreme Court outlawed school segregation in *Brown v. Board of Education*, ethnic segregation is still prevalent in schools. Disparities in incarceration and mortality rates between ethnic minorities and Whites symbolize the continuing deleterious effects of racism. Although Whites are more than twice as likely as Blacks to be arrested and charged with a criminal offense, more Blacks than Whites are imprisoned.

Despite the overwhelming evidence that race continues to matter in America, many people continue to believe that our nation has virtually eliminated racism. If it is believed that racism has ended, there is no need for affirmative action. If it is believed that equality has been achieved, the concern shifts from taking responsibility for the perpetuation of White supremacy to discrimination against White males.

The racist slur continues to be one of the most pervasive channels through which discriminatory attitudes are communicated. These types of messages cause harm to the dignity and self-esteem of the target or victim of the message. They continue the myth that distinctions of race are distinctions of merit, self-respect, status, and personhood. Not only does the listener learn and internalize the messages contained in racial insults; these messages also influence society's institutions and are culturally transmitted to succeeding generations.

The psychological harms caused by racial stigmatization are often much more severe than those created by other stereotyping actions (Delgado, 1995b). Race and ethnicity is an ascribed, vis-à-vis achieved, status. That is, the stigma of race is something that cannot be self-induced or overcome; poverty can be eliminated, a junkie can come clean, a drunk can sober up, but skin color is permanent.

WELCOME TO THE KLAN

> We are the oldest, largest, and most professional white rights organization . . . we are the real thing.
>
> The entertainment industry backed by individuals with a Marxist agenda have waged an attack upon the consciousness of white Christians.
>
> —KKK Web site welcome

The Knights of the Ku Klux Klan equates itself with U.S. patriotism and Christianity—and as victims of integrationist mass media and government that is toppling Southern cultural pride and favoring Blacks, Latinos, Jews, and Asians:

> If you are proud of your country and have nationalist feelings than surely you must be a racist or bigot of some sort. Yes, the world has indeed gone crazy when you can't even be proud of your ancestors. In America our flag is still flown with pride. (KKK Web site)

The Klan is media-savvy enough not to directly propagate feelings of hatred or violence toward minorities. Consequently, its public restraint from making statements against minorities discourages litigation from civil rights activists and aims to appeal to less extremist Whites. Instead of overt racism, White pride is supported:

> We do not endorse hatred. It is hypocritical for one to think a black, Asian, Mexican or any other person should be praised for being loyal to their heritage. Yet a white person can feel the same sense of pride and be criticized for it. It doesn't make sense. (KKK Web site)

In terms of the developmental stage model presented in Chapter 1, the Klan Web site is Stage 2, intentional discrimination. The Klan intentionally excludes ethnic minorities, non-Protestants, and gays and lesbians from its membership:

- Membership in The Knights is reserved for white Christians.
- We don't care who is superior and who isn't. God made us all. We simply believe that the United States of America was founded as a white Christian nation. (KKK Web site)

During the turbulent times of Reconstruction, the Ku Klux Klan justified its reign of terror as necessary to control newly freed Black men, whom it labeled as a sexual threat to White women. Many of these ideas found expression in the compelling, insensitive, and significant writings of Thomas Dixon, whose work simultaneously provided income and spread racism. He believed that all Whites were called upon to preserve Anglo-Saxon heritage. Dixon (1905) wrote *The Clansman*, causing a sensation, especially in the South. Ten years later, filmmaker D. W. Griffith used the plots of *Clansman* and *The Leopard's Spots*—another Dixon (1902) novel—for an epic three-hour film, *The Birth of a Nation*.

The film transformed Dixon's novels into vivid visual images, featuring Uncle Toms, mammies, buffoons, an interfering mulatto mistress, and a scene in which a Black man (actually a white actor in "black face" since

Blacks were not yet permitted on the silver screen) with primitive manner-isms chases a young White woman until she jumps to her death from a cliff's edge rather than submit to the lustful predator.

Audiences across the nation viewed this insurgent film. Recent immi-grants from southern and eastern Europe watched *Birth* in movie houses in indigent, densely populated urban neighborhoods, where it played for almost a year. It played in the South for 15 years (Delgado and Stefancic, 1992). President Woodrow Wilson—a former classmate of Dixon—hosted a special screening at the White House for guests, including the Supreme Court. Wilson later characterized the film "like writing history with light-ing." Blacks could not stop the vast attractiveness of *Birth*. The film's mo-mentum was relentless. Liberal film critics blasted the racism, yet praised the film for its path-breaking technical and artistic merits.

The Klan was a key influence in American life in the 1920s. The Klan had resurrected in 1915 and developed into a large national organization with 3 million to 6 million members (Walker, 1994). Besides its traditional power based in the Deep South, the Klan was a major political power in California, Ohio, Oregon, Indiana, and other states. The Klan was big in both rural and urban areas. There were even chapters at Harvard and Princeton.

The Klan was also a violent organization using vigilante violence and lynching as a form of social control. An atmosphere of terror characterized much of the South as well as some northern and midwestern cities. Even supposedly peaceful demonstrations by hooded Klansmen were intended to intimidate victims.

In 1920, the American Civil Liberties Union (ACLU) was established, committing itself to defending free speech, including hateful and offensive speech. In 1921, the NAACP unsuccessfully lobbied the Postmaster Gen-eral to ban KKK propaganda in the mail (Walker, 1994). The NAACP es-tablished its own newspaper and was partially successful in attempting to have *The Birth of a Nation* banned in local communities because of its racist content.

The ACLU opposed this type of censorship, and the conflict between these two civil rights organizations continued intermittently over the years. In the 1940s, however, the NAACP opposed a bill to restrict racist propa-ganda from the mail. This reversal represented a strategy that constitutional litigation to protect individual rights was the most promising avenue for advancing the rights of Blacks (Walker, 1994). This shift by the leading civil rights organization in the United States was a major indicator of the trend in American law and social policy.

By 1990, 16 states and Washington, D.C., had passed laws outlawing Klan members' parading in masks. The anti-mask laws bring up a recur-ring phenomenon throughout the history of the hate speech: the disregard for laws banning expressions of hatred and bigotry. There seems to have been little use of these laws in the nearly 80 years they have been codified. One survey (*Washington Law Review*, 1991) found only 12 reported cases. This raises the question whether, entirely separate from concerns of constitutionality, hate-speech laws have any useful effect as a deterrent.

The contemporary Klan aspires to be a dominant political party and claims to be nonviolent. Violent Klansmen are portrayed as renegades:

> Unfortunately, there are some small Klan groups who play right into their hands. . . . Maybe they lost a job due to affirmative action or were victimized in some other way. They will then grow hateful. Without really learning any thing about the true Ku Klux Klan, they proceed on their own, start a little Klan group and then vent their rage by saying the most idiotic things on TV talk shows. This gives the true believers a bad name and they in no way whatsoever represent the thousands of good men and women of The Knights.
>
> Q. Why do you kill black people?
>
> We don't kill black people. This is another misconception about the Klan. What is true is that there have been men in the past who joined the Klan in order to benefit from the wearing of the robe and hood—to be able to commit a crime against some one they did not like. This was not the objective of the Klan, but only the prerogative of some misfits in the 60's. (KKK Web site)

In the Freedom Summer of 1964, the local Ku Klux Klan near the town of Philadelphia, Mississippi, murdered two White and one Black voter registration volunteers (Magee, 2002). All three were members of the Student Non-violent Coordinating Committee (SNCC).

NATIONAL ALLIANCE AND OTHER VIOLENT RESISTANCE WEB SITES

> *Stormfront is a resource for those courageous men and women fighting to preserve their White Western culture, ideals and freedom of speech and association—a forum for planning strategies and forming political and social groups to ensure victory.*
>
> —stormfront.org (National Alliance Web site, 2001)

In 1995, the nation's largest neo-Nazi organization, National Alliance, emerged in cyberspace. The group's leader, William Pierce, published *The Turner Diaries* under the pseudonym Andrew Macdonald. The book is a puffed-up, fictional account of an antigovernment race war by a band of White supremacists who commit atrocities against government officials, Jews, intellectuals, and Blacks. After Pierce declared the novel a "handbook for White victory," neo-Nazi skinheads adopted it as a battle cry.

A group of neo-Nazis, including National Alliance and Aryan Nations members from the American Northwest, organized the terrorist group the Order, named for the fictional criminal group featured in *The Turner Di-*

aries (Macdonald, 1978). National Alliance's Pacific Northwest division declared war against American government and society. The rebels' activities culminated in the largest armored car heist in American history and the assassination of a prominent Jewish radio personality, Alan Berg, in 1984 (Levin, 2003). After the robbery, Pierce paid $95,000 in cash for 346 acres of land in rural West Virginia as the new site for the National Alliance's headquarters (Southern Poverty Law Center, 1999: 15).

Pierce followed *The Turner Diaries* with another racist novel, *Hunter* (Macdonald, 1989). The book was dedicated to a violent racist, Paul Franklin, who murdered two innocent Black joggers in Salt Lake City (Levin, 2003). Pierce received further notoriety when media reported that Oklahoma City bomber Timothy McVeigh was enamored with *The Turner Diaries* and had made telephone calls to the National Alliance in the period prior to the bombing. The book glorifies an antigovernment terrorist who blows up a federal building in an early morning bomb detonation. This qualifies as Stage 4 (Inciting Discriminatory Violence) since it demonstrates how to be violent and encourages violence against minorities.

Pierce (1994) has promoted White revolution against government, Jews, Blacks, and other minorities. Besides the Web site, the National Alliance promotes its ideology through magazines, newsletters, leaflets, radio broadcasts, comic books (targeted at youth), and hate-rock compact discs.

Although national hate groups were among the first extremists to use the Internet, there are now many others that target America for propaganda or attack. Hate groups also use the Internet to access private message boards, e-mail, research, hacking, hidden instructions, listservs (closed e-mail networks), and chat rooms where conversations occur in actual time.

Leftist environmental and animal-liberation extremists have dozens of Web sites that provide information on legal activism, news, and disfavored institutions, as well as downloadable sabotage manuals—accompanied by carefully worded disclaimers. While their philosophies are different from those of online bigots, their use of the Web as a tool for propaganda and violent leaderless resistance is noticeably similar.

A radical anti-abortion Web site, the Nuremberg Files, which has been on the Internet intermittently during the past several years, proposed future Nuremberg-style trials for abortion providers. The organization posts a list of doctors who perform abortions, with slash marks through the names of those who have been murdered (Christian Gallery, 2001; *Planned Parenthood v. American Coalition of Life Activists*, 2001). The site has provided extensive personal information about them that included driver's license information, social security numbers, home addresses, vehicles, and their travel information. Clearly, this information could assist and encourage identity fraud, expressions of hate, or ambushes for assault or even murder.

In November 2001, an Internet-savvy armed fugitive on the FBI's 10

Most Wanted list, Clayton Waagner, allegedly went to the home of the publisher of the Nuremberg Files site, Neal Horsely. Waagner was allegedly staking out abortion clinics when he was previously arrested. Waagner talked about the Nuremberg Files Web site when he was captured. Moreover, he confessed to authorities that he used a variety of e-mail accounts to conceal confidential information. Waagner's goal was to force Horsley to use his Web site to post proof that 42 abortion clinic employees—whom Waagner had targeted for attack—had quit their jobs in order to be removed from his hit list (Roddy, 2001b). Upon his arrest in December 2001, it was documented that Waagner had posted threats to abortion clinic workers on the Internet and supervised the Web site with a laptop and computers at Kinko's copy stores (Roddy, 2001a).

THE FIRST AMENDMENT

> *In an open democratic society the streets, the parks, and other public places are an important facility for public discussion and the political process.*
>
> —W. Cohen and D. Danelski, 1997: 375

The use of the Internet by individuals and groups to disseminate controversial and hateful messages has reignited debate on the status of the First Amendment. Over the past century, the Supreme Court has established new standards relating to the protection of expressive rights from governmental interference, and these rulings have a direct impact on Internet expression. Specifically, the Court has identified various conditions in which the government has greater leeway to intervene with or punish expression. These include:

- The time, place, or manner (vis-à-vis the content) of the expression in the context of a particular setting;
- Whether the expression's character falls into an area of speech the Court has labeled "unprotected" (see below);
- Whether the expression constitutes behavior traditionally regarded as criminal;
- Whether there is a compelling governmental interest in restricting the message.

The legal classification of the medium on the Internet is the major issue regarding the government's capacity to regulate free speech or expression. The Supreme Court addressed the legal status of the Internet and the regulation of controversial content on it in *Reno et al. v. American Civil Liberties Union et al.* (1997). This decision nullified two parts of the Communications Decency Act of 1996 that restricted the display of sexually oriented material. In relevant parts, the act punished the intentional communication to minors of "obscene or indecent" messages. It also banned the intentional communication of messages to minors or the display of messages that could be viewed by minors. The prohibited messages related to material that was "patently offensive as measured by contemporary community standards, sexual or excretory activities or organs" (223 [d]).

The judgment was significant for two reasons. First, the Supreme Court gave extensive First Amendment protection to Internet-based communications, rejecting government assertions that they should be restricted in the same manner as radio and television frequencies. The Court also set aside the idea that the government can ban communications between adults on the grounds that minors might receive messages for which they are unfit. In conclusion, the ruling represents an important conceptual and legal distinction between the Internet and television or radio.

On the Internet, there are unrestricted numbers of outlets, there is no precedent of governmental restrictions, and the recipient of a message actively searches for it with some notion of its substance. The government can restrict speech from the Internet only when it is necessary to develop an important governmental interest (i.e., equal protection under the law, freedom from discrimination) and is narrowly modified to attain that objective.

In *Reno v. ACLU* (1997), the Supreme Court ruled that the Internet is basically a public forum—a place, albeit open-ended—where speech is most protected from governmental regulation. After this ruling, the government's strategy was to focus on more narrow issues on the Internet. For example, in the Child Online Protection Act (COPA) (47 U.S.C., 23), restrictions apply only to commercial Web sites. COPA makes it a criminal offense to provide material that is "harmful to minors" and defines such as "patently offensive" material involving lewd nudity or sexuality.

The Internet is home to wide-ranging fields of subject matter. Governmental regulations based simply on the content of the thought expressed will typically be upturned. If the expression falls under an "unprotected" area of speech, the government has far greater power to regulate or outlaw it. When speech falls into a category that is unprotected, it can be prohibited outright as long as the government can demonstrate a sound parallel between the regulation and a legitimate governmental purpose. Unprotected areas of speech include fraudulent commercial speech, obscenity, and incitement to criminality. Defamation is largely protected, albeit in varying degrees, depending on whether the allegedly defamed person is a public or a private figure (*New York Times v. Sullivan*, 1964; *Gertz v. Robert Welch, Inc.*, 1974). Technically, another unprotected category called "fighting words" exists but is considered by many to be dormant because for five decades the Court has refused to invoke the category in upholding a speech restriction.

Controversial content that causes anger, disgust, or offense in many viewers has a home on the Internet. A series of Supreme Court decisions has set forth standards relating to the government's capacity to regulate controversial content. In 1942, the Supreme Court created the unprotected category of fighting words and defined them as those words that by their very expression would arouse a violent response from the receiver of the message (*Chaplinsky v. State of New Hampshire*, 1942). Although theoretically, extremely offensive speech could be banned as fighting words, the Supreme Court has failed to identify any fighting words fit for governmental prohibition for over five decades and has consistently held that the mere offensiveness of speech is not a basis for restricting it. This policy seems to weaken the purpose of the fighting words exemption in the first place.

In *Texas v. Johnson* (1989), the Supreme Court ruled that the Constitution protects even the most unpopular and offensive kind of speech in a case involving flag-burning. While protesting outside city hall near the site of the 1984 Republican National Convention in Dallas, Gregory Johnson set fire to an American flag. Johnson was arrested and convicted for desecrating a "venerated object." Included under the Texas law: "a state or national flag." The statute states that desecration means to "deface, damage, or otherwise physically mistreat [it] in a way that the actor knows will seriously offend one or more persons likely to observe or discover his action." During the trial, several prosecution witnesses testified that they had indeed been "seriously offended" by the flag-burning (*Texas v. Johnson*, 1989: 400).

On appeal from the Texas state courts, the Supreme Court ruled that the law was unconstitutionally applied to Johnson. The Court stated that offensiveness was protected speech, unlike the unprotected categories of incitement to criminality or fighting words. The court affirmed that government may not "ban the expression of certain disagreeable ideas on the unsupported presumption that their very disagreeableness will provoke violence" (409). Justice William Brennan, speaking for the five-person majority, stated, "If there is a bedrock principle underlying the First Amendment, it is that the government may not prohibit the expression of an idea simply because society finds the idea itself offensive or disagreeable" (414). However, there is an important distinction between dissent of popular political opinion and bigoted expressions of hate that injure minority group members.

In light of *Texas v. Johnson* and other cases, the unprotected speech category of fighting words no longer exists in practice. It does exist, technically, because the category has never been officially and explicitly overruled by any Supreme Court decision. In practical terms, however, conceptual support for the fighting words category has been undercut to the point at which current controlling case law is in direct conflict. That is probably why the Supreme Court has failed to identify and punish the expression of fighting words. The *Texas v. Johnson* case was a waymark for free-speech analyses on the Internet. It represents the notion that the government cannot single out the nonviolent expression of even the most offensive and disturbing thoughts.

HATE SPEECH AND GENOCIDE IN RWANDA

On November 22, 1992, before a large crowd in the prefecture of Gisenyi, a Rwandan leader named Léon Mugesera delivered a notorious hate speech that would result in the murders of approximately a million people (Eliadis, 2003). Rambling—at times even incoherent—Mugesera urged his audience to prepare for a rapidly arriving war. He called the people of the rival faction *Inyenzis* (cockroaches) and essentially said that attacking them is really self-defense.

The *cockroaches* were expatriate Rwandan rebels known as the Rwandan Patriotic Front. They were supported by neighboring Uganda, comprised largely from the Tutsi minority tribe, and had been competing for power since 1990. Mugesera then aimed his hateful speech at the Tutsi civilians who might support the rebels:

> Those are the people who pushed us into allowing ourselves to be invaded. . . . Why do [our leaders] not arrest these parents who have sent away their children and why do they not exterminate them? Why do they not arrest the people taking them away and why do they not exterminate all of them? Are we really waiting till they come to exterminate us? . . . Do not be afraid, know that anyone whose neck you do not cut is the one who will cut your neck. Let me tell you, these people should begin leaving while there is still time and go and live with their people, or even go to the *Inyenzis*, instead of living among us and keeping their guns, so that when we are asleep they can shoot us.

Mugesera and his family had already fled the country by the time police tried to arrest him three days later. Regrettably, his incendiary message did not leave with him. In 100 days starting in April 1994, between 800,000 and a million people were hacked, shot, and burned to death (Eliadis, 2003). The majority of the victims were unarmed men, women, and children of the Tutsi ethnic group. They were killed because they were Tutsi, in an ethnic cleansing of inconceivable violence and cruelty.

When the international community began to hear reports about the atrocities, it did not stop what has been called the fastest genocide of the twentieth century. In the aftermath of the human disaster and political embarrassment in Somalia in 1993, Americans and other members of the U.N. Security Council vigorously opposed official use of the term "genocide" for fear of appealing to a moral as well as legal obligation to intervene. The U.S. administration had trouble even locating Rwanda on a world map and confused the names of the two warring tribes (Eliadis, 2003).

Mugesera became a permanent resident of Canada on August 12, 1993. Survivors of the genocide have sought his deportation on the grounds that his 1992 speech incited murder and hatred and was a crime against humanity. Apparently, Mugesera's hate speech left Rwanda in a killing frenzy; it stirred up ethnic divisions. This type of hate speech represents Stage 4, the highest level in my model of severity of hate speech (see Chapter 1) because it encouraged and justified genocide against the Tutsi people.

In Canada, individuals can be deported if they commit criminal offenses before or after obtaining permanent residence—but hate speech in another country and in another language is nebulous. After seven years of hearings, the Federal Court of Appeal unanimously refused to hear the case against Mugesera, who continues to live freely in Canada. The role his words played in the genocide is now at the center of the issue.

Jean-Paul Nyilinkwaya, who lost virtually his entire family, was enrolled at Eastern Michigan University in 1994 when the genocide broke out. After anxious calls to home, he discovered that his family's house had been burned to the ground and the Rwandan military had shot everyone inside. Approximately 30 family members had been slaughtered. His father died in his sister's arms. His mother was left for dead; she survived, but is partially paralyzed. Jean-Paul abandoned his studies soon after the killings and moved to Montreal. A father of two, he is struggling to rebuild his life, seeking peace and justice.

He and his Tutsi community have hit upon neither as yet. Mugesera's lawyer, Guy Bertrand, successfully argued the case against the Minister for Citizenship and Immigration. The case hinged on four key issues: first, whether the extreme and violent words used in the speech were justified as self-defense; second, whether there is such a crime as hate speech; third, whether the speech should be assessed in light of the subsequent genocide in 1994; and fourth, whether the right of free speech protected Mugesera's words. The Minister lost on each point.

The Court of Appeal gave shrift to evidence of racist labels and threats of violence. Prior to the mass murders, there was a carefully orchestrated plan to demonize, dehumanize, and destroy an entire population. Tutsi were regularly labeled "cockroaches" and under attack as "vermin." The Court of Appeal, however, concluded that Mugesera's speech is not hate speech because technically it refers mainly to insects (i.e., cockroaches) rather than people (i.e., Tutsi). Yet, in its cultural context, *inyenzi* is synonymous with *Tutsi*. The Court of Appeal's decision in essence excuses the genocide.

Clearly, the Clinton administration and the international community were unwilling to intervene in the ethnic slaughter in Rwanda. America remained passive in the face of some of history's worse crimes. Rwanda represents the human costs of indifference and passivity.

In April 1994, a program of massacres began in Rwanda that ended up claiming the lives of 800,000 in a hundred days, 333⅓ murdered every hour, and 5½ lives every minute as this occurred. People were murdered at a rate that exceeded by three times the speed of the extermination of Jews during the Holocaust (Gourevitch, 1998). It happened in our time, in front of our noses, somewhat before our cameras, and it vanished very quickly. As soon as the blood was dry the story disappeared from the newspapers.

Media explanations of the bloodshed were not coherent or convincing. The cause of the problem was mislabeled as anarchy and chaos. This account was improbable plainly because to be able to murder at that high rate requires organization, method, and mobilization. That is just the opposite of anarchy and chaos. Genocide is neither random nor accidental. The media simply reported the story incorrectly and carelessly—perhaps even with a bit of arrogance. A great tragedy occurred and Americans seemed fairly content to be badly informed.

It is ironic that the genocide in Rwanda occurred at a time in our history when the Holocaust was in the public consciousness—not long after the opening of the Holocaust Museum in Washington, DC, and the premier of *Schindler's List*. The rhetoric for the Holocaust commemoration was powerful and pervasive: vigorous opposition to hate speech and intolerance guaranties that genocide would never happen again. The Holocaust Museum was dedicated in 1993 with this notion that it somehow had a preventative function. Denouncing evil makes everyone feel righteous, but that does not even come close to being righteous.

It was not difficult to take the right position on the Holocaust in 1993. There had been 50 years of moral uncertainty. Evidently, it was much more difficult to know how to respond to what was happening before us. By convincing our collective conscience that it could not happen again, we were ignoring it as it took place right in front of us.

Following Mugesera's hateful and inciting words and the militia's leadership, Hutus—young, middle-aged, and old—quickly took up the grisly mission. They began organizing and killing. Neighbors hacked neighbors to death in their own houses. Colleagues hacked colleagues to death in their workspace. Doctors killed their patients. Teachers killed their students. Within only a few days, the Tutsi populations of many villages were virtually eliminated. In Kigali, prisoners were temporarily released from prison in work gangs to collect the corpses that lined the roadsides.

Opposing Hate Speech and Genocide in Rwanda

There was some resistance to the Rwandan hate speech and genocide. A radio announcer had decided not to participate in the genocidal radio rhetoric; he thereby made himself an enemy of the regime. The announcer had found shelter at the Hotel des Mille Collines during the genocide. Many people who were scheduled to be killed ended up at this hotel—this sanctuary. At that time, Hotel des Mille Collines was the only first-class hotel in Kigali, Rwanda's capital. In a third-world nation stricken with poverty, the Hotel des Mille Collines charges about twice as much as the annual average per capita income—$80—in Rwanda. It cost approximately $150 a night.

Nearly a thousand people who had been running for their lives found refuge at the hotel. Many Tutsis as well as Hutus who were persecuted by the regime also sought refuge at the Sainte Famille Church down the street. But the fate they met was not fortunate. Father Wenceslas, from the parish, betrayed their trust and handed them over to the militia. The militia were allowed in the church, resulting in genocide victims being taken away little by little. The same phenomenon happened in schools.

But the hotel was different. Paul Rusesabagina, a Hutu, and newly appointed acting manager of the Hotel des Mille Collines, responded to events humanely and rescued some people. He worked for Sabena, a large corporation that owned the Belgian national airlines and a hotel chain. He had worked for them for most of his career. He was the first Rwandan to attain the rank of director general of a hotel and was a sophisticated businessman. Paul was actually working at another hotel, but during the turmoil he was recruited as manager when the foreign manager—presumably a refugee—left the country.

Rusesabagina used the cards he was dealt to save lives. He used his influence through the hotel's extensive liquor closet and basement wine cellar. His successful strategy was to bring in the enemy, loosen them up with alcohol, and persuade them to overlook some of those on the death list. Would you like a little drink? Why don't we talk? Why don't you leave these people alone? Instead of trying to shut them out, he brought in the generals and heads of the militia.

Rusesabagina had a secret phone line that he and his noticeably prominent guests used to call the White House, the French foreign ministry, the King of Belgium, and Sabena national headquarters in Brussels (Gourevitch, 1998). This outlet was very helpful because it continuously drew attention to the plight of this particular pocket of refugees. Father Wenceslas, the priest down the street, also had a phone line but never used it. Instead he enthusiastically embraced the genocide as he cooperated with the militia.

Rusesabagina had assumed that many people all across Rwanda were behaving as he was, because it was the only rational and humane behavior. He does not even want to be thought of as a hero because the only standard by which he was exceptional was in comparison with the terrible actions of murderers. He did not believe that he was extraordinary merely for not becoming a murderer. After all, it was they who were extraordinary for their murderous behavior. Rusesabagina clearly saw right from wrong in his everyday life and simply began to confront what was happening.

It was the conventional people who had crossed the line and cooperated with the genocidal order without much resistance. What does this say about the "moral progress" in the world since the Holocaust? Some Holocaust Museum visitors empathize with Jewish victims and feel bad about themselves or sorry for themselves; others relate to the liberators (Gourevitch, 1998). During the Holocaust, a sizable portion of people in Europe were either bystanders, collaborators, or in some other way in morally reprehensible positions.

Virtually none of the Holocaust Museum visitors would admit to supporting or participating in genocide. Yet the world stood by as the most rapid genocide in the twentieth century occurred. Even though touring the museum may leave the visitor feeling that this could not happen again, the Rwandan genocide flies in the face of that fantasy.

The killings began during the night of April 6, 1994, continuing through the next morning. Very quickly it became clear to Tutsis across the country that Armageddon had come; each was slated for murder—as were the Hutus who opposed the genocide. Throughout the country the Tutsi sought refuge in places that they thought would be sanctuaries—civic buildings, stadiums, schools, hospitals, and especially, churches.

Traditionally, churches have been sacred ground—a sanctuary. When there had been political violence in Rwanda in the past, places of worship had been respected. Instead, during the genocide, churches became the largest slaughterhouses, because the killers did not defer to any sanctuary.

Mugonero is a town in the province of Kibuye in Western Rwanda. Although Rwanda is predominantly (65–70 percent) Catholic, this area had been evangelized by Seventh Day Adventists and was the site of an Adventist campus headquarters (Gourevitch, 1998). People began arriving in Mugonero from around the country. Approximately 2,000 Tutsis came to Mugonero in the first 10 days to two weeks of the genocide.

Seven Tutsi pastors were among the church refugees. As time went by, conditions became increasingly bleak inside. As the moral and community authority, the priests assumed the role of leaders of the flock. On April 15, when a message arrived that there would be a massacre the next day, the leaders of the flock wrote a letter to the church president.

The church president was a Hutu named Elizaphan Ntakirutimana, who was in his late sixties at the time. He was the authority figure in the town and had been directing people to go to the church. So they wrote to him, begging him to intercede on their behalf. But instead of helping, Ntakirutimana ended up supervising the massacre. He was typical of Rwandan authority figures. They believed in the prevailing political order. There was a close alliance between leaders of the military, state, and church. There was a prevalent belief in ethnic cleansing.

He is under indictment from the U.N. Tribunal for Rwanda. He did find refuge in Laredo, Texas, and then managed to get former U.S. Attorney General Ramsey Clark, who likes to defend political criminals, to defend him, claiming that the U.N. Tribunal was not legitimate. Finally, the Supreme Court authorized his extradition and criminal trial in Rwanda.

In Nazi Germany and late-twentieth-century Rwanda, people did not participate in genocide as if it were a terrible crime. Instead, ethnic cleansing became normative through hate speech. It is not disorder, but rather a perverted type of social order. It is a strange attempt at utopia. Genocidal extremists believed that ethnic cleansing and elimination would result in purification and harmony. It is merely an exercise in community building. If everyone in a particular society is caught up in genocide, being implicated is void. An ideology of ethnic superiority had become institutional, permeating the mind-set of Rwandans during 35 years of Hutu dictatorship. The hateful speech and genocide attitude had been simmering over generations.

Poverty was not the major cause of the genocide in Rwanda. It was a mechanism of genocidal logic in Rwandan life. A small elite class that seized control of the state designed the genocide through hate speech and fear. The Rwandan population, uneducated, economically disadvantaged, fearful, impoverished, ignorant, was ripe for manipulation. Still, why was there virtually no moral resistance to slaughtering one's neighbor? Most of the killing was done between people who knew or were at least acquainted with each other. It was not anonymous slaughter.

The genocide in Rwanda varied in another significant way from the Holocaust. The Industrial Revolution and the Enlightenment were blamed for providing the infrastructure that made the Holocaust possible. After all, science and technology had made possible the sanitary extermination of massive numbers of people. Under the pretense of taking showers, Holocaust victims were manipulated into a gas chamber. Pellets discharging poisonous gas were dropped from ventilation ducts in the ceiling. No guns. No knives. Not even guilt from face-to-face contact with victims. Bodies burned to ashes. It was virtually an assembly line between the ghettos and the camps. The Holocaust exposed the irrationality of rationality (Bauman, 1989; Ritzer, 2000) and was based on the principles of efficiency, calculability, predictability, and control—the same principles that are coming to dominate more and more sectors of American society as well as the rest of the world.

Rwanda demonstrated that technological underdevelopment was no barrier to genocide. The killings were generally done by hand with machetes and knives. Moreover, the murderers generally knew their victims. It is cynical yet correct to recognize that the same mechanisms that shape people toward agreement can also be used to drive a society to genocide.

Rwandan Media Tribunal

For publishing and broadcasting hate speech and images that produced and promoted ethnic atrocities, three Rwandan media leaders were found guilty of genocide, incitement to genocide, and crimes against humanity (extermination and persecution) in April 2004, by Trial Chamber I of the International Criminal Tribunal for Rwanda (ICTR) (Mackinnon and Caron, 2004). *Kangura* and Radio-Television Libre des Milles Collines (RTLM) were found to be media puppets for the Coalition pour la Defense de la Republique's (CDR) Hutu power combination of politics and ethnicity, civilians and combatants.

Continuous media drumming led to a self-identification of the Hutu tribal members based on ethnic superiority and contempt for the Tutsi. Moreover, the Rwandan Patriotic Front, a largely Tutsi military force, was equated with the Tutsi people as such, essentially defining the enemy as the entire Tutsi tribe. *Kangura* provoked fear with hate speech, whipping the Hutu population into a killing rage and paving the route to genocide in Rwanda. The newspaper used a multipronged attack, publishing hit lists, death warrants, ethnically condescending and misogynist cartoons, and inflammatory editorials and letters.

The requisite element of discriminatory intent was verified in the hate speech used by RTLM, *Kangura*, and CDR. Some of the hate speech was misogynist, aimed at persecuting Tutsi women by characterizing them so as to articulate a predatory framework that made the sexual attack on them imminent.

This case is notable and relevant to my model of hate-speech severity since the conviction was based on hate speech (in particular, Stage 4: Inciting Discriminatory Violence). The courts held a newspaper editor and a broadcast executive criminally accountable not only for the crime of what they said, but for the crimes their words *did*: the genocidal acts that resulted from what they said, or were responsible for saying, to their pubic audiences.

The case charged violations of international humanitarian law in the context of the ethnic genocide in Rwanda in 1994, in which approximately 800,000 members of the Tutsi ethnic group and their supporters, most of them civilians, were slaughtered within three months. The first defendant was Ferdinand Nahimana, an academic who founded and was the major player in RTLM. The second accused was Hassan Ngeze, the founder, owner, and editor-in-chief of the newspaper *Kangura*. Both of these men were sentenced to life in prison. The third and final defendant, Jean-Bosco Barayagwiza, a lawyer by training, RTLM executive, and leader in the political party Coalition pour la Defense de la Republique (CDR), was sentenced to 35 years, reduced from life because his procedural rights had been violated.

Close examination of facts presented at the nearly three-year-long trial with over 100 witnesses takes up most of the Tribunal's more than 350-page report known as *The Media Case*. *Kangura* and RTLM were called a common media front and partners in a Hutu coalition, of which CDR was also a part. The goal of the alliance was to mobilize the historically subordinated Hutu majority population against the historically dominant Tutsi ethnic minority.

The seditious newspaper, *Kangura*, was widely circulated and even more widely talked about in this poor African nation where only 30 percent of the population is literate. The Tribunal found that *Kangura* described the Tutsi people as hypocrites, thieves, and killers marked by malice and dishonesty. The Tutsi were declared essentially evil and symbolized by a snake or cockroach. Portraying Tutsi men as criminal and dangerous is characteristic of the predator stereotype of Chicano and African American men (see Cortese, 2004).

On the other hand, editorials portrayed the Hutu as generous and naïve. The Tutsi were portrayed as devious and aggressive. *Kangura* suggested that Tutsi women intentionally used their sexuality to lure Hutu men into sex in order to promote the ethnic dominance of the Tutsi over the Hutu. Political cartoons, especially, sexualized the underlying political message that Tutsi women involved with Hutu men were untrustworthy spies.

Kangura also demonized individual members of the Tutsi tribe. When this occurred, they would often lose their jobs or sometimes even their lives. This was a significant point in deliberations for the Tribunal. In general, the newspaper's message of hatred, prejudice, and fear cleared the way for massacring the Tutsi ethnic group. For example, the published statement that an imminent attack by Tutsi militants would trigger the slaughter of innocent Tutsi was found to be a threat, particularly in light of the strong, violent language used in conveying the message. The hate speech of *Kangura* poisoned the minds of the Hutu readers. The newspaper often called for direct action against the Tutsi minority.

In Rwanda, radio is truly a mass medium. Its access is pervasive. In the context of Tutsi privilege and Hutu disadvantage, RTLM broadcasts exploited the fear of armed attack to mobilize the population, thus creating a frenzied atmosphere of fear, hatred, and violence against the Tutsi and their Hutu supporters. RTLM broadcasts stereotyped Tutsi as the enemy, promoted contempt and hatred for them, and called on listeners to attack them. Youth wing and other Hutu militia at roadblocks paid attention to RTLM and, in fact, acted on the information it broadcast.

RTLM actively encouraged the Hutu people to kill, relentlessly driving the message that the Tutsi were the enemy and had to be permanently eliminated. RTLM intentionally ignited hatred in the Hutu, consequently establishing a very hostile atmosphere. RTLM was found to have initiated and ordered attacks on individuals, who were hunted down and killed according to its instructions. The Tribunal often found that the victims' deaths were causally linked to the broadcast of their names.

The RTLM was called "Radio Machete" and engaged in ethnic stereotyping that promoted contempt and hatred for the Tutsi. The station then called on listeners to seek out and take up arms against the "enemy"—labeled as the Tutsi population. Both *Kangura* and RTLM persistently targeted the Tutsi population for destruction with hate speech that demonized the Tutsi as having inherently evil qualities, equating the ethnic group with "the enemy." Describinging Tutsi women as seductive enemy agents is consistent with America's advertising images of Chicanas and African American women as sexual predators (Cortese, 2004).

Rwandan media also called for the extermination of the Tutsi by playing up the political threat that they associated with Tutsi ethnicity. The hate speech from the media helped to develop and maintain a Hutu mind-set in which ethnic hatred was conventional political ideology. The Tribunal evaluated what the defendants personally said and did, what they encouraged others to say and do, and what others whom they controlled said and did. From these findings, the Tribunal judged the newspaper editorials and radio broadcasts to be genocidal and to constitute conclusive evidence of defendants' intent to systematically kill all Tutsi.

The Tribunal acknowledged that murder through mass media necessitates a separate adjoining cause. That is, for communication, both a messenger and receiver are necessary. Likewise, for every role, there is a complementary role—in this case, leaders and followers. The Tribunal concluded that just because the media moguls may not have actually taken part in the actual slaughters, it not diminish the responsibility the media, or the criminal accountability of those responsible for the communication.

Hate speech, regardless of its source—television, radio, or newspaper—was essentially the bullets in the gun that triggered the genocide. The trigger had such a lethal effect since the gun was loaded. Hate speech inciting ethnic cleansing was the ammunition that was clearly and efficiently disseminated through RTLM, *Kangura*, and CDR. Hate speech encouraging—in fact, demanding—violence against the Tutsi (Stage 4) was the act that instigated the killing of Tutsi civilians. The Tribunal found the three defendants unequivocally guilty of genocide.

Tactless references to the physical and personal traits of Tutsi ethnicity and constant stereotypical descriptions of the Tutsi as evil were pervasive in *Kangura* and the writings and oral statements of Negeze. This, in addition to his commands to attack Tutsi civilians, provided convincing evidence of Ngeze's genocidal intent. Nahimana, the leader of RTLM, used hate speech in newspapers and radio stations to bring about the slaughter of Tutsi civilians.

The media-based hate speech was successfully designed to exterminate the Tutsi. At public meetings, Barayagwiza, in fact, often articulated statements about exterminating the Tutsi. The Tribunal found Barayagwiza guilty of genocide based on CDR members' killing of Tutsi civilians according to his orders, for failing to stop them, and for the ultimate responsibility for RTLM broadcasts of hate speech resulting in ethnic cleansing.

The Tribunal separately convicted the defendants for direct and public incitement to commit genocide. Ngeze used *Kangura* to inspire hatred, encourage fear, and stir up genocide. Barayagwiza, the leader of CDR, used hate speech heavily sprinkled with genocidal ideology and neglected to stop his assistants from pushing for extermination. Nahimana and Barayagwiza basically urged the mass murder of the Tutsi through indoctrination that the extraordinary power of radio, which used the influence of the human voice to add an indescribable quality and dimension to the message conveyed. The media fundamentally poisoned the minds of the public.

Nahimana, without a gun, machete, or any physical weapon caused the deaths of thousands of innocent victims. There also had been an alliance between the three media voices; Barayagwiza was recognized as the leader among them. The trio conspired to commit genocide by organizing the numerous links among them as well as the institutions they commanded. The shared purpose and the common objective of the cartel was the destruction of the Tutsi people.

The Tribunal defined hate speech as a discriminatory form of aggression that destroys the dignity of those in the group under attack. It creates a lesser status not only in the eyes of the group members themselves but also in the eyes of others who perceive and treat them as less than human. Building on a Nuremberg precedent, persecution was seen to include "conditioning" a population, and the establishment of persecution was not seen as a provocation to cause harm: it is in *itself* the harm. Consequently, the tribunal also convicted the three men of persecution on political grounds of an ethnic character—a crime against humanity.

This settlement is the first since Nuremberg to expose the responsibility of the media under international criminal justice principles. Since that time, on those rare occasions where media were held legally accountable for hate speech, it has virtually always been under laws regulating certain types of words and pictures, focusing more on the content of the hate speech than its consequences. In this case, the international Tribunal is significant for holding a newspaper editor and a broadcast executive criminally accountable not only for the crime of hate speech, but for the genocidal crimes that resulted from them. In other words, successful incitement to genocide is genocide.

The spreaders and entrepreneurs of ethnic cleansing, subversive journalism, and hate speech radio were found guilty of using hate speech as a deadly weapon—just as guilty as if they had personally hacked innocent civilians with machetes. The judgment holds them responsible for the hate-speech crimes of incitement to genocide that resulted from their targeting victims, conditioning victimizers, and ethnically polluting Rwandan society. In particular, the defendants incited others to persecute Tutsi and commit genocide.

Nevertheless, the greatest implication of the case for hate-speech policy and law is the decision that media committed genocide by prompting it. Consequently, media leaders were held accountable and successfully prosecuted. The Tribunal was forced to make a delicate distinction between the development of ethnic pride and the production of ethnic hatred—speech that results from the stereotyping *and* denigration of a particular ethnic background.

The Tribunal had to sensitively distinguish between protected speech and discrimination. Ethnic stereotyping occupies a precarious and contested area somewhere in the middle. For example, much of the indicted material was judged to be legally protected speech. Examples include historical information, political analysis, and the advocacy of ethnic consciousness.

The Tribunal's theories, methodology, and procedures are likely to become models for hate-speech and hate crime policy, laws, and court proceedings. For example, the Tribunal used conventional judicial techniques to evaluate the content of written and oral communication, carefully considering what was said as well as basics like the positioning and composition of visual images. For example, the machete on the cover of *Kangura* (Number 26) was found to answer the question there: "What weapons shall we use to conquer the *Inyenzi* once and for all?"

The Tribunal also used contextual interpretation in order to discern code and innuendo. Trustworthiness calculations affected the credence of a defendant's offered explanation. For example, Nahimana and Ngeze attempted to dissociate themselves from their hate speech, but did not try to create such crucial distance at the time the words were spoken. The intent and consequences of the materials were gauged within a particular context. Ultimately, the Tribunal determined the fundamental impact of the hate speech on the violence it produced. The perceptions of causal associations by simultaneous witnesses, participants, and observers were particularly influential.

The Tribunal did not try to force the sometimes complex relationship between expression and action into a single formulation. Rather, it utilized the facts of the case and acknowledged the numerous dynamic relations between hate speech and hate crime that a complex social disaster like a genocide expectably generates. Sometimes there was a "call to action" against "dangerous" people. Other times individuals were named or listed and later murdered. In some instances, there was not enough evidence to show a clear link between the words and the killings. In others cases, there was sufficient evidence that media-motivated listeners acted violently.

Killing sprees were often found to have been triggered by false forecasts of imminent attacks on the Hutu by the Rwandan Patriotic Front, a largely Tutsi military force. The media voice pieces used hate speech to ignite aggression, violence, and even murder under the guise of self-defense. The media disseminated hatred and violence. The dangerous writings of *Kangura* and incendiary broadcasts of RTLM functioned to brainwash the Hutu population. The media's subversive stereotypical portrayals of Tutsi women as conniving and predatory easily regressed to a rationalization for the genocidal rape that was committed on a mass scale.

The human rights principles expressed in *The Media Case* are relevant to several legal areas of hate-speech regulation. They, undoubtedly, will make an impression throughout the global community. People are listening even in countries that have been inclined to see themselves as exempt from atrocities such as Rwanda's. Even in the United States, where such an attitude has been common, more practicality about the harms of hate speech has been evident since the terrorist attacks of 9/11. Judges, policymakers, and legal scholars will carefully examine the Rwandan media Tribunal. It is likely to be used in cases of incited violence even when the crime is ostensibly far removed from hate speech.

The ICTR's decision is a model for justice, demonstrating that equality and free-speech rights can be harmonized when courts encounter the media's power to take life. Specifically, any person or group that plans, instigates, orders, commits, or otherwise aids and abets in the planning, preparation, or execution of a crime is responsible for the crime. Moreover, Barayagwiza and Ngeze took on physical acts of ordering, aiding, and abetting the killing of Tutsi, for which they were also found guilty.

The ICTR statute holds managers responsible if they knew—or had reason to know—that the subordinate was about to commit such acts or had done so and the supervisors failed to take the necessary and reasonable measures to prevent such acts or to punish the perpetrators. The three defendants were also convicted of extermination in large-scale killings of Tutsi, variously for their own acts or as responsible bosses.

In spite of the Tribunal's premium investigative methods and success in convicting the defendants, there is one glaring injustice. As early as 1996, Nowrojee, a human rights watchdog group, documented mass rape in the Rwandan genocide. Sexual violence during the Rwandan genocide and its aftermath devastated the lives of the Tutsi women. Yet the rapes themselves were not part of the charges in the tribunal.

CONCLUSION

The Internet is a technological innovation that has deeply impacted society, in both good and bad ways. It increases the power of groups, whether they are troubled citizens, leftist radicals, or even White supremacist terrorists. Social activists can pressurize social and political organizations that have Web sites with "virtual" marches, protests, or demonstrations. More extremist groups accomplished in computer "hacking" may find that their adversaries are more susceptible in cyberspace than in the actual physical world. The Internet has made available a venue for millions, and it has amplified their right to be heard.

It has permitted the quick recruitment of people across expansive areas, as has been shown in the 1990s with use of the Internet to coordinate protests against the World Trade Organization meetings and political party gatherings. Anybody outfitted with a computer and a modem or Ethernet connection can send e-mails or start a personal Web page. Online he or she can access the world audience with views, photos, or e-mail messages. Others can contact that same Internet user. Separating the legality and effectiveness of regulating speech on the Internet has become one of the most urgent concerns of government and society in the new millennium.

Unlike most of the actions for which tort law provides redress to the victim, racial labeling and racial insults directly harm the perpetrator as well as the victim (Delgado, 1995b). Bigotry harms the people who harbor it by reinforcing rigid thinking, thereby dulling their moral and social senses (Allport, 1958). There is little evidence that racial insults serve as a "safety valve" for anxiety that would otherwise result in violence.

Racist hate speech and racial stigmatization hurt not only the victim and the performer of individual racist acts but also society as a whole. Racism is a violation of the principle of social equality. A society in which some members habitually are subjected to degradation because of their race flies in the face of this principle. The failure of our legal system to intervene in the injuries of racism, and of racial insults in particular, communicates the message that social equality is not a basic principle of society. The law, through inaction, implicitly teaches that respect for individuals is of little importance. Additionally, unchecked violations of the egalitarian ideal may demoralize all those who prefer to live in a truly equal society, making them unwilling participants in the perpetuation of racial inequality.

The Internet has become the latest technology to be exploited by extremists and bigots. After a series of disastrous criminal and civil judgments over the past two decades, postmodern American racists have refined both their message and their methods. For a variety of reasons, including legal developments and technological advances in communications, many contemporary hate leaders are more willing to just inspire violence than their predecessors were. In the past, groups like the Klan believed they shared the goals, if not the tactics, of their overall community. Today, a collection of ideological and religious extremists view their role as changed from the enforcers of the status quo to warriors in a guerrilla insurgency called "leaderless resistance."

Technological innovations such as the Internet have allowed extremists to inexpensively spread their ideologies and strategies to a wider audience of potential would-be terrorists without the necessity—and legal risks—of maintaining a more direct relationship with them. Violence or property destruction directed by hate groups and other terrorists is no longer protected from punishment by a *laissez-faire* legal system. The Supreme Court and lower courts have sculpted an important position to protect the rights of bigots and other extremists who vigorously promote hateful and distasteful views, in cyberspace and other public venues. Because American law is more protective of speech than laws elsewhere, there will be continued litigation to determine which nation has jurisdiction over cyberspeech that breaks the law.

American law protects offensive content on the Internet. More secretive foreign terrorist groups such as Al Qaeda, hampered by a lack of Internet access to much of their impoverished potential audience, rely on the Internet as a tactical tool, bypassing its marketing efficiencies. The most successful domestic purveyors of hate, however, are people like William Pierce, who uses the Internet as a gateway marketing device to expose people to a variety of messages from other media including hate-rock compact discs, radio broadcasts, books, and periodicals.

Although the Internet is important in bringing extremist messages to the public, it is only the beginning of the recruitment process. No one becomes a neo-Nazi simply by entering a hate Web site. Ultimately, it is through White-power music concerts, speeches by charismatic leaders, and face-to-face interaction that the movement actually brings in new participants (Mark Potok, cited in Levin, 2003). The FBI has observed that a new twenty-first-century terrorist threat has emerged from the use of computers and the Internet. Terrorists are known to be using information technology and the Internet to devise plans, raise finances, distribute propaganda, recruit new members, and communicate securely. However, there have also been cases of terrorists using cyber-based attack. The threat of cyberterrorism will grow in the new millennium, as the leaders of hate groups are increasingly filled with younger, Internet-savvy individuals (FBI, 1999).

Although technological advances such as the Internet have made it easier for hate groups to spread their intolerance and hatred, recruit new members, and provide support and encouragement for lone haters, Rwanda clearly indicated that technological underdevelopment was no obstacle to genocide. The weapons were typically machetes and knives, as mentioned above.

The same mechanisms of group identity, consensus-building, and bonding that hold society together like glue can also be used to drive a society to genocide. There is also an important psychological distinction that must be drawn between killing an enemy in war, even suicide bombers killing strangers, and murdering acquaintances, perhaps even friends or lovers.

Genocide is propagated by hate speech that is trusted by conventional people who cooperate without much forethought or inner struggle. We are not making moral progress in the new millennium. The fastest genocide in the twentieth century happened virtually in front of us in Rwanda. After the Holocaust, it was agreed—never again. The genocidal rhetoric and mass murders in Cambodia, Serbia, Croatia, and Rwanda awakened us from that dream. Through the continuous drumming of anti-minority hate speech, ethnic cleansing becomes ordinary in a distorted social order. It is a strange attempt at utopia and an exercise in group identification. But in the end, hate speech was, and remains, a tool for genocide.

3

Religion and Hate Speech

Islam is a religion which God requires you to send your son to die for Him!

—John Ashcroft, U.S. Attorney General
(www.crosswalk.com)

On February 13, 2004, the Democratic National Committee (DNC) called on President Bush and Republican leaders to repudiate remarks made by Representative Peter King (R–New York) accusing American Muslims of "extremist leadership," and saying that most American Muslims are unwilling to cooperate with law enforcement officials on homeland security issues. Representative King made these comments—viewed by the Muslim community as hate speech—in an interview on a nationally syndicated radio program where he was promoting his new novel about future terrorist attacks by "Muslim extremists" in New York, and the fact that the content is "half truth and half fiction."

Democrats attacked the poor fit of these remarks with the White House's official line. President Bush had previously informed Muslim Americans that his administration would not excuse bigotry. Muslim Americans are teachers, lawyers, physicians, educators, civil servants, and entrepreneurs who have made invaluable contributions to the United States. President Bush has said, "those who feel they can intimidate our fellow citizens and take out their anger . . . represent the worst of humankind." The DNC called on President Bush and the Republican leadership to denounce this latest example of hate speech.

The DNC also argued that Representative King was using bigotry for financial gain. The problem is stereotyping Arab and Muslim Americans as terrorists. The reality is that most are decent, patriotic citizens. In the immediate aftermath of 9/11, President Bush had urged Americans not to strike out against their Arab and Muslim neighbors. Yet too many members and supporters of his own administration have undercut that message using anti-Muslim and anti-Arab hate speech to create fear and suspicion.

In failing to repudiate and demand apologies from John Ashcroft, General William Boykin, televangelist Pat Robertson, and Christian leader Franklin Graham for their bigoted remarks, President Bush had sabotaged his own message and created a dangerous atmosphere where some in his administration now believe they have presidential permission to disperse a message of hate. The DNC called on President Bush to rebuke those in his administration and his supporters who continue to emit anti-Muslim and anti-Arab bigotry.

Completing this pattern, President Bush was accused of hate speech for "praising the Southern Baptist Convention" (SBC). A former SBC president made disparaging comments about Mohammed, the founder of Islam, and also suggested that many of America's social problems could be blamed on religious pluralism. (Freedom of religion is one of the core values on which this democratic nation was founded.) Such anti-Muslim comments register either Stage 2 (Conscious Discrimination) since the SBC president's discriminatory statements are intentionally rebuffing Muslims, or Stage 3 (Inciting Discriminatory Hatred) because blaming Muslims for wide-scale social problems exhibits an irrational and overgeneralized animosity and lack of goodwill.

In the period following September 11, 2001, Muslims and Arabs (as well as people who were perceived to be Muslims or Arabs) became the targets of hate speech, xenophobic anger, and violent crime (American-Arab Anti-Discrimination Committee [ADC], 2002; American Broadcasting System, 2001; Arab American Institute, 2003; Ibish, 2003; Idupuganti, 2001; Public Broadcasting System, 2003; United Methodist Women, 2003; Zogby International, 2001). Within 10 days, at least three Muslim or Arab Americans were killed in vengeful hate crimes. Within nine weeks of the terrorist attacks, the ADC had received over 600 reports of violent incidents and direct threats of violence (McLemore and Romo, 2005). In several cities, Arabs and Muslims were forced to leave airplanes after they had cleared the security checkpoints and been seated. ADC recorded 60 such cases in which either other passengers or members of the airplanes's flight crew refused to fly if those suspected of being Muslim or Arab stayed on board the aircraft.

The Islamic Institute of New York, soon after the attack of 9/11, was a victim of hate speech. The Institute received a phone call threatening to paint the streets red with the blood of Muslim children. As a Lebanese American man searched for survivors in the rubble of the World Trade Center, he was cursed and told: "go back to your country." A mosque in Denton, Texas, was firebombed. Another in Cleveland, Ohio, was damaged when an automobile was intentionally driven into it. In Huntington, New

York, a man attempted to run over a Pakistani woman in a parking lot. In Seattle, Washington, a man approached a mosque, doused a parked car with gasoline, and tried to shoot the car's owner.

This chapter addresses anti-Muslim and anti-Semitic speech, images, and expressions and whether they should be regulated. This chapter will also consider some of the contemporary anti-immigration or anti-minority movements in France, the Netherlands, Belgium, Germany, and Austria.

POST-9/11 HATE SPEECH AGAINST MUSLIMS

> *I feel power in my religion, but I don't feel hate. I feel only love and power. And everything that I need is in my religion. So I am happy with my religion, but there are people that see it like a terrorist religion, a bad religion, a hate religion.*
> —Fekre Tayardi (Muslim man)

After 9/11, the religious right or fundamentalist Christian movement used anti-Islamic hate speech, calling for the conversion of Muslims to Christianity and identifying Islam as "evil." For example, Minister Franklin Graham professed that Islam is "a very evil and wicked religion." Pat Roberston and Jerry Falwell have also articulated anti-Muslim sentiments. According to Reverend Richard Cizik of the National Association of Evangelicals, a very large group that represents 43,000 congregations, "Muslims have become the Modern-day equivalent" of Communism and, thus, of a new "Evil Empire" (Goodstein, 2003: A22). Most Christian denominations, however, responded to the 9/11 attacks by sponsoring various interfaith meetings and efforts to demonstrate solidarity with Muslims in the United States and around the world.

Hate attacks in wake of 9/11 were generalized to include any person whom the perpetrators associated with Muslims or Arabs. For example, in Richmond Hill, New York, an elderly Sikh man was beaten with a baseball bat. In San Diego, California, two men attacked a Sikh woman and shouted "this is what you get for what you've done to us." Sikhs may have been targeted because of the men's turbans and beards. Two Spanish-speaking women in Los Angeles were attacked and told, "You foreigners caused all this trouble." In Minneapolis, Minnesota, three young men punched an Asian Indian woman in the stomach and told her, "this is what you people deserve." The rates of hate crimes against Asian and Pacific Island peoples approximately doubled during the first three months after 9/11 (McLemore and Romo, 2005).

Such confrontations point to the overall tensions in ethnic relations that erupted nationwide in the period following 9/11. A sizable minority of the U.S. population (43 percent) was "personally more suspicious" of people who looked Muslim or Arab than they had been before (Public Broadcasting System, 2003). Nearly half of Arab Americans surveyed a month after 9/11 knew "someone of Arab ethnicity or Arab-speaking background who [had] experienced discrimination since the September 11 attacks" (Zogby, 2001).

The violent attacks described above occurred despite a vigorous effort by Muslim and Arab Americans to demonstrate their patriotism and loyalty to America and despite some timely efforts by federal and local officials to prevent such attacks. Muslim and Arab American organizations moved quickly to condemn the 9/11 attacks and to make evident that Muslims also had lost relatives and loved ones in the attacks. They joined all other Americans in mourning and stated their hope that those responsible for the attacks would be found and held responsible. They also urged their fellow Americans not to "rush to judgment" and place collective blame on all Muslims or Arabs (Arab American Institute, 2003: 2).

The coalition of Chicago Arab Organizations, Muslims and Arab American leaders, and the ADC issued similar statements. Muslim members in law enforcement, firefighting, and the National Guard were part of the rescue efforts at Ground Zero in New York. These people contributed their work while dealing with their own grief and relationships. In addition, Muslim and Arab groups across the United States donated hundreds of thousands of dollars to the Red Cross Disaster Relief Fund, the Twin Towers Relief Fund, and other organizations bringing help to those most directly affected by the terrorist attacks (Arab American Institute, 2003: 2-5).

On September 12, 2001, the U.S. Congress adopted a resolution stating "that the civil rights and civil liberties of all Americans . . . should be protected" and condemning "any acts of violence or discrimination against any Americans." President George W. Bush reminded the country that Muslim and Arab Americans love the United States and deserve to be treated with respect. On September 17, 2001, Robert Mueller, the Director of the FBI, stated that the FBI already had "initiated 40 hate crime investigations" regarding attacks on Muslim Americans or their institutions. Moreover, mosques and Islamic institutes in several cities were given around-the-clock protection by law enforcement. Evidently, these measures paid off. Nine weeks after 9/11, the rate of attacks against Muslims and Arabs declined rapidly (Ibish, 2003). The swift and reassuring words of President Bush and other officials are likely to have prevented even more violence. At the same time, however, there was a sharp rise in the termination of Muslim and Arab workers and the level of employment discrimination remained high (Ibish, 2003).

The widespread hate speech against Muslims allegorically knocks us in the head, forcing us to remember that religious intolerance, racism, and xenophobia are not dead; instead, they remain quite potent in the United States. Simultaneously, anti-Muslim hate speech has been drowned out by expressions of compassion, prayers, and material support for the needy.

Thousands of Americans posted signs on their property calling for tolerance and unity or opposing the blaming and hating of Muslims. Others
sent electronic, facsimile, or phone messages to spread the word. An interfaith group of Muslims and Jews convened a peace pilgrimage in Albu-
querque, New Mexico (Public Broadcasting System, 2003).

People were asking their fellow Americans not to stereotype or discriminate against Muslims. At the same time, however, under the guise of national security, the U.S. Department of Justice used ethnic or racial profiling
to pinpoint young adult Muslim males. This type of discrimination is based
on the stereotype or prejudiced notion that virtually all Muslims who fit
that description are terrorists. Accordingly, Muslims are primarily viewed
as members of a terrorist or religious group and not as individuals.

The federal government ordered wiretapping and monitored the mass in-
terrogation and detention of young Muslim men, unwittingly displaying
the stereotype that Arab and Muslim Americans were "by definition, suspicious and possibly dangerous" (Hamad, 2001). These actions also
aroused the fears of many people that America's democratic institutions
might fail in this crisis to protect the civil liberties not only of Muslims and
Arabs, but other immigrants, ethnic minority citizens, and other Americans
as well.

Two of the primary red flags raised by civil libertarians and humanists
around the globe have been the consequences of the USA Patriot Act of
2001, aimed "to deter and punish terrorist acts" in the United States and
elsewhere, and various administrative policy changes. The Patriot Act
granted the federal government broad new powers to detain noncitizens indefinitely without due process. The Patriot Act also reduces the standards
that law enforcement officers must meet to conduct searches, seizures, and
surveillance. The major policy changes allow the government to try accused
terrorists in military tribunals without counsel. The political controversy
continues on this issue.

However, in 2004 the U.S Supreme Court ruled that the president is not
given blanket power to indefinitely detain prisoners of the war on terror
incommunicado at Camp X-Ray on Guantanamo Bay, Cuba. The federal
government's recent policy to eavesdrop on client–attorney communications has also been challenged.

Do these new laws and policies actually increase the nation's ability to
fight terrorism and increase the safety of Americans and other victims of
terrorism in the international community? Or have they themselves become
the greater threat to the democratic process? For many Americans, there
may have been a collective sigh of relief after the U.S. government increased
its powers to fight terrorism in the wake of 9/11. However, the result of
ethnic or racial profiling is discriminatory to Muslim and Arab Americans
and does little to curb the organization, mobility, and threats of violence
by terrorists. If a particular religious or ethnic group is targeted for close

inspection, it seems likely that official policy and action may reproduce the ethnocentrism and racism that has gone along with the expansion of our nation since its inception.

In 1942, parts of the federal government fostered the belief that the Japanese internment was a matter of "military necessity," but this rationale was later revealed to be only a thin veil covering the interlocking assumptions of racist and nativist thought (McLemore and Romo, 2005). Let us learn from our previous mistakes. The call for "national security" should not act as a thin veil for hate speech and discriminatory treatment as we wage war on terror.

Shortly before and during the one-year anniversary of the terrorist attacks of September 11, 2001, there was a major thrust to condemn anti-Muslim hate speech and hate crimes to prevent violence against ethnic minorities. A group letter was sent to President George W. Bush, Governor George E. Pataki, and New York Mayor Michael R. Bloomberg. The letter was multiculturally dated: September 10, 2002/Rajab 3, 1423. The letter was written on behalf of 7 million Muslim Americans and 3 million Arab Americans.

The letter to the local, state, and federal officials asked for

clear condemnation of the anti-Muslim hate-speech uttered by some fellow Americans. Such anti-Muslim rhetoric, if not condemned by you now, will continue to lead a small number of bigoted individuals to turn hate-filled words into violent attacks against innocent Muslim and Arab Americans.

It went on to recognize the distinction between terrorism and Islam and mentioned the hate crime in Selden, New York, where a woman and her 15-year-old son were beaten outside their family's restaurant.

Following are examples of hate speech and their evaluation according to the four-stage developmental model of hate-speech severity as presented in Chapter 1. Even the religious right has used hate speech for political purposes.

1. U.S. Attorney General John Ashcroft stated that "Islam is a religion which God requires you to send your son to die for Him!" (www.crosswalk.com). Clearly, Mr. Ashcroft would be aware that his comments purposively offended Muslims. Thus, it does not meet the criteria for Stage 1 (Unintentional Discrimination). This sentence perhaps most solidly represents Stage 2 (Conscious Discrimination) since, structurally, it represents intentionally slighting Muslims. One could also argue that Ashcroft's comments approach Stage 3 (Inciting Discriminatory Hatred) since images of suicide bombings could easily propagate feelings of hatred for Muslims.

2. Televangelist Pat Robertson's continuous defamation of Islam represents perhaps both Stage 2 (Conscious Discrimination) since he is intentionally

rebuffing Islam, and Stage 3 (Inciting Discriminatory Hatred) since he is likely generating feelings of hated for Muslims in his television audiences.

3. The Reverend Jerry Vines, former president of the Southern Baptist Convention, made disparaging remarks about Mohammed, the founder of Islam, in a speech before the Southern Baptist Convention. His description of the Prophet Muhammad as a "demon-possessed pedophile" seems to clearly generate feelings of hatred for Muslims by appealing to his audience's conservative values and loathing of sexual sinners (Stage 3: Inciting Discriminatory Hatred). He also claimed that many of America's problems could be attributed to religious pluralism.

4. Franklin Graham, the son of Reverend Billy Graham, claimed that Islam is a "very evil and wicked religion." This also characterizes Stage 3 since Graham is demonizing Islam.

5. Free Congress Foundation's William S. Lind's allegation that "There is no such thing as peaceful Islam." This could fit either Stage 2 (Conscious Discrimination) or Stage 3 (Inciting Discriminatory Hatred).

6. Syndicated columnist Ann Coulter's call to "invade Muslim countries and convert the populations to Christianity." This is clearly Stage 4 since invading is violent, whether human lives are taken or religious tolerance is abandoned. Attitudes that aspire to convert nonbelievers to Christianity may also represent Stage 1 (Unintentional Discrimination) since believers may be unaware of the intolerance that characterizes their religious dogma.

7. The suggestion by an editor of the *National Review* that "nuking Mecca" would send a "signal" to Muslims ostensibly is Stage 4 (Inciting Discriminatory Violence). However, it also calls for linguistic analysis for possible double meaning. The implied meaning is sarcasm and comedy. However, comedy may be a front for hate speech. Moreover, even if sarcasm or comedy was intended, the receiver may still be encouraged to discriminate, hate, or do violence against social minorities (including gays and lesbians, women, physically handicapped, and ethnic and racial minorities).

8. Fox News Network talk-show host Bill O'Reilly's comparison of the Koran to Hitler's (1939) *Mein Kampf* is clearly Stage 3 (Inciting Discriminatory Hatred). This comparison seems to be designed to promulgate feelings of hatred for Muslims.

9. Former Special Counsel to President Nixon, Chuck Colson's claim that "Islam is a religion which breeds hatred." This statement justifies the spawning of hate for Muslims as self-defense (Stage 3—Inciting Discriminatory Hatred).

10. Media reports in South Carolina revealed that a Republican congressional candidate said that Islam is not "a true religion, it's a cult . . . there's nothing peaceful about that religion. It says kill and be killed." (http:// www.thestate-com/mid/thestate/news/politics/3921214/htm) This testimonial also justifies hate as self-defense (Stage 3—Inciting Discriminatory Hatred).

In August 2002, Robert J. Goldstein was arrested in Florida after authorities found a stash of explosives and weapons, including .50-caliber machine guns and sniper rifles, in his home. Police also found more than 30 explosive devices, including hand grenades and a 5-gallon gasoline bomb with an attached timer. Officials also discovered a list of 50 Florida mosques and, chillingly, detailed plans for bombing an Islamic education center for Muslim children.

ANTI-MUSLIM HATE SPEECH ON CAMPUS

Police say intruders entered student's suite, left message, then exited without incident.
                                                                —Laura Hess, 2003

On the evening of March 27, 2003, on the campus of Yale University, several male students, one wielding a wooden plank, broke into the suite of an anti-war activist (Katherine Lo) and wrote a hateful note on her bedroom message board (Hess, 2003). The incident occurred a day after Lo hung an American flag upside-down from her bedroom window to protest the war in Iraq.

Yale Police confirmed that a group of students entered Lo's suite, wrote a message on her whiteboard, and left without altercation. After unsuccessful attempts to enter her bedroom, the students wrote an inflammatory message that was targeted at Muslims and anti-war protesters. The message contained a sadistic call for the killing of Muslims and Iraqis. The message ended with the words, "I hate you, GO AMERICA." This hate speech contains meaning that entails both Stage 3 (Inciting Discriminatory Hatred) and Stage 4 (Inciting Discriminatory Violence). It meets Stage 3 criteria because it propagates feelings of hatred toward minorities (i.e., "I hate you"). Additionally, it satisfies Stage 4 criteria because it encourages the use of violence against minorities (i.e., the killing of Muslims and Iraqis).

Yale University affirmed Lo's right to freely express opposition to what President George W. Bush called "the Battle of Iraq." At the same time, the university did not view the written hate message as free speech. Rather, it was interpreted as harassment. Dean of Student Affairs Betty Trachtenberg described the incident as heinous. She added: "People have a right to express themselves, People do not have a right to break in and harass students where they live" (Castillo, 2003).

Prior to the incident, Lo anticipated others would disagree with her act of protest and would search out her room in order to debate her. Consequently, she left a message on her bedroom door, defending her right to express her opposition to the war and dissent with official U.S. policy. Lo, who attended anti-war demonstrations during spring break, hung the flag partly out of frustration with President Bush's not paying attention to anti-war demonstrations.

Lo used her right to dissent and hung the flag as "a symbol of distress" (Castillo, 2003). She was very upset about the U.S. war "against the Iraqi people," and that "President Bush ignored public opinion of the nation and of the world." On the evening of the incident, Lo was working in her bedroom when she overheard a group of male students who had entered her common room say, "This is the room." She immediately locked her bedroom door and remained silent so as not to attract attention from the trespassers. After she locked her door, the intruders approached her bedroom door and attempted to open it. The intruders remained in her suite approximately 7 to 10 minutes.

Out of fear for her safety, Lo did not leave her room until the next morning when she contacted authorities. Lo, responding to a Yale Peace mailing list, then urged students to hang upside-down flags outside of their windows. Accordingly, some students used this action as a symbol of their right to dissent—to exercise free expression through a collective political voice.

In solidarity with Lo and as a symbol that freedom of speech will not be shut down by violent intimidation, approximately 30 other students all over the campus hung American flags upside-down outside their windows (Hess, 2003). But, once again, freedom of expression had been attacked. Someone had entered the common room of a dormitory suite, uninvited, and turned a flag right side up.

AOL Hate Speech Lawsuit

A federal lawsuit was filed against AOL Time Warner for allowing and not condemning anti-Muslim hate speech, and sought class-action status for the case (Weisman, 2001). The lawsuit was filed in August 2001, and charged that the Dulles, Virginia–based company permitted anti-Muslim speech to continue unabated in chat rooms catering to the Muslim demographic. This is in violation of federal civil rights laws.

The suit is based on the 1964 Civil Rights Act that prohibits discrimination in places of public accommodation such as restaurants, hotels, and recreation facilities. In light of the growing significance of the Internet, the suit alleged that a public chat room should be classified as a site of entertainment and, therefore, should be free of hate speech and ethnic harassment.

The lawsuit, filed on behalf of Saad Noah of Oak Crest, Illinois, sought an injunction that would make AOL enforce its self-generated standards preventing members from transmitting offensive messages. Noah cancelled his AOL service in July 2000, after AOL ignored his repeated requests to monitor anti-Muslim hate speech that occurred virtually daily in such Islam-centric chat rooms as "Beliefs: Islam" and "Koran."

AOL considers the case without merit, claiming a zero tolerance for any hate speech on the service. When a complaint is brought to their attention, AOL staff reviews it and can take action ranging from a reprimand to cancellation of service. AOL policy also calls on members to report hate speech when they read it. AOL is the world's largest Internet access provider with over 30 million subscribers using its online service.

Nevertheless, the lawsuit alleged that Noah always forwarded each example of hate speech or injurious or harassing statement to AOL along with his requests for help, which AOL ignored.

The 27-page lawsuit contains over 20 pages of hate speech Noah documented and reported to AOL between 1998 and 2000. For example, "If Muhamm[a]d [is] your 'Prophet', then Larry Flynt [is] your 'Prophet' too," and "MECCA is a GARBAGE DUMP." This represents Stage 3 (Inciting Discriminatory Hatred) in my developmental model, since comparing the blessed founder of Islam to a notorious icon and publisher of pornography certainly encourages hatred and ridicule of Muslims.

While a substantial number of the obscenities came from such posters as "Vulgar Jew" and "JEWNPROUD," several posts denigrated both Muslims and Jews with comments such as: All Muslims and Jews are terrorists. The suit alleged that AOL inconsistently removed postings of purely anti-Semitic comments in chat rooms catering to Jews. In 2000, the topic of anti-Semitism was pulled into the national spotlight with Democratic presidential candidate Al Gore's decision to pick Senator Joseph Lieberman of Connecticut to be his vice-presidential running mate.

Apparently, there has been a significant inconsistency between AOL's zero-tolerance policy and the plethora of hate speech in its chat rooms and message boards. One type of gainful intervention is to seek consultation from Muslims to help monitor hate speech on these communication networks. This would help to address some of the concerns of the Muslim community.

Muslim Woman Sues to Wear Veil for Driver's License

Is revoking the driver's license of a Muslim woman—after she refuses to remove her veil for her driver's license photo—a violation of her rights of religious freedom and free expression? In May 2003, the ACLU, who is representing Sultaana Freeman, the Muslim woman, in court, filed suit against the state of Florida for threatening to revoke her driver's license. The legal issue is whether Florida has a compelling interest in regulating drivers that overrides the religious protections afforded one of its citizens. Since Florida routinely issues driver's licenses without photos, it certainly appears that there is no compelling interest. Therefore, the possibility of hate speech or anti-Muslim discrimination comes into play. Similarly, in

France, the federal government has prohibited wearing head scarves in schools (see next section).

From 1998 to 2003, Florida issued more than 800,000 temporary licenses and/or driving permits—without photographs—to individuals for a range of various reasons. For example, convicted drunk drivers with revoked licenses are legally allowed to drive in Florida using only driving permits without photographs. Other photo-exempt categories include foreign nationals, those who failed their eye or written exams, and military personnel.

A driver's license may serve as a substitute for identification, but if truth be told, it is nothing more than a license to operate a motor vehicle on government highways. Consequently, this type of license does not require suspending religious freedom or assaulting the privacy of someone who wishes to preserve it. After all, a driver's license is not, for example, a passport. A passport functions as a form of identification and requires the means to physically identify the person in question. However, one must also consider that DNA or fingerprint samples are better verification of identity than a photograph.

As a postscript to the story, Sultaana Freeman, formerly Sandra Keller, is a convicted felon. Following her 1997 conversion to Islam, she was arrested in Decatur, Illinois, for battering a foster child. Freeman pleaded guilty in 1999 to felony aggravated battery and was sentenced to 18 months' probation. As a result of the conviction, state officials removed two foster children from Freeman's care. Illinois, it ends up, already has an unveiled government portrait of Freeman.

ANTI-MUSLIM HATE SPEECH IN EUROPE

> *You don't know me, but you are afraid of me! And we live in the same country. For me, that is a very big problem.*
>
> *I don't want to be tolerated in this country. I have lived here for 32 years. I'm a citizen of Holland. I want to be accepted.*
>
> —Samira Abbos (Muslim woman and writer)

> *If you say, "I reject the Western lifestyle, and I don't want to fit in your way," I say, "keep away!"*
>
> —Barry Madlener (Rotterdam City Councilman
> speaking against Muslim immigration)

Anti-Muslim hate speech is prevalent and tensions between Muslims and non-Muslims continue to increase in Western Europe. In Germany, police raided two Islamic centers and mosques looking for signs of terrorism or hate speech but made no arrests (*Religion & Ethics Newsweekly*, 2004). In France, there is a ban on head scarves in schools. In the Netherlands,

Muslim clerics are now required to use the Dutch language in religious services.

For decades, Muslims from the Middle East and North Africa have emigrated to Europe to find work. Low-skill employment, however, is difficult to find. The terrorist attacks in America on September 11, 2001, the Spanish train bombings on March 11, 2004, and the London terrorist bombings on July 7, 2005, have heightened ethnic tensions and anti-Muslim fears in Europe.

The Netherlands has long been a country recognized for its peace and prosperity; its 16 million citizens enjoy one of the highest standards of living in the world (*Religion & Ethics Newsweekly*, 2004). The country is known internationally for its liberal social values. Prostitution is open and legal. Marijuana and hashish are bought and smoked in coffee houses. Hallucenogenic mushrooms are also legal.

Like other European nations, the Netherlands' reputation for tolerance is being tested as the country struggles with how to welcome and integrate its growing immigrant Muslim population—many of them refugees. The Muslim community is 900,000 strong, who are increasingly vocal in demanding equality in Dutch society. Muslims, especially the younger generation, are trying to reconcile their identities as both Muslims and Europeans. The synthesis is a loud cry for freedom.

As the Netherlands and other European nations struggle to assimilate their growing Muslim populations, some fear there is a fissure developing between Muslims and non-Muslims—a division characterized by mutual suspicion and hostility. The Dutch port city of Rotterdam is a metropolis where nearly 50 percent of all residents are foreign-born, with most of them from Muslim countries. Many Europeans support restrictions on immigration and argue that Muslims living in Europe are unwilling to accept European cultural values, such as equality for women and gays and lesbians.

More than a third of Dutch citizens feel threatened by Muslims, according to a recent national poll. Fears of terrorism also contribute to Europeans' ambivalence toward the continent's more than 12 million Muslims, especially in the wake of the Madrid train bombings in March 2004 and, more recently, with the London bombings. Those attacks, designed and executed by Islamic militants, killed over 250 people. Clearly, the actions of a small number of extremists make it easier for Europeans (and Americans) to demonize all Muslims. For example, the London bombings were followed by attacks on local locations where Muslims gather, such as mosques.

Many European Muslims keep a traditional lifestyle, while at the same time rejecting a Western one. Thus, the conflict quickly emerges when fundamentalist Muslims immigrate to Europe, wishing to retain their traditional lifestyle in a liberal society. Problems exasperate when second-generation Muslim children are unable to assimilate in schools and in society, in general. Consequently, is there cause for concern if a generation of poor Muslim adolescents, alienated not only from their host society but from parents and extended family as well, mixes its feelings of rejection with Islamic extremist ideology freshly transmitted from the Middle East?

Young Muslims have been stereotyped by a Dutch legislator as antagonistic: "You see that these individuals have now gone through a complete mental change and take a hostile attitude towards Europe and Europeans" (Ayaan Hirsi Ali in *Religion & Ethics Newsweekly*, 2004). It is not surprising that many European Muslims complain of hate speech as suspicion of them grows. Muslims cannot be political without being viewed as extremist.

Using race relations theory as a comparative model, the predicament of Muslims in twenty-first-century Europe is perhaps no better than that of African Americans during the days of segregation. European Muslims have high unemployment, low educational attainment with high dropout rates, and acute problems in obtaining decent, affordable housing.

Laws that require acculturation are averse examples of forced cultural assimilation that send a clear message to Muslims: "We don't want you to stay here. But if we must have you, you must change. We don't like people who are different. We want you to be exactly like us. Only when you are exactly like us, we will accept you."

As the Muslim immigrant populations increases, what Western Europe is currently experiencing is not dissimilar to what is happening in America, where dealing with newcomers has always been a challenge. But if you only accept people who are just like you, how tolerant is that?

ANTI-SEMITIC HATE SPEECH

The unremitting violent conflict between the Palestinians and Israelis over the Gaza Strip and West Bank has been exacerbated by an increasingly deadly series of suicide bombings resulting in harsh vengeance, including assassinations of terrorist leaders and financiers, by the Israeli government. Such ruthless reprisals have been generally denounced, even by the United States, Israel's staunchest ally. In the United States and throughout the international community, there have been protests against Israel and in unity with the Palestinian people. Some protestors wield signs directed at all Jewish people. They are strongly in opposition to Israel and those who back the Israeli cause. Demonstrators yell anti-Semitic slogans and chalk or paint them on the streets and walls.

Malaysia's Mohamed: "Jews Rule the World"

On October 15, 2003, Malaysia's prime minister, Mahathir Mohamed, was widely criticized for comments that "Jews ruled the world by proxy." In a speech opening the Organization of Islamic Conference (OIC) summit in Malaysia, he said the Jewish people had an influence in the world that far outweighed their numbers, because of their relationship with the United

States. He claimed that "Jews rule this world" and "[Jews] get others to fight and die for them" and called on Muslims to use brains, not brute force, to fight them.

The United States condemned the remarks. U.S. State Department spokesman Adam Ereli said, "The remarks are offensive, they are inflammatory, and we view them with the contempt and derision they deserve." Italy's foreign minister, Franco Frattini, says his country, which currently holds the European Union presidency, included a condemnation of Mohamed's comments at the conclusion of a two-day EU summit. "What he said was very strongly anti-Semitic. [His comments] run strongly counter to the principles of tolerance and dialogue between the West and the Islamic world," Frattini said.

The head of the Jewish human rights organization, the Simon Weisenthal Center, Efraim Zuroff, said the enlightened world should silence Mohamed for his remarks. "It is time that the democratic, enlightened, liberal world mobilizes to stop him from continuing to openly call for the hatred of Jews," Zuroff said. Australia's prime minister, John Howard, told Southern Cross Radio that Mohamed's remarks are offensive and unhelpful. "Any suggestion from anybody in the world of dividing the world into Jewish and non-Jewish groupings is historically indefensible and wrong and something most Australians would regard as quite repugnant," Howard said.

Critical race theorists (Delgado, 2004b) have suggested that this type of hateful speech must be restricted. Australia's Labor Party's foreign affairs spokesman, Kevin Rudd, agreed: "You actually need governments to respond to this sort of outrageous offensive and dangerous language." Mohamed, Malaysia's prime minister of 22 years, stepped down from power only two weeks after delivering this infamous verbal assault on Jews and the United States. By all accounts, he was a complex figure, leading Malaysia on an amazing advance toward modernization and industrialization while simultaneously rejecting Western influences and keeping a dictatorial hold on political and military power.

Malaysian papers generally heaped praise on the firebrand leader on the occasion of his retirement and glossed over his frequently outrageous remarks. A fawning editorial in Malaysia's *New Straits Times* focused on Mohamed's extensive economic accomplishments, which would have him "go down in history as a great leader and go up in the eyes of his people as the greatest Malaysian alive." Other Malaysian papers had a more balanced assessment of the country's virtual godfather. The *Harakah Daily* alluded to his political corruption.

Mohamed earned fainter praise abroad, though even his critics applauded his economic feats. Most international pundits were less impressed with his tarnished political record: authoritarianism, reliance on party cronyism, failure to curb corruption, and the abuse of judicial and human rights. Most infamous is the case of Anwar Ibrahim, Mohamed's likely successor until a falling out between the two. Ibrahim is currently in prison on what is generally believed to be false charges.

U.N. Resolution on Anti-Semitism Withdrawn

In December 2003, a United Nations (U.N.) draft resolution on anti-Semitism was withdrawn in the face of Arab and Muslim opposition. This is ironic considering that the United Nations is an organization whose core human rights principles were drafted from the lessons of the Holocaust. The moral principles embracing its founding charter are "tolerance," "the dignity and worth of the human person," and "equal rights." The resolution would have been a first in U.N. history.

Daily incidents of anti-Semitic violence around the globe are reported in the media. While world leaders condemn synagogue bombings in Turkey, fire-bombings of Jewish schools in France, and the hate speech of Malaysia's former president, the United Nations seems unable to successfully oppose anti-Semitic speech.

The United Nations seems to be more effectively opposing anti-Islamic speech. For example, the U.N. Commission on Human Rights requires reports to be submitted regularly on discrimination against Muslims and Arab peoples in various parts of the world, including any physical assaults and attacks against their places of worship, cultural centers, businesses, and properties. Also, a 2003 Commission resolution combating defamation of religions mentions only prejudice against Muslims, Arabs, and Islam.

Condemnation of all hate speech, including anti-Semitism, ought to be self-evident to an organization that espouses tolerance, the dignity and worth of the human person, and equal rights. From ancient times to the modern age, genocidal persecution of Jews has been justified by any label that served the perpetrator's interests: religion, race, ethnic origin, or nationality have all functioned, at one time or another, as grounds for anti-Semitism.

Restitution for Anti-Semitic Remarks

When anti-Semitic speech is adversative to the fundamental democratic principles that base the First Amendment as well as the equal protection clause of the Fourteenth Amendment, it should be constrained. There is a robust connection between hate speech and hate crime; hate speech typically precedes hate crime. Hate-speech victims lose a bit of their freedom and some geographical space where the incident occurred. It is clear that there are tensions between First Amendment absolutism and the democratic ideals of liberty and equality. Hate speech is not dissent. Hate speech virtually always attacks individuals or groups that are defenseless to those who are dominant in society, predatory, and bigoted. There has been a thrust for a formal, legal-structural response to hate speech and it has had some success. Hate speech goes against our tradition of tolerance; when it is restricted and its messengers jailed, fined, or otherwise punished, this displays a social commitment to tolerance as a value and recognition of cultural diversity.

In *Imperial Diner, Inc. v. State Human Rights Appeal Board* (1980), a restaurant owner had sarcastically told a waitress that she thought she was something special, "Just like all the other fucking Jewish broads around here." The owner repeatedly refused to apologize for his comments. The New York Court of Appeals affirmed the State Division of Human Rights ruling that the petitioner discriminated against the waitress by reviling her religion in a matter related to her working conditions and enforced the division's award of $500 to the waitress for "shock, humiliation, and outrage."

Attempted Nazi Rally in Skokie

During 1977 and 1978, a small group of neo-Nazis, led by Frank Collin, tried to hold a rally in the village of Skokie, Illinois. Village officials vehemently resisted Collin's attempts to demonstrate in Skokie, first by passing a series of ordinances aimed at preventing distribution of hate materials, parading in military costumes, and then obliging parade organizers to obtain an insurance bond before a permit would be issued.

Collin's decision to target Skokie was particularly detestable because Skokie was home to a large population of Jewish people, including many survivors of the Holocaust. Village officials, citizens of Skokie, religious leaders from the surrounding communities, and people from all over the United States offered support and advice on the best way to put a stop to the impact that a neo-Nazi demonstration would have on the community.

The ordinances were ultimately overturned following a series of state and federal lawsuits and the neo-Nazis were eventually issued a license to demonstrate in Skokie. "On May 23, 1978, standing squarely in the center of the path leading directly to Skokie, Frank Collin turned and marched in the opposite direction" (Hamlin, 1980: 163). He couched his decision in terms that he must have thought were face-saving, and he did not entirely eliminate the possibility of a demonstration in Skokie. Nevertheless, Collin made it quite clear to anyone interested that he would much prefer not to demonstrate in Skokie. As typical of producers of hate speech, instead of facing the growing number of organized counter-demonstrators, Collin and his group held demonstrations in Federal Plaza in downtown Chicago and in Marquette Park in south Chicago.

Only twice after his brief demonstrations in Chicago did Frank Collin generate any media attention. First, several months after the Marquette Park demonstration, it was reported that Collin had threatened a suburb of Cleveland in the same manner he had threatened Skokie. The press accounts of that minor event imply that Collin was simply ignored—after the laughter had ended. Collin was merely the butt of jokes and returned to Chicago without further word.

Then, early in 1980, Collin was arrested in Chicago on a morals charge involving the taking of indecent liberties with underaged boys. He was brought to trial and subsequently convicted. He was sentenced to seven years in an Illinois prison and began serving that sentence immediately. At approximately the same time, Collin was kicked out of the National Socialist Party of America.

KKK Rally in Skokie in the New Millennium

More than two decades after Collin's Nazi group threatened to march in Skokie, another White supremacist group applied for a permit and held a "White Pride Rally" in the village in December 2000. The demonstration's sponsor was the Mercer, Wisconsin–based chapter of the Ku Klux Klan. About 250 people attended the rally on the steps of the Cook County Courthouse. While about 20 Klansmen demonstrated, clashes broke out with counter-protesters and about 20 people were arrested. The weekend was fraught with anger, frustration, and pain for Skokie's citizens.

Skinheads attacked a Black couple leaving the rally, punching the woman and knocking her down. Several police officers were also hurt in the scuffle. Police confiscated baseball bats, knives, and crowbars from members of the crowd. One man was charged with unlawful use of a weapon and unlawful possession of ammunition after police found a semiautomatic handgun in his car. If we apply the four-stage model of severity of hate speech or discriminatory statements (see Chapter 1), the hate speech at the KKK rally was characteristic of Stage 4, the most severe: inciting discriminatory violence and encouraging the use of violence against minorities.

The KKK rally appeared to strengthen the resolve of Skokie residents in their fight against bigotry and hate speech. In the wake of the Klan's rally, 1,400 people gathered at Niles West High School the next day to celebrate their diversity. While Skokie's rich cultural patchwork is a source of strength and pride, it also makes the village a target of hate speech. Still, Skokie residents empowered themselves with more force and power than any KKK group could have. Skokie residents seem to do whatever it takes to preserve the welcoming character of the northern Illinois suburban village.

The rally gave residents a chance to express their feelings about the weekend's events—and to peacefully fight back. Skokie residents let it be known that when one or a group of them is attacked, the community considers it an attack on everyone.

Under village ordinances governing assemblies, the Klan was required to obtain $1 million in liability and $1 million in bodily injury insurance, and show proof of the insurance to the village. The ordinance also required the group to pay any additional costs for police officers, firefighters, or other village services. The permit was approved despite the right to reject the rally for "potential to disrupt the peace or create a riot." Even though the rally went forward, there was vigorous response by Skokie residents to show opposition to hate groups like the Klan.

Advertising for the rally had been posted on several White supremacist Web sites, claiming that it was co-sponsored by the Klan, Aryan Nations, and Aryan National Alliance. The notice referred to Skokie as "Jew town" and used the intentionally inflammatory term "parasitic Jewry" (Stage 2). The same Web pages also offered other anti-Semitic hate speech, including a downloadable Nazi computer game. The Mercer chapter of the Ku Klux Klan originated in 1997 and held similar rallies in Wisconsin and Michigan. They are on the Anti-Defamation League's radar.

For longtime residents of Skokie, the rally brought back memories of 1978 when Collin's Chicago Nazi group planned a march in the village. As mentioned above, the group finally dropped its plans following a lengthy court fight in which the group was supported by the American Civil Liberties Union. But Skokie demographics changed vastly from 1978 to 2000. A smaller percentage of the population of the village is Jewish and it had lost many of its Holocaust survivors, the target of the Nazi march.

The effect of the rally was not nearly as chilling as in the late 1970s. Still, it showed a media-savvy resurgence of White supremacy. And the temptation to minimize the potential effect of any hate group is almost certainly self-delusional. For example, a racially motivated shooting spree by Benjamin Smith in Skokie in July 1999, left two people dead, including former Northwestern University basketball coach Ricky Byrdsong, who was gunned down near his Skokie home. Smith was a member of the Peoria, Illinois–based World Church of the Creator, another White supremacist group. Byrdsong's widow decided to stay, indicating that Skokie is a community that values racial and ethnic differences.

ANTI-SEMITIC HATE SPEECH ON UNIVERSITY CAMPUSES

As mentioned in the introductory chapter, hate speech has reached near-epidemic proportions on American college campuses. One out of every four college or university students is subjected to ethnoviolence (threats or overt violence on the grounds of a social, cultural, or physical characteristic). This section addresses and evaluates three prominent examples of anti-Semitic hate speech at universities. The hate speech–free speech issue and the efficacy of campus speech codes are fiercely debated. Is a hostile environment, perhaps leading to ethnoviolence, worth absolute free speech?

University campuses are recognized historically for their spirited debate, countercultural dissent, and forums for free speech. This section demonstrates how they are appearing more and more like legal battlegrounds. The central issue is the intersection of free speech—First Amendment rights— versus hate speech that is discriminatory and incites anti-Semitic hatred and even violence. There are examples of discomfort among both absolutist civil libertarians, who believe that the range of restrictions of campus speech creates a risky disturbing effect, and those who insist that there is no place for hate speech in educational institutions.

In addition to the three examples that follow, I would also like to note a "vituperatively anti-Semitic speech" at the University of Washington and a Ku Klux Klan rally at Stockton State College, New Jersey (Marcus, 1996: vii). The three examples are from Harvard University, Stanford University, and Kean College. Let us start at Harvard.

Preventing Anti-Semitic Speech at Harvard

Speech grounded in argument is clearly a major component of higher learning. It certainly seems to be part of the essence of what makes a university. Academic freedom and free expression are passionately safeguarded almost always, regardless of content. Yet in November 2002, the English Department at Harvard University withdrew its invitation to the poet Tom Paulin to deliver its annual Morris Gray Lecture.

The withdrawal of the invitation to speak was based on mounting protests over Paulin's anti-Semitic comments during an interview for a Cairo-based newspaper, *Al-Ahram Weekly*, in which he said of "Brooklyn born" Jewish settlers on the West Bank: "They should be shot dead. I think they are Nazis, racists, I feel nothing but hatred for them." He also said, "I never believed that Israel had the right to exist at all" (Rothstein, 2002). Moreover, in a poem published in *The Observer* in 2001, he referred to the Israeli army as "the Zionist SS." These comments represent Stage 4 (Inciting Discriminatory Violence) severity of hate speech; clearly, they encourage violence against minorities.

First Amendment activists, in a new round of protests, then criticized the English Department for its cumbersome reversal. In a letter to *The Harvard Crimson*, Patrick Cavanagh, a Harvard psychology professor (who signed a petition urging that Harvard disinvest in Israel) accused Harvard's president, Lawrence H. Summers, of bigotry for his support of the department's retraction. Summers' action was viewed by free-speech advocates as censorship, especially in light of his recent criticism of anti-Semitic hate speech on American campuses.

First Amendments absolutists maintained that, despite the unpopularity of Paulin's opinions, he was simply making controversial arguments that should be protected by free-speech rights. Evidently swayed by the protests, the English Department met and again changed its collective mind.

Paulin has even attempted to defend his notorious poem, "Killed in Crossfire," with its reference to the "Zionist SS" killing a "little Palestinian boy." But that poem's language is loaded with hate speech including talk of the "weasel" language of Zionists and insinuations of Jewish arrogance, lies, and cheating based on ancient stereotypes that are still in use.

In addition to hate speech, Paulin's comments are moral and historical distortions and lack context. In short, when murders are explicitly encouraged and then carried out, this corresponds to the most severe level of hate speech (Stage 4—Inciting Discriminatory Violence).

The free speech–hate speech issue is also of concern to Harvard's Law School, which debated enacting a "speech code" that would bar certain forms of hateful speech in the classroom. Would incitements to murder and allusions to the Zionist SS qualify? Certainly, this most severe form of hate speech (Stage 4) goes beyond the principles of the First Amendment (dissent, free expression).

Opposing Hate Speech at Stanford

The commotion over hate speech also surfaced in another controversy. The Stanford University Law School invited attorney Lynne Stewart to mentor in the Mills program aiming "to provide public-interest students the opportunity to meet and learn from practitioners and scholars in public service."

But Stewart, who unsuccessfully defended Sheik Omar Abdel Rahman for his responsibility in the 1993 World Trade Center bombing, was indicted in 2001 on charges of aiding a terrorist organization and illegally passing messages from the sheik's prison cell. In particular, in June 2000, she publicly confirmed for the sheik's fundamentalist followers in Egypt that he had called for an end to a cease-fire between those followers and the Egyptian government.

Stewart believes in violence directed at the institutions which perpetuate capitalism, racism, and sexism, and at the people who are the appointed or elected guardians of those institutions. In reacting to the civilian deaths of 9/11, she has hardened and simply accepted them as part of a necessary struggle against the evils of capitalism.

Stewart is part Maoist, part Stalinist, and part Castro Communist. She supports Castro's imprisonment of political dissidents whom she accuses of undermining a people's revolution. Alternately, Stewart views Muslim fundamentalists as forces of national liberation presumably entitled to violence. After Stewart's violent ideology became public, the dean of Stanford's law school stripped her of the title: Mills Mentor. Yet her lectures occurred and her mentoring of students continued.

Stewart's hate speech signifies Stage 4 (Inciting Discriminatory Violence); her words have encouraged violence against Jews and other nonbelievers. Stewart's public lectures and proclamations have resulted in violence. For example, her declaration of the end of that cease-fire was indeed followed by killings in Egypt. It also encouraged violence against American targets.

Hate Speech at Kean College

Kean College, near Newark, New Jersey, was the scene of a series of hate-speech events in the early 1990s. The first was a controversial speech by Afrocentrist Leonard Jeffries in February 1992. This was the ultimate event in the celebration of Black History month. Then on November 29, 1993, Khalid Abdul Muhammad delivered a speech on campus that would vault him into the national spotlight. During the following spring, Louis Farrakhan also spoke at the college.

The fallout was tremendous. The president resigned amid the tensions. There was internal conflict between multiculturalists and First Amendment advocates on one side and those who sought to restrict or control hate speech. Enrollments and fundraising were also adversely affected.

Leonard Jeffries was on the faculty of City College of the City University of New York. He created quite a stir when he professed that Europeans and Americans of European descent are "ice people" instilled with overwhelmingly negative characteristics. He also taught his students that there was a Jewish conspiracy behind the slave trade. Jeffries attacked Jews and Italians for allegedly producing negative images of racial stereotypes in Hollywood films to maintain the oppression and racial stratification of African Americans. Thus, he soon became labeled as anti-White and anti-Jewish.

When some Jewish students, staff, and faculty—including some of Kean College's most enthusiastic advocates of multiculturalism—tried to get into the event, they were not allowed entrance. It was a Blacks-only "private dinner" open only to the sponsoring student organization and guests. Consequently, the banned Jewish students, staff, and faculty protested the function and picketed in front of it, much to the dismay of the dinner's sponsors. A compromise ensued, allowing a few Jewish students in as observers.

Jeffries then stigmatized the Jewish students by telling the audience that now he could not deliver his complete message because of their presence. He added that for those who wanted to receive the entire message, he would subsequently be speaking at a Black church. A political conflict emerged in February 1992 soon after the incident.

There was turmoil on campus. Jewish students, staff, and faculty were indignant that the college administration would allow a man who had openly used anti-Semitic hate speech on previous occasions without having to face those whom he denigrated. The African American students and faculty who attended the dinner were angry that their cultural event and their revered elder had been disrespected. It was clear that there is a fine line between free speech and hate speech. Many members of the campus community, including people from a wide range of ethnic and racial backgrounds, were upset that a student group had been permitted to use campus facilities for a venue at which admission was restricted on the basis of race.

When classes resumed in September 1993, the campus was troubled. There were messages announcing that Jeffries was returning to speak on campus at a conference of a regional academic association. The college president announced a new campus speakers interim policy shortly before Jeffries' arrival. It banned events that restricted admittance on the basis of race or ethnicity. It also required that outside speakers be videotaped. Moreover, advance notice was required.

Given its timing, the change in policy invited criticism from African American students that it was driven by retaliation for damage caused by Jeffries' earlier Blacks-only event. Several Black student leaders called for the president's termination. Jeffries' second talk occurred without incident. However, it resulted in the final dissolution of the U.S. Justice Department's mediation initiative, which had stagnated during the summer of 1993, and likely led to the invitation to Muhammad (Trustee Subcommittee, 1994).

An African American Kean College student leader successfully sought funds to establish an alternative multicultural series. The first speaker was Khalid Abdul Muhammad, national spokesperson for the Nation of Islam (Black Muslims). The title of his talk was provocative: "The Secret Relationship between Blacks and Jews."

As members of the audience arrived for the speech, Muhammad informed the college that unless each person was searched by Fruit of Islam, his bodyguards, before entering the auditorium, there would be no talk. College officials feared the negative ramifications of having to cancel the event at the last minute. Seeking advice from the U.S. Attorney General's Office, college officials suggested requesting that people agree to be searched. Those that did not consent to a search could be given a refund and barred admission. As Muhammad's security force frisked the audience, campus police stood nearby.

Muhammad spoke for three hours, setting himself up as a major hatemonger. He prefaced his comments with a warning that he came to take no prisoners. Muhammad disparaged Jews for criticizing his boss, Louis Farrakhan. He insulted them with scatological references and a simulated Yiddish accent. Muhammad evoked a plethora of Jewish stereotypes (money hungry and in control of the Federal Reserve Board) and accused Jews of being murderers behind the slave trade. He indicated that they deserved the Holocaust and termed Hitler "wickedly great." These comments are Stage 3 (Inciting Discriminatory Hatred) since they are aimed at generating hatred for Jews.

Muhammad's hate speech was not limited to anti-Semitic comments. He also disparaged Christians and made homophobic statements. Muhammad even vulgarly criticized prominent Blacks (e.g., Spike Lee, David Dinkins, Tom Bradley, Henry Louis Gates) whose views were less radical than his as "Uncle Toms." He used Stage 4 (Inciting Discriminatory Violence) to condemn South African Whites and Nelson Mandela's non-vengeance policy:

> We don't owe the white man nothing. . . . If we want to be merciful . . . we give him 24 hours to get out of town. . . . If he won't get out town . . . we kill everything white . . . we kill the women. We kill the children. We kill the babies. We kill the blind. We kill the crippled. We kill the faggot. We kill the Lesbian. We kill them all . . . kill the old ones, too. . . . If they [are] in a wheelchair, push 'em off a cliff. . . . Kill the crazy . . . and when you get through killing 'em all, go to the . . . graveyard and dig up the grave and kill 'em . . . again, cause they didn't die hard enough. (Muhammad in Marcus, 1996: xvii)

Muhammad was an effective speaker. His hate speech was well received by many of those in attendance, including Kean College students, staff, and faculty, who laughed in response to his portrayals and cheered him on with supportive and appreciative comments and applause, even for his most heinous speech. Muhammad even put down a Black student who was courageous enough to challenge him. One of the few Whites in the audience, a faculty member who had been encouraged to attend the speech by some of his African American students in order to learn an Afrocentric perspective, wrote the trustees that he was shocked to see "the leading Kean College faculty and student exponents of Afrocentrism [sitting] in the front row cheering" (Nordheimer, 1993: B6).

CONCLUSION

This chapter examined anti-Muslim and anti-Semitic speech, calling for the restriction of speech that results in or incites discrimination, unfair treatment, hatred, and violence. There has been a plethora of hate speech and hate crimes against Muslims, Arabs, and those perceived to be either since 9/11. In addition, U.S. federal policy of racial profiling young male Muslims has resulted in further hate speech and discrimination against Muslims. What the government fails to realize is that in order to compensate for racial profiling, terrorists will change their profile. Since terrorism is an ideology, anyone can be taught to hate, to be violent, and to sacrifice his or her life for the cause. Consequently, racial profiling will not defeat or even significantly reduce terrorism.

Anti-Muslim hate speech has appeared at institutions of higher learning under the guise of patriotism and nationalism. Colleges and universities have enacted codes restricting hate speech or any activity that interferes with the education of other students or creates a hostile environment for learning. There is often a fine line between academic freedom and speech or symbols that degrade religious or other types of minorities or incite discrimination and hatred.

The Internet has also been a site for anti-Muslim hate mongers, both in terms of hate speech and xenophobic cartoon images. Clearly, the Internet is a frontier that defies the normal range of legal activities regarding free speech and free expression because enforcement is so problematic, especially due to conflicting laws between countries.

Anti-Muslim hate speech and attacks on Muslim people and their institutions has also become a major problem in Europe following the train bombings in Madrid in 2004 and the subway and bus bombings in London in 2005. This chapter also looked at some of the contemporary anti-immigration or anti-minority movements in France, the Netherlands, Belgium, Germany, and Austria.

I also described and analyzed inflammatory anti-Semitic hate speech by foreign heads of state and anti-Semitics around the world. Hate speech also includes anti-Semitic demonstrations by the Ku Klux Klan. Parallel to the rising anti-Muslim speech on college campuses, anti-Semitic hate speech has also been spread at institutions of higher education by scholars and instructors who claim that academic freedom excuses their odious statements. In agreement with critical race theory, I have maintained that this type of hate speech should be restricted.

4

Gender and Hate Speech

We are going to protest because this is just a massage parlor by any other name.

—Sandra White, feminist protester

It's exploitative to women and just a bit cheap and nasty. All it is really is a cheap publicity stunt for someone's business.

—The Scottish Coalition Against Sexual Exploitation

On April 14, 2004, feminist groups and anti-porn campaigners met to plan their protest against the launch of Scotland's first topless barbers (Gallacher and Murray, 2004). Fundamentalist Christians and Scottish Women Against Porn were scheduled to demonstrate against the opening of the aptly named "A Bit Off the Top" in Paisley. When the Glasgow-based Urban Group publicized its plans to kick off its combination massage parlor/semi-nude barber shop, the city erupted. The firm recruited former lap-dancers who are also trained as hairdressers to work for the new venture on Canal Street.

Male customers may choose between a massage in a private booth or a haircut for £25 (currently equivalent to $47.37 American currency). Previously, the company's owners created controversy by hanging a huge banner with an image of a woman cupping her breasts outside the shop. The banner displays body-chopping or dismemberment (Cortese, 2004: 38); the woman has no face. Accordingly, women's bodies are often shown dismembered or hacked apart in advertising and other public images. When their bodies are separated into parts, women cease to be seen as whole persons. This perpetuates the notion that a woman's body is not linked to her mind, soul, or emotions.

Women's body parts are sometimes portrayed as inanimate objects such as mannequins, ice cream cones, hills, and flowers (Cortese, 2004). Depictions of dismemberment or body-chopping appears to occur much more frequently for women than men. The implication is that women are objects and therefore less than human. Public images that depict women's bodies without faces, heads, and feet imply that all that is really important about a woman lies between her neck and her knees. The lack of a head symbolizes a woman without a brain. A faceless woman, such as the image in the banner, has no individuality. A woman without feet is immobile and therefore submissive.

Protestors promised to closely monitor the barber shop for signs of indecency. Others call it disgusting, shocking, and degrading to women. It profits from immature men who view women as sex objects and subordinate to men. The men pay for the women, whom they control. Despite the widespread opposition, the courts are powerless to stop it from opening. In such venues as strip-clubs with lap-dancing, the male patrons denigrate the women through their words, gestures, and other actions. They make a distinction between the dancers and those women they would ask out on a date. The shop's owners, the Urban Group, have indicated that they have already taken many reservations and expect the salon, which they contend is harmless fun, to be popular.

This chapter examines gender and hate speech. In particular, it focuses on pornography as hate speech and its possible links to rape, sexual harassment, and child molestation. Then expansion of sexual harassment on the Internet is analyzed as pornographic hate speech. There are two subsequent sections on the child sex industry—one on child prostitution, the other on child pornography—to establish that pornography harms children as well as women. Feminist protests and demonstrations have been used as a technique for securing equal rights and protection under the law. We will discuss the Take Back the Night movement and look at a first-person narrative of a repentant rapist. Hate speech in anti-feminist demonstrations is looked at from a critical perspective. There are also a brief sociohistorical background of hate radio and a case study of misogynist and racist hate radio on a university campus.

PORNOGRAPHY AS HATE SPEECH

> *As a clinical psychologist, I have treated, over the years, approximately 350 sex addicts, sex offenders, or other individuals (96% male) with sexual illnesses. This includes many types of unwanted compulsive sexual acting-out, plus such things as child molestation, exhibitionism, voyeurism, sadomasochism, fetishism, and rape. With several exceptions, pornography has been a major or minor contributor or facilitator in the acquisition of their deviation or sexual addition.*
> —Victor B. Cline,
> http://www.moralityinmedia.org/clinepage.htm

Your violation his arousal, your torture his pleasure.
—Catharine MacKinnon, 1993: 4

Is pornography free speech that should be protected by the First Amendment? Or is pornography hate speech? Or perhaps, it is not speech at all, but rather harmful action in itself that also leads to predatory sexual activity. This section begins by evaluating the damage done to women and children, directly and indirectly, through pornography. A robust link from pornography to rape, violence, sexual harassment, and child molestation is highlighted, developed, and revealed.

The feminist orientation guides the conceptual framework for this chapter. Accordingly, hardcore pornography is "not a celebration of sexual freedom [but] a cynical exploitation of female sexual activity through the device of making all such activity and consequently all females 'dirty'" (Brownmiller, 1976: 446).

There are social processes (e.g., gender socialization, advertising) whose underlying dynamic is the sexual objectification of women as a means to maintain male dominance and female subordination. The dehumanization of women in pornography is part of a continuum of female submission that starts with the visual appropriation of women in misogynistic pornography and the malignity of women in musical lyrics, then moves on to the verbal and physical abuse of women in sexual harassment, then the misappropriation of women as prostitutes, then as rape victims in forced sex, and finally to sexual murder. This continuum is also evident in the dehumanization of children in child pornography, molestation, child prostitution, rape, and eventually, the sexual murder of children. This scale parallels the four-stage theory of hate speech severity presented in Chapter 1.

Does the First Amendment provide pornographic filmmakers with unlimited freedom of expression? How does one resolve the tensions between the pornographic filmmakers' right of expressive freedom with the rights of women and children to be protected from visual images that humiliate, dehumanize, injure, torture, and incite hatred, violence, and murder?

We turn to an examination of the connection between pornography and rape.

PORNOGRAPHY AND RAPE

No one learns respect for women from pornography.
—Catharine MacKinnon, 1995: 7

Technological advances have provided relatively inexpensive home video cameras and VCRs, increasing the ease of making and viewing pornographic features, in turn spawning more hardcore materials. The number of hardcore video rentals increased from 75 million in 1985 to 665 million in 1996. Americans now spend $8–$10 billion a year on hardcore videos, peep shows, live sex acts, sexual devices, adult cable programming, computer porn, telephone sex, and sex magazines—more than they spend on Hollywood movies or on music recordings (Macionis, 2002; Parrillo et al., 1999). Americans now spend more money at strip clubs than at all Broadway, off-Broadway and regional, nonprofit theaters, and at opera, ballet, and jazz and classical music performances combined.

Since violence is endemic in American culture, it is not surprising that rape is a more prevalent problem than in other countries. There is a strong relationship between the amount of money spent on pornography and rates of sexual assault. The United States spends the most on pornography and has the highest proportion of rapes. Girls and women in the United States run a much higher risk of being raped than women in Europe (United Nations, 1995).

Estimates are that from 17.6 percent (Tjaden and Thoennes, 1991) to 28 percent (Koss et al., 1987) to nearly half (Russell, 1982, 1986) of all women are victims of rape or attempted rape at least once in their lives, many more than once, especially women of color, many involving multiple attackers, mostly acquaintances, friends, lovers, or husbands. Twenty-four percent of women are raped in their marriages (MacKinnon, 1993).

In 2001, 90,491 completed or attempted rapes were reported to the police; 64 of every 100,000 females in the United States were reported victims of forcible rape (Federal Bureau of Investigation, 2002). This amounts to one every six minutes. The FBI statistics do not include attempted rape, nor do they include consensual sex with a minor (typically, a person under age 18—a crime known as "statutory rape"). Partly because most victims know their attackers, police make arrests in half of reported rape cases (Macionis, 2002).

Most rapes go unreported to the police. The National Crime Victimization Survey discovered 147,000 rape incidents during 2001—almost two attempted or completed rapes for every 1,000 residents age 12 or older (Bureau of Justice Statistics, 2002). The National Violence Against Women Survey—considered to be the best current measure of the prevalence of rape (Schmalleger, 2004)—reveals that there are slightly more than 300,000 rape victims and 876,064 rape incidents annually (Tjaden and Thoennes, 1991).

Almost 60 percent of all rapes take place in the victim's home or at the home of a friend, relative, or neighbor; in 80 percent of all cases, the victim and the offender know each other. Sixty-one percent of all rape victims are less than 18 years old (Federal Bureau of Investigation, 1995; Greenfeld, 1997; National Victim Center, 1992). Date rape—also referred to as acquaintance rape—comprises more than half of all cases of (Bachman and Saltzman, 1995).

In the international arena, rape has been chillingly linked to mass murder. Nowrojee (1996), a human rights organization, documented mass rape in the Rwandan genocide in 1994. Sexual violence during the Rwandan genocide and its aftermath shattered the lives of the Tutsi women. It is a miscarriage of justice that the rapes themselves were not part of the indictments in the Rwandan tribunal (see Chapter 2).

PORNOGRAPHY AND VIOLENCE

> The question "Who is the typical rapist, wife beater, incest offender, etc.?" is raised constantly. The answer is simple: men.
> —Carol J. Sheffield, 2004: 414

Is pornography free expression that should be protected under the First Amendment? Or does the production and viewing of pornographic film result in significant psychological or physical harm to women and children? It depends on how you define it. The word "pornography" comes from the Greek term *porne* and means "sexual slave" (Dworkin, 1991; MacKinnon, 2001). Let us start with an important distinction between eroticism and pornography. *Eroticism* is the vivid depiction of sexual passion and love. *Pornography* is the depiction of brutal sexual behavior resulting in female or male dehumanization, degradation, and exploitation (Millett, 1983). Much of pornography fits in to Stage 4 (Inciting Discriminatory Violence) because it encourages violence against women. This includes rape, physical and psychological abuse, by both individual men and gangs. It also includes "snuff" films where women are actually killed in the film in the name of violent eroticism.

Some of pornographic film accommodates to Stage 3 (Inciting Discriminatory Hatred) since the sexual objectification of women is a natural precursor in generating feelings of hatred for women. As Catharine MacKinnon (1995: 7) has stated: "No one learns respect for women from pornography." Some of pornography fits Stage 2 (Conscious Discrimination) because treating women as subordinate sex toys seems to be, at the very least, a conscious attempt to discriminate and deny women equal treatment.

What harm is a little porn video? It provides men and women with exploiter or exploited roles and *scripts*—cultural messages that teach us how to behave—for their relationships and marriages. There is a causal relationship between viewing violent pornography and sexual violence. In this sense, the most graphic pornography is equivalent to Stage 4 (Inciting discriminatory Violence) because it stimulates violence against women. Viewing pornography that contains violence makes people more accepting of violent acts such as rape (Attorney-General's Commission on Pornography, 1986). This conclusion, which found support among both conservatives and liberals in government, also has wide public support. In a recent national survey, approximately half of U.S. adults think pornography does encourage people to commit rape (NORC, 1999: 237)

Like MacKinnon (1995, 2001) and Dworkin (1991), I oppose the absolutist view that pornography is a form of speech protected by the First Amendment. Denigrating, sexually explicit images of women should not be legally different from denigrating, sexually explicit images of children. Disparagement of women appears to be a logical step to the development of feelings of hatred for women (Stage 3: Inciting Discriminatory Hatred).

The U.S. Supreme Court allows communities to ban sexual material as obscene if it violates community standards of decency and lacks any redeeming social value. There is prevalent concern about the effects of pornography on individuals and society as a whole. Almost 60 percent of U.S. adults claim "sexual material leads to a breakdown of morals" (NORC, 1999: 237). Even so, in any community, not everyone will agree about standards of decency, making the issue of pornography difficult and often disruptive.

Other kinds of offensive expressions are also subject to government regulation. For example, signs indicating, "No Mexicans allowed" is an act of ethnic discrimination. Saying "I'll terminate your employment if you don't have sex with me" is an act of sexual harassment. One cannot sensibly claim that ethnic discrimination or sexual harassment deserves First Amendment protection or that their prohibition restricts individual rights.

SEXUAL HARASSMENT

She was seductive. She misunderstood. I was just being friendly.
—Myth of sexual harassment

The idea of using a paycheck as a license for sex seems ludicrous, if not sick, but it happens all the time. Men who would never think, or at least never follow through on, the idea of pinching a woman's breast in a bus or on the street, feel free to subject their secretary to this humiliation as if it were a job-given right.
—Patti Giuffre and Christine Williams, 1994: 70

Sexual harassment, like pornography, is based on an assumption of entitlement to sexual privileges. Sexual harassment is any unwelcome sexual advances, requests for sexual favors, and other verbal or physical conduct of a sexual nature when submission is made a condition of employment, or rejection of the advance is used as the basis for future employment decision, or interfering with the individual's performance or creating an intimidating, hostile, or offensive working environment.

Because men hold most positions of power and authority, most sexual harassers are men, and most victims are women. Sexual harassment is typically a power play committed by bosses against underlings, by professors against students, by more secure colleagues against weaker co-workers. However, this is not always the case. Seventy-seven percent of women physicians surveyed have been sexually harassed by their own male patients, usually in their own offices (Phillips and Schneider, 1993).

In 1976, a federal court (in *Williams v. Saxbe*) ruled that sexual harassment amounted to illegal sex discrimination. At this point, sexual harassment began receiving public attention and was soon considered a serious problem. That same year, a survey by *Redbook*, a women's magazine, found that 90 percent of the women respondents reported that they had been sexually harassed at some time in their work lives. Findings from later studies are fairly consistent with that figure. Eighty-five percent of women who work outside the home are sexually harassed at some point by employers or co-workers (United States Merit Protection Board, 1981, 1988).

Many thousands of complaints of sexual harassment are filed each year in agencies at all levels of government; of these, less than 10 percent are filed by men Richmond-Abbott, 1992). These formal complaints are but a small fragment of the total number of occurrences of sexual harassment in workplaces, community associations, and public settings (Hippensteele and Pearson, 1999).

Sexual harassment is also extremely common in schools and other educational institutions. A recent random sample survey of 2,064 public school students in the eighth through eleventh grades (American Association of University Women, 2001) discovered that for many students, sexual harassment is an ongoing experience: more than 1 in 4 students experience it "often."

On October 11 and 12, 1991, all the major television networks preempted their afternoon soap operas and much of their evening and weekend schedules to broadcast the real-life political soap opera of the all-male Senate Judiciary Committee's investigation of Anita Hill's accusations of sexual harassment against Supreme Court justice nominee Clarence Thomas. Hill, at the time a University of Oklahoma law professor, dropped a bombshell into the middle of Senate Supreme Court confirmation hearings for Thomas: Hill alleged that Thomas had harassed and embarrassed her with repeated requests for dates and discussions about pornography while supervising her at the Equal Employment Opportunity Commission.

In a calm and dignified manner, Hill reported to the Committee that while in his employ, Thomas allegedly handed her a can of soda with a pubic hair on it, talked about pornography and videos starring Long Dong Silver, and repeatedly advised her of his sexual prowess (Hill and Jordan, 1995). There was testimony that Justice Thomas had an obsessive interest in pornography and had often rented pornographic movies when Hill worked for him (Abramson and Mayer, 1994). The graphic testimony entertained and shocked many, but mostly it brought to the forefront the topic of sexual harassment in the workplace.

Hill's allegations introduced a volatile mix of sex, race, and scandal into the proceedings, deeply dividing both the Senate and the entire country. More than 40 million U.S. households watched the two-day televised hearings and the networks lost an estimated $15 to $20 million in advertising revenue. The testimony by Hill and others enlightened the public about how lewd and crude remarks constitute sexual harassment. The four-stage model of hate speech severity presented in Chapter 1 is also applicable to the various types of spoken or written sexual harassment.

In the end, the Senate Judiciary Committee voted to approve Thomas's nomination to the Supreme Court, much to the chagrin of feminists and many other Americans. The hearing galvanized public awareness, and the formal complaints filed with the Equal Employment Opportunity Commission (EEOC) charging sexual harassment nearly doubled (Ingrassia, 1993). Finally, the hearing also bore witness to the close relationship between sexual harassment and pornography as hate speech.

PORNOGRAPHY AND THE SEXUAL ABUSE OF CHILDREN

> *Confucius say, "if rape is inevitable, relax and enjoy it."*
> —Tex Antoine, weather forecaster, after hearing a
> report of the rape of an eight-year-old

> *May all your troubles be little ones.*
> —One child molester to another in William
> Burroughs's *Naked Lunch*

Until relatively recently in our nation's history, U.S. law has not protected children against sexual abuse. Children have consistently been considered the property of their fathers and could be legitimately exploited, sold, or even killed by their parents or masters (de Mause, 1974). Since children were also sexual property, sexual relations between male adults and minors has been permitted, or at least accepted, in American institutions of marriage, concubinage, slavery, and—as emphasized in the present analyses—in prostitution and pornography.

Current laws on the sexual abuse of children are complex and often contradictory. Generally, the sexual abuse of children includes statutory rape, molestation, carnal knowledge, indecent liberties, impairing the morals of a minor, child abuse, child neglect, and incest. Each of these is defined, interpreted, and punished independently in each state.

The theory underlying statutory-rape legislation is that a child below a certain age (arbitrarily assigned by state law) is not able to give meaningful consent to sex. Thus, sexual intercourse with a child below a certain age, even with ostensible consent, is rape. Punishment for statutory rape is rarely imposed—even though the law permits *life imprisonment*. Parallel to laws on statutory rape are laws on criminal incest. Incest is commonly viewed as sexual activity, most often intercourse, with a blood relative. The difference, then, between statutory rape and incest is the relation of the offender to the child.

Statutory rape is committed by someone outside the family; incest is committed by a member of the family. The sentencing for incest, also rarely imposed, is more often than not no more than *10 years* in prison. This stark contrast between statutory rape and incest implicitly suggests that sexual abuse of children is tolerated when it occurs within the family and that unqualified protection of children from sexual assault is not the intent of the law.

In the new millennium, we expect mothers, caretakers, and the legal system to protect children from sexual abuse and exploitation in the sex industry. However, American law enforcement officers, judges, and policymakers have all neglected to deprive men of their sexual privileges. Consequently, prohibitions depict a double standard based on gender. The typical approval of sex between young females and older males is reflected in law and social custom in the United States.

In 1962, the American Law Institute recommended that the legal age of consent to sex—that is, the age below which sex is defined as statutory rape—be dropped in every state to age 10 (Katchadourian and Lund, 1972: 439). In fact, until the mid-1960s, the legal age of consent in Delaware was 7 (Kling, 1965: 216). So a 50-year-old man could legally have sexual intercourse with a 7-year-old boy or girl. The current ages for consent range from 16 to 18 and are set into law arbitrarily by each state.

There is no doubt that men's sexual attraction to children and child pornography feed off each other. Magazine publishers, film producers, entrepreneurs, and advertisers have successfully captured this growing market. The value being sold is a long-awaited, forbidden sexual desire. The repeated images of the young girl–woman provocatively posed in conjunction with various products and services is a direct appeal to male sexual interest in little girls (Cortese, 2004). A prime example is the 1960s British fashion model, Twiggy, who stood 5 feet, 6 inches, but weighed only 90 pounds. It was evident that small, infantile, and childish was considered the cultural standard of feminine beauty and sexuality. More recently, supermodel Kate Moss has continued this tradition. There is a double threat here: the male testosterone surges from the visual stimulation and the waifish images colonize the dreams of young girls who recognize the power and popularity via sexual allure of these idealized bodies. The display of more and more skin and sexually explicit posing by young models pushes the envelope and blurs the distinction between advertising and soft pornography.

The child as sex object has become a commodity not unlike the products that her body is used to sell (Cortese, 2004). Another more acceptable technique used to display and stimulate the sexual abuse of children is art. The prominent photographer O.G. Rejlander, the painters Jules Pascin and

Balthus, and the photography of David Hamilton have depicted the female child as either sexually aggressive, sexually unrestrained, or uninhibited, or sexually depraved and harlot-like (Rush, 1980).

In the 1970s, the film *Taxi Driver* featured a then very young Jodie Foster who portrayed a 12-year-old street prostitute who gladly pleased any male urge so as to satisfy her malicious pimp. The adolescent prostitute character was so popular that Foster gave an encore performance in *The Little Girl Who Lives Down the Lane*, in which she performed as a 13-year-old imp of maturing sexuality.

The relationship between pornography and the criminal sexual assault against children is direct and cannot be disregarded. Law enforcement records across the United States archive reports of both adult men and juvenile offenders who have been found with pornographic material either on their persons, in their cars, or in their rooms (Rush, 1980). Law enforcement officers, district attorneys, judges, and social workers are consistently drawing links between sexual assaults against children and pornography. Here is an example from the San Antonio, Texas, police force:

A 15-year-old boy grabbed a 9-year-old girl, dragged her into the brush and was ripping off her clothes. The girl screamed and the youth fled. The next day he was picked up by the police. He admitted that he had done the same thing in Houston, Galveston, and now in San Antonio. He said his father kept pornographic pictures in his top dresser drawer and that each time he looked at them the urge would come over him (Gallagher, 1977: 20).

In Jacksonville, Florida, in each of four cases in criminal courts where adults were charged with felonies with various sexual offenses involving minor children, obscene literature and other pornographic materials were used to entice the children.

THE CHILD SEX INDUSTRY: PROSTITUTION

> *A person comes up to you, and he asks you if you want something to eat, or if you want a soft drink. Then he asks you how old you are, and he asks you if you've had sex before. And that's how it begins.*
> —A young Acapulco man who worked in male
> pornography and prostitution

> *There's a lot of child prostitution, and there's a lot of child pornography . . . there are 10-year-olds who are in the business.*
> —Miguel Lopez Sotelo, child-welfare official,
> Guerrero, Mexico

Child molestation has been clearly linked to pornography. An estimated 40 percent of child pornography consumers also sexually abuse children (Sadowitz, 2003). A recent crackdown on the child sex industry in Mexico, with pressure from the U.S. Department of Homeland Security, seems to show a connection between pornography and child molestation for both child victims and their adult molesters. Thousands of Mexican girls and boys work in prostitution or pornography (Azaloa, 2000). Many work in both arenas. The typical scenario involves a poor young boy fleeing a broken home. Often he becomes addicted to crack and turns to both prostitution and posing nude for photos and videos to pay for his drugs.

The attack on the child sex industry resulted in the closing of Castillo Vista del Mar, a scenic inn offering room and board, stunning cliff-side views, and boys as young as 6 years old for $1,000 a week (Edgerton and Case, 2003). Indigent Mexican boys are recruited by entrepreneurs—often themselves pedophiles—promising food, shelter, and money. The inn targeted travelers from the United States, Canada, and Europe and was located in Acapulco, a major center for the thriving child sex industry. Acapulco, like Bangkok, Thailand, is ideal for the child sex industry—what street kids call *el business*—because of its strong tourist venue and large numbers of indigent children.

There appears to be a strong connection between pornography and molestation. Men who molest children are typically heavy pornography viewers and sometimes even producers. For example (Edgerton and Case, 2003):

- In the 1990s, two Americans moved to Guadalajara, Mexico, began molesting young boys and making child pornography. They had gained access to the boys under the guise of teaching them English.
- Robert W. Decker, manager of Castillo Vista del Mar, was convicted of child sexual abuse and later arrested for possession of child pornography.
- In April 2003, Mexican federal police arrested 20 men for child sexual abuse. (Ten children were rescued in the process.) Some defendants were found with stashes of child porn, cameras, and video equipment.

The Mexican child sex industry also has female victims. Smugglers have lured girls as young as 12 across the border with promises of housekeeping jobs, then forced them into prostitution in Southern California migrant labor camps.

THE CHILD SEX INDUSTRY: PORNOGRAPHY

The most exotic ten-year-old you'll ever meet!
—*Lollitots* (child pornography magazine) introduction
of "Patti"

Pedophilia is outside the interests of pornography.
—The Commission on Obscenity and Pornography,
1970

Some parents appeared in the [porn] movie with their children; others merely allowed their children to have sex. One little girl, age 11, who

ran crying from the bedroom after being told to have sex with a man
of 40, protested, "Mommy, I can't do it."
    "You have to do it," her mother answered. "We need the money."
And of course, the little girl did.

—Robert Sam Anson, 1977

Child pornography is big business and has been recognized as a growing social problem since the late 1970s. Child models are easy to recruit
for pornographic film and video. Many magazine publishers and film producers use their own children; others advertise to parents (Rush, 1980). To
be sure, it is less problematic for us to express outrage against child pornography than adult pornography. However, young girls grow up to be women.
What legal protection there is dissipates as they reach the age of consent.
Thus, the legalized exploitation resumes.

It is not coincidence that cultural standards of feminine beauty are images and concepts of infantilized women. A big part of female attractiveness to men is the defenselessness of a child. Advertising images make the
child look and act like a woman and the woman look and act like a child.

Child pornography is a booming enterprise. The profits are large, the
overhead minimal. The production has become routine, using the principles of "McDonaldization": efficiency, calculability, predictability, and control (Ritzer, 2000). The industry is a virtual kiddy porno factory. The
standard formula has not changed over the last several decades: "emphasis on the innocence of children and the lechery of adults. Boys from six
to thirteen and girls from six to fifteen. Emphasize hairlessness—tiny pri-
vates, lack of tits" (Sproat, 1974).

Children who run away from their homes often end up in prostitution
or pornography. The most comprehensive study done in 1989 by the Government Accounting Office indicates 1.3 million kids are on the street each
year. According to the Children's Defense Fund, approximately 1,200 youth
run away each day. An estimated 2.8 million youth living in the United
States reported a runaway experience during the prior year (Greene et al.,
1995).

Anti-pornography laws have existed since the eighteenth century, but
have rarely been enforced. By the mid-1950s, a series of Supreme Court
decisions led to progressively more lenient attitudes toward sexually explicit material. In 1970, the Commission on Obscenity and Pornography
published a report, concluding that pornography is not harmful, but even
educational and encourages frank communication between parents and
children. The report also found that pornography releases inhibitions, is
not a factor in the causation of crime, and is, therefore, not a matter of
public concern.

Perhaps the best example of the commission's apparent apathy is its re-
fusal to contend with the exploitation and victimization of vulnerable children in pornography. The commission reported such gross inaccuracies as

"Pedophilia is outside the interests of pornography," or "the taboo against pedophilia remains inviolate," and "the use of prepubescent children is almost nonexistent" (Barnes, 1970: 147).

Pornography and Child Molestation

Sexual predators scar children psychologically by molesting them. *Child molestation* is the legal term for child sexual abuse, which occurs when an adult engages in sexual activity such as exposure of sexual organs, fondling, intercourse, oral sex, or pornography with a minor (Parillo et al., 1999). Pornography is linked to child molestation in several ways. First, sexual predators often expose children to it. Other times, pornographic filmmakers and photographers force children to have sex with adults to produce images for commercial use. Finally, perhaps viewing child pornography may trigger an urge or create a *modeling* effect for the viewer to actually molest a child.

Child molestation cuts across all socioeconomic levels, although a disproportionate number of child molesters are White (West and Templer, 1994). Many child molesters experienced sexual abuse during their own childhood, and most often the victim knows the offender (Romano and DeLuca, 1997). The ratio is about even for heterosexual and homosexual child molesters.

Approximately 140,000 child molestation cases are reported each year in the United States, but the number of unreported cases is far greater, because children are often afraid to tell anyone what happened (U.S. Department of Health and Human Services, 1995). Estimates are that from 12.5 (*Maclean's*, 1997) to 33 (Hopper, 2003) to 38 percent (MacKinnon, 1993; Salter, 1988) of girls are sexually molested before age 18. Approximately 11 (Salter, 1988) to 17 percent (Dorais, 2002; Hopper, 2003) of boys are sexually molested during childhood or adolescence—and yet this abuse remains a taboo subject, even among victims. Dorais (2002) provides boy victims a voice, offering sensitive analyses of their traumas, self-doubt, and coping strategies.

From 1980 to 1984, 33 percent of all reported child sexual abuse incidents involved a babysitter or day-care worker; 22 percent involved a family member. From 1985 to 1990, babysitter and day-care cases remained at the same level, but family member involvement rose dramatically to 55 percent. From 1991 to 1994, virtually no cases involved babysitters or day-care workers and cases involving family members dipped to 39 percent, but the clergy were prominent at 26 percent (Becker, 1996).

HATE SPEECH AND SEXUAL HARASSMENT ON THE INTERNET

The Internet has become an important global resource and has an estimated 20 million users (Rosenberg, 2003). Consequently, a number of concerns have emerged that create tough questions for both users and system administrators. For example, the Internet has become another avenue of easy access to pornographic materials, with at least 10,000 out of 25,000 sites on the World Wide Web devoted to various forms of pornography (Harmon, 1997).

Internet Environment

Men appear to dominate the Internet; they set the agenda and the style—and women who want to partake must play by male-generated rules. This situation constitutes sexual harassment because it creates a hostile environment for women to participate in. Regulatory steps should be taken to eliminate sexual harassment and even the playing field.

There is also a glaring connection between pornography and sexual harassment on the Internet. Use of public computing facilities does not license anyone to display material that, for example, women may find offensive. Disregarding the articulated uneasiness of women may expose one to charges of sexual harassment.

Whereas electronic networks such as the Internet have brought huge benefits to scholarship, research, business, and, to be sure, communication, their use has been accompanied by a variety of issues that are apt to compromise, even to disrupt, these significant uses. Rosenberg (1993) has dealt extensively with free speech and pornography and has continued and extended this discussion in new directions. Recent developments include attempts to either restrict or ban certain Usernet newsgroups.

In addition to pornography, the problem of sexual harassment raises free-speech issues. There is concern with sexual harassment over the Net. There are a variety of offensive postings with sexual themes. Moreover, women may be directly harassed in a variety of ways: offensive e-mail, "flamed" or just put down in newsgroups, and insulted in IRC (Internet Relay Chats) interactions.

Solution: Sexual Harassment Procedures

Rosenberg (2003), a strong supporter of free speech, opposes the censorship of potentially offensive material on networks and instead encourages the use of sexual harassment procedures, if appropriate. Sexual harassment procedures could be used to redress gross insensitivity or sheer malicious behavior.

The consequences of viewing certain material in public places—including the Internet—may well be detrimental to the well-being of some people. Women who find it offensive and whose feelings are ignored in attempts to improve unpleasant situations can initiate sexual harassment procedures. Such actions may not be easy, however, and may subject women to further abuse. In addition, what constitutes sexual harassment in the workplace is still being defined and the burden placed on women to voice their displeasure is typically arduous.

Use of public computing facilities does not license anyone to display material that others, not necessarily women, may find offensive. Ignoring the expressed discomfort of others may open one up to charges of harassment, sexual or otherwise. However, First Amendment absolutists argue that private reading or viewing of material that some might find offensive is not sufficient cause to deny ready access to all. Nevertheless, since the law and the judiciary protect people from discrimination and sexual harassment, one may rebut that this takes legal precedence over the free expression of obscene and offensive materiel.

TAKE BACK THE NIGHT

> *Seven years ago I raped someone. I did not use a knife, a gun or a fist. I did not threaten her and she did not scream for help, but I had sex with a woman who did not consent—and that is rape.*
>
> *I never want to rape again. And until I understand more about my own power, I will do everything I can to make sure I do not express it as rape.*
>
> —Jack M., 2002

Take Back the Night is an international protest rally and march that is organized in local communities in order to make people aware of violence against women, children, and families. The event is a collaboration of community and campus and other interested persons to take a stand against violence and reclaim the darkness, making the night safer for everyone. The first Take Back the Night originated in Germany in 1973 in response to a series of sexual assaults, rapes, and murders. Rallies and marches soon followed in England as a protest against the fear that women encountered walking the streets at night. The first Take Back the Night in the United States occurred in San Francisco in 1978.

There are chapters across the country, and in these venues it is an annual event that brings together organizations, civic leaders, and the public to protest violence against women and to promote awareness of the attitudes, beliefs, and behaviors which perpetuate this type of violence. Local chapters of Take Back the Night often team with local chapters of the National Organization for Women to sponsor the events. The events showcase organizations that offer assistance to women and educate the public and private sectors on the characteristics of these crimes. These events and programs often coincide with September's Sexual Assault Month or October's Domestic Violence Awareness Month.

Today, marches are held in numerous cities in the United States, Canada, Latin America, India, and Europe. While different organizations and agencies may sponsor this event, the message is always the same. The purpose of the march is to demand that the perpetrators of this violence—the batterers, the rapists, the murderers—be held responsible for their actions and be made to change (Lederer, 1980). As a sign of unity, it is not uncommon for 200 or more groups to sponsor an event that offers assistance and educates the public and private sectors on the characteristics of these crimes.

What follows is part of a graphic depiction of a sexual assault from the perspective of the perpetrator—Jack M (2002). This segment is not meant to reproduce, justify, or validate the rape—but rather to provide information on and understanding of the twisted reasoning of a sexual predator and to emphasize the strong correlation between alcohol consumption and sexual assault. It is also meant to stimulate understanding of what happened and how, and to evaluate the extent to which the rapist now understands what he did and accepts responsibility for his actions. This is an edited version of an article that appeared in *Manhattan Spirit* newspaper, a weekly in New York City owned by News Communications, Inc. (text in italics indicates earlier reflections on the incident).

Seven years ago I raped someone. I did not use a knife, a gun or a fist. I did not threaten her and she did not scream for help, but I had sex with a woman who did not consent—and that is rape. I don't think of myself as a bad guy. I have a college degree in the arts from a prestigious school, and my parents, still married, are very supportive. I do not hate women or the world, or myself for that matter. My female friends here in New York, as well as many of my ex-girlfriends, think I am a bright, caring, understanding person. But none of that kept me from raping.

I did not understand that what I did was rape until about a year ago. What made me finally realize my crime was the recent surge in media coverage of the phenomenon of "date rape." The St. Johns University and Palm Beach rape cases, as well as other highly publicized scenarios where the alleged assaults were more ambiguous than a knife to the throat and a demand for sex, made me think about what date rape really is, as I relived that night.

I went to an upper West Side bar "scamming" with some of my friends. We had already been drinking steadily and by the time we got there, we were still coherent, but basically numb.

Through the entire night, even though I was drinking, I remained in control of my body. The booze accentuated my confidence and made me feel invincible—immune to rejection. Tonight, whatever I wanted, I was going to take, and nothing was going to stop me.

I met her at the bar. She was from England and had come to New York for a short time to tour with a theater company, I think. When I walked in, I knew I wanted to bed this woman. I wanted to have sex that night and she looked like an inviting prospect.

This was a period of my life where I was "slutting" heavily. I would pick a woman up at a bar and sleep with her the same night. I started to think I was entitled to sex. After talking a woman up and buying her a few drinks, I would do everything I could to make her go to bed with me. Usually she was willing. Sometimes, however, it took a little more work to convince her.

I was often cruel to these women. If the sex was good, I might see them again, but I would quickly get bored, and after gaining their trust and having them fully confide in me, I would abruptly blow them off. They would be shocked and hurt, and would call me in the middle of the night to cry and call me names and demand an explanation. I would tell them, "I don't have to give you an explanation. Good night"; or I would be brutally straightforward, saying, "I'm bored with you," "I don't like your body" or "You don't turn me on anymore."

She had only recently arrived and did not know much about the City. We talked for awhile and a mild seduction took place. I made her believe I was interested in what she was saying, and she thought I really cared about her. Our thighs rubbed together, my arm brushed against her breast.

I was getting to her.

We drank some more and I grew confident that I was not going home alone tonight. She was staying at a friend's place in midtown, and I assumed that when we left together, it meant she was going over to my place.

This was exactly the kind of assumption which often leads to a date rape. She had no idea that I wanted to sleep with her that night, but from my point of view, it was a given. Why else would I leave the bar? If I was not going to have sex with her, I would much rather drink more and try my hand at someone else. So it was understood on my part that we were going to sleep together. That understanding was not mutual. There was no understanding.

I asked her if she wanted to leave the bar, saying, "Do you want to take a walk?" I told her that I would take her back to the bar or to her friend's place. She believed me, and I was on the road to getting her to sleep over.

I have always had a secret agenda with women. I would do anything I could to seduce them. I would use empathy, understanding, humor, even my deepest secrets to get them on my side. I would show that I was a "sensitive guy" and use that for the sole purpose of bedding them.

This time I used a woman's drunkenness and unfamiliarity with the City for my purposes. Now that she was out of the bar, she had no friends to help her, no one to call, nowhere to go except where I wanted her to go.

We started walking and she asked, "Where are we going?" I said, "Just walking," all the time knowing that we were walking in the direction of my apartment.

We would stop sporadically and make out. During one heavy session I said to her, "Come back to my place." She refused. I said, "What do you mean, no? This is New York City. You don't leave a bar with a guy and not sleep with him. C'mon, this isn't England. This is the big city! This is how we do things."

She still refused, but I could tell I was influencing her with that ridiculous line. So we walked some more and made out some more, all the time getting closer and closer to my apartment. I used that "New York code of etiquette" line time and time again as I took her through unfamiliar streets.

We reached my apartment and I asked her if she wanted to come up. She said no, and I said, "Just come up for a little bit and then I'll take you back." That sat better with her and I congratulated myself for the brilliant sell.

To use language as I did is abusive and irresponsible. I took advantage of someone's innocence for my own ends. I was so confident that I could manipulate her that I did not understand where seduction ended and abusive behavior began.

Before I admitted to myself that I raped this woman, I would say, "She deserved it. If she was gullible enough to fall for that line, then I am not responsible for what happens." But I am responsible. I know I have a command of the language, and I can make some people do what I want by shaping my speech in a certain way and charging it with emotion.

We got up to my apartment and I began kissing her, but now she was not responding as she had on the street. I asked her, "What's the matter?" But she just stared blankly past me into the wall. I gave up on kissing her and began to touch her in ways that would appear lewd on the street. Still no response. I felt like I was fondling a rag doll.

Not that I cared. I did not need any response on her part to get what I wanted.

I tried to take her blouse off and she locked her arms to her sides. I was stronger than her, so I pulled and forced her arms until I got it off.

If the rape did not start when I verbally manipulated her, it was certainly starting now. Now I was forcing her to do something against her will. I was using my strength as well as unfamiliar surroundings to my advantage—and completely disregarding her signals to stop.

I eased her down on the bed and she moved like dead weight. She did not resist me, but she did not hop onto the bed in anticipation either. She just stared straight ahead and began grinding her teeth furiously.

Grinding her teeth and tensing her body were the only ways she could safely express her fear. Here was a girl in a dark apartment with a man she never met before who could easily kill her, in a city which I described to her as a moral vacuum. She did not cry, scream, or fight. Only recently have I put myself in her place and realized the terror she must have felt. To me she was a source of sex and that was all. Getting the sex was a little more challenging than I was used to, but it was still a game.

I got the rest of her clothes off the same way I got her shirt off—I forced them off. There she was, naked on her back with her knees locked firmly together, staring at the ceiling and grinding her teeth. Not a word was spoken during this struggle. It was just me trying to get her legs apart and her trying to get them back together . . .

The sex lasted about a minute or two, and when I was done, I had the familiar aftertaste of unsatisfying sex. My power, so active five minutes before, was spent. All of the manipulative force I'd used left me empty.

I did not want this woman sleeping in my bed. I also did not want to walk her home, but is was dark and she did not know the area. She sat up in bed and again said she wanted to leave. By now it was 4 a.m. and I could not let her go out alone, even if she did know how to get back. I still find it amazing that after raping her I could feel concerned for her safety.

"Just sleep over," I said reluctantly. "You can leave when it's light out."

She did sleep over, and she never stopped grinding her teeth through the entire night.

When we awoke the next morning, I insisted she wait and walk out with me, since I had to leave for work anyway. I guess I still wanted to be a nice guy. The last thing I said to her when we reached the street was, "You have to walk that way to get back to your friend's place."

I've talked to my male friends about this and there is a fair amount of denial. "I did something like that once, but I don't think it's rape. It isn't like you forced her to have sex with you."

But I did force her! What constitutes force? Does it require that I threaten her life? Does it require physical injury? If I were walking in a dangerous and unfamiliar neighborhood and a man twice my size walked up to me on a deserted street and said, "Give me your money," I would probably hand it over. The thought going through my head would be, "This guy could easily kill me. He did not threaten me, but merely demanded I give him something. I could run, but I would not know where to go for help. I may lose my money and feel violated, but it is better than having him kill me."

I do not remember her name but I think about her now. It hurts me to know that I damaged someone like that. Have I caused her to mistrust men, to be more confused about sex than she needs to be, to fear that she might have AIDS? (I did not use a condom when I assaulted her.)

Maybe she blamed herself for getting into that situation with me and allowing herself to be taken advantage of. Maybe she buried it deep in her subconscious for years until she could deny the pain no longer and had a nervous breakdown. I have an image of her in long-term therapy, my face conjuring up awful memories as she recounts the events of that night. I am responsible for her realization that a man can steal from you something that belongs to you, that you are supposed to be able to share with someone only when you desire to. It can be stolen from you as easily as someone might snatch a chain from around your neck.

I am aware that the power to rape is inside me. Now, when I meet a woman and see that she likes me, here's what I'm learning and wanting to do. I'm more cautious about making unwanted moves. I am learning to interact nonaggressively. I'm learning to talk *with* her, not *to* her, possibly about intimacy with her, but speaking and listening with genuine interest. If the interest is not there, I know something's wrong.

Most of all, I will not seduce. I will not try to pull desire out of her whether or not it is there. Even if she initiates sexual contact, I want to proceed more slowly than before. I don't want to rely on body language or guesses or assumptions about what we *should* be doing. I want consent, without any coercion, if we're going to be intimate.

I never want to rape again. And until I understand more about my own power, I will do everything I can to make sure I do not express it as rape.

SOCIOHISTORICAL BACKGROUND OF HATE RADIO

Call-in radio shows have been on the air since the 1950s. The number of talk radio shows increased from 75 to 1,350 between 1980 and 1998 (Talk Radio Research Project, 2002). Rush Limbaugh, a popular conservative, is the king of talk radio. He is heard on more than 600 radio stations, five days a week, three hours per day, and attracts over 20 million listeners a week. Eighteen percent of all adults listen to at least one call-in radio show at least twice a week (Capella et al., 1996: 12). Fifteen million people a day listen to at least part of a radio talk show (Owen, 1996: 127). Three basic reasons have been advanced to explain this apparently explosive trend—technology, demographics, and the demise of the Fairness Doctrine (Delgado, 2004b).

Beginning in the 1960s, AM radio stations started losing listeners because of the rising popularity of FM stations, which were capable of supplying stereophonic music. Over the next few decades AM stations began replacing their "Top 40" pop music formats with talk shows in order to make profits. Technological advances such as the tape delay (available since the 1950s), inexpensive 800 numbers, cellular telephones, and satellite communications contributed to the popularity of the call-in format and the countrywide syndication of programs at a relatively low cost (Capella et al., 1996: 6). The huge number of baby boomers delivered a growing audience base as well.

The dramatic rise in the number of so-called "shock jocks" began with the repeal of the Fairness Doctrine in 1987 (Delgado, 2004b). This doctrine was implemented by the Federal Communications Commission (FCC) and essentially required radio stations to provide a forum for opposing views on controversial topics. The doctrine was eventually retracted subsequent to a series of legal tests. The FCC reversed policy dating back to the 1920s in justifying its decision. Accordingly, the Fairness Doctrine meant that the control of the airwaves belonged to the listeners, not the speakers (Donahue, 1989). In consequence, repealing the Fairness Doctrine gave talk show hosts the right to say whatever they wanted without regard for an opposing or minority position—thus, opening the door for hate radio.

In 1987 and 1993 Congress tried—albeit unsuccessfully—to restore the Fairness Doctrine. President Reagan vetoed the bill in 1987. In 1993, the legislation fell short of passing. Bringing back the doctrine would take the edge off hate radio—also known as *cringe* radio, a broadcasting program devoted to using hate speech and other negative information and attitudes about targeted social categories based on ethnicity, race, religion, gender, and sexual orientation. If hate speech is simultaneously presented and then rebuked within the same radio program, listeners receive a more balanced perspective. Listening to both sides of the issue means that the audience is less likely to be taken in by persuasive hate speech. Bigoted persons, however, are still unlikely to change their views even in the face of overwhelming evidence.

Requiring ideological balance in radio programs provides helpful types of information in pursuant of social welfare. Prescribing a balanced approach also guarantees that media-savvy upper-class individuals or elitist groups do not monopolize editorial time on the radio. Moreover, it prevents censorship by media gatekeepers. Necessitating fairness on the radio promotes the public's access to the airwaves. If, in the future, Congress reestablishes the Fairness Doctrine, it would provide an effective legal procedure for countering hate speech, including racist, misogynist, xenophobic, and homophobic messages.

First Amendment absolutists believe that the Fairness Doctrine would restrain rather than encourage the free surge of news and other types of information. This argument assumes that broadcasters would typically reject advertising that graphically presents contentious issues rather than provide an open forum—a rather dubious assumption. Russ Limbaugh spun the 1993 bill to restore the Fairness Doctrine as the "Hush Russ" bill (Cohen, 1994), setting the tone for his listeners' fervent opposition to the proposed change in policy. The legislation, however, was not aimed at talk show hosts, nor did it necessitate that stations offer equal time to discuss controversial topics. It merely would have prohibited stations from continuously producing and broadcasting programs with the same point of view, without *any* opposing perspective.

The conservative Heritage Foundation met with a panel of talk show hosts to evaluate the merits of the Fairness Doctrine. Not surprisingly, the panel concluded that the explosion of talk shows since 1987 demonstrates the benefits of the "unfettered exchange of information" that has given rise to "millions of Americans [achieving] a level of political sophistication the country hasn't know before" (Berrigan, 2002: 9). According to the Heritage Foundation (1993), the Fairness Doctrine would be political censorship disguised within the Trojan horse of ideological balance.

Fairness and Accuracy in Reporting (FAIR), a liberal media watchdog, posits a more menacing rationale for the rise in the number of hate radio shows. Accordingly, it is "a deliberate process in which major broadcasters like ABC/Cap Cities [currently Disney/ABC] have chosen to narrowcast to conservative audiences by stoking prejudice and fear" (Cohen and Solomon, 1994). To the degree that this interpretation is correct, gainfully opposing hate speech is that much more urgent.

HATE RADIO AND MISOGYNIST DISCOURSE

> *I once was in China.*
> *wanted to see some vagina*
> *I love when strippers give me lick, to my dick*
> *I said babe, touch my chopstick . . .*
> *she said "me love you long time."*
> —*The Men's Room*, WBRS, Brandeis University,
> November 20, 2001

The last line in this improvised and misogynist song refers to Asian women as submissive sex objects (Cortese, 2004: 104). These and other sexist and racist comments were broadcasted by five male Brandeis students known as *The Men's Room* on the university's radio station. WBRS is Brandeis University's noncommercial radio station, broadcasting 25 watts at 100.1 FM in Waltham, Massachusetts. The station reaches virtually all of Waltham, and most of the adjacent communities to the north, east, and south.

In December 2001, concerned Brandeis University students rallied in front of the Student Center, spurred by misogynist hate speech on the radio as well as harassment targeting Asian American women on campus (Brugge, 2001). The demonstration provided a safe space for students' voices to be heard and solidarity in the fight against all forms of intolerance and discrimination.

The harassment included a November 20, 2001, incident where WBRS broadcasted *The Men's Room*. The hosts of the show made sexist and racist remarks over the air specifically targeting Asian Americans. Hate words such as Chink and Gook were used synonymously for Asians. They laughed during a song they improvised on Asian female strippers. They disparaged and stereotyped Asians as "slanted," ridiculing the almond-shaped eyes distinctive to Asians. *The Men's Room* undermined the integrity and humanity of Asian American women, with verses like "she was hot and yellow and showed us her tits."

Students quickly notified university administrators of this broadcasted hate speech against Asian Americans. In response, an open forum on racism was aired on WBRS, on *The Men's Room*. The open forum did not end the hate speech; instead it intensified. In less than a week after the event, two separate student housing areas had been vandalized with the phrases "me love you long time," "black dicks too big," and "me fuck you long time." The graffiti appeared to be hostile responses to the courage with which many Asian American women on campus had immediately and vigorously defended themselves in the wake of their public humiliation.

Brandeis' president, Jehudah Reinharz, announced that if the perpetrator(s) to these hate crimes were discovered, they would be appropriately penalized. Reinharz also issued a broad statement condemning hate speech and acts of intolerance, including *The Men's Room* radio show. However, the Intercultural Center Programming Board at Brandeis was not satisfied with the president's response and issued a statement calling for specific discourse on the types of insensitivity the hate radio exposed. They further criticized the generic response for lacking any actual meaning to many of the minority students.

The statement included larger community concerns—valid concerns about no longer feeling comfortable or safe in a hostile and hateful environment on campus. Asian women—who dared to break their stereotype of passive and submissive sexual objects—were disparaged, disempowered, and terrorized by the hate radio and follow-up sexual harassment.

The demonstrators demanded that the university create two new senior administrative positions for addressing the concerns of population diversity among the student body, faculty, staff, and administration. The proposed office would provide a central location for confidential reporting of homophobic, sexist, racist, and other types of intolerance behavior, creating a safe space for ethnic and social minority students to talk about their concerns.

The administrators would implement programs of sensitivity training for students and faculty to include concern for issues of difference within gender, race, class, age, disability, religion, nationality, and ethnicity. The show has long since been canceled, although some members of the radio station's executive board remain on board. WBRS's current programming supports an all-genre block format, with a policy of playing everything received.

CONCLUSION

This chapter has looked at gender and hate speech. In particular, it focused on pornographic materials as hate speech and their robust relationship to rape, sexual harassment, and child molestation. It is concluded that pornography is not a free speech issue. Rather, it is an issue of protecting women and children from emotional and physical damage and sexual homicide. The emphasis is on equal protection under the law for women and children.

We also addressed how sexual harassment has expanded on the Internet through e-mail communication, chat rooms, and instant messaging. The courts have been much less likely to restrict sexual harassment and other forms of hate speech on the Internet based on the primacy of the First Amendment.

The strong link between the child sex industry and pornography was discussed in detail, both in terms of child prostitution and child pornography. Consequently, it is evident that pornography harms children as well as women. Feminist protests and demonstrations illustrated the use of the First Amendment right to free speech for securing equal rights and protection under the law, with concentration on the international Take Back the Night Movement. We were able to see the elements of gender privilege and violent masculinity in the narrative of an apologetic rapist.

A sociohistorical background to hate radio was provided. This was followed by an example of misogynist and racist hate radio on a university campus.

Pornography is one way in which gender inequality and stratification occurs and is maintained. Consequently, pornography both symbolizes and actualizes the distinct social power of men over women (MacKinnon, 1994). Pornography is part of the social world that constructs, defines, and reinforces gender traits that we believe to be either "male" or "female."

The problem of reconciling rights is tricky and often results in apparent unfairness, especially when it is free speech versus the violation of the civil rights of women by the ready availability and viewing of pornography. Pornography does not cause rape, molestation, prostitution, or sexually related murder. It does, however, support and enhance a culture in which the dehumanization, degradation, and violent abuse of women and children is something to be sought out, attained, and even celebrated. Aggression is a learned behavior. Pornography teaches us aggression. Since aggression is learned, it is possible that it can be unlearned or, better yet, never taught in the first place.

The porn industry produces, reproduces, and distributes aggressive, violent, intimidating, or coercive images and scripts. This pattern of pornographic violence, continuously repeated and often extreme, creates a cumulative effect that often numbs the viewer to human suffering and brutality. Pornography legitimizes such violence and, in doing so, glamorizes a type of violent masculinity.

Why is violent, hateful aggression and humiliation more objectionable than using conventional sexual images to stimulate conventional appetites? Because it trivializes conduct that lacerates the bodies and psyches of unwilling victims, and obliquely excuses those who inflict the wounds. Instead of being seen as deeply shameful, which it is, sexual violence has become stylish through pornography. Pornography's use of sexual violence corresponds to Stage 4 (Inciting Discriminatory Violence) since it provides a model for and clearly promotes violence against women.

Violent pornography is not really about free speech. In order to make pornographic images, real acts must be performed by men upon women (MacKinnon, 1995: 7). Perhaps more important, as a consequence of viewing and internalizing the message in pornographic films, real men inflict violence and aggression on real women.

The empirical evidence, including testimony from experience, is clear (MacKinnon, 1995). Not all viewers of pornography become violent. However, many of them do—not only those inclined so. Not all men and boys believe that women are inferior to men and live to be sexually dominated and raped, but many do—including clinically psychologically normal men. It is clear that no man learns respect for women through the consumption of pornography.

The United States has been characterized as a "rape culture." The American media link sex and violence. American vernacular does the same. Take, for example, the phrase, "Fuck you!" It has both sexual and aggressive connotations. Moreover, most young men grow up learning a violent and sexually aggressive form of masculinity.

Pornography teaches boys and men cultural scripts of sexual violence. To the extent that American culture can be characterized as "rape culture," the problem of sexual violence is not loners on the fringes of society, but rather, men who are well adjusted to a defective cultural system that equates sex and violence. In conclusion, when we combine males brought up to think this way and females brought up to submit to males, we have a formula for widespread sexual violence.

The growing anti-women sentiment culminated in the creation of the Promise Keepers—the men's "Christian" organization which advocates the violent "taking back" of men's authority over their wives—all for the little woman's good, of course. During and immediately after this group's rallies, many women have reported being accosted by members and new recruits.

5

Sexual Orientation and Hate Speech

Ideally, it would have been nice to have a few phalanxes of policemen with machine guns and mow them down.
—Bob Grant, former Disney/ABC broadcaster,
following a gay pride march (Naureckas, 1995)

The Office of Civil Rights (OCR) of the U.S. Department of Education ruled that a nontenured lecturer in the English Department at the University of North Carolina illegally subjected a student to "intentional discrimination and harassment" because he was "a white, heterosexual Christian male" who expressed disapproval of homosexuality (*Washington Times*, 2004). Professor Elyse Crystall violated student Timothy R. Mertes's civil rights, the agency said, by improperly accusing him of "hate speech" in an e-mail sent to students after a class discussion in which Mertes said he was a Christian and felt "disgusted, not threatened" by homosexual behavior. In February 2004, Crystall, in response to the student's expressed objections to homosexuality, sent an e-mail message to the students in her "Literature and Cultural Diversity" course, stating:

> That a white, heterosexual, Christian male, one who vehemently denied his privilege last week insisting that he earned all he has, can feel entitled to make violent, heterosexist comments and not feel marked or threatened or vulnerable is what privilege makes possible . . . [W]hat we heard [T]hursday at the end of class constitutes "hate speech" and is completely unacceptable. [I]t has created a hostile environment.

She encouraged the students to use the course's online discussion forum to debate the issue, but warned that anonymous postings would not be allowed and that "NO HATE SPEECH will be tolerated."

Soon afterward, she apologized for her remarks. The chair of the English Department had indicated that he would monitor the course. But the "damage" had already been done. The message had already captured the attention of conservative students at the university and Internet activists who lamented that the case was further proof of an underlying liberal bias in academia.

U.S. Representative Walter B. Jones (R-North Carolina) made a federal case of this incident by encouraging OCR's investigation. Moreover, he complained directly to the university's chancellor, James Moeser, in February 2004: "Had Ms. Crystall substituted the word 'black' for 'white,' 'homosexual' for 'heterosexual,' or 'Muslim' for 'Christian,' she would have been suspended or fired immediately."

For her part, Crystall says she has been the victim of "a harassment campaign" since the incident became public. She said that the student's comments, made at the end of class—that homosexuality was sinful and "disgusting"—had made other students upset. She noted that while the government could investigate her remarks as racist (anti-White) or sexist (anti-male), it would not investigate the student's as homophobic. Crystall said, "By claiming that there may have been a violation of racial discrimination, that because I called the student 'white,' seems to be a perversion of what the civil-rights laws were meant to protect."

Accordingly, a student effectively calls homosexuality a disgusting perversion. Furthermore, the instructor calls the student a violent, White, privileged heterosexist and a "neutral," colorblind application of civil rights laws "a perversion." The Office of Civil Rights of the U.S. Department of Education is brought in to investigate. Perhaps hate speech regulations are not the most efficacious way of gainfully opposing hate speech. Maybe the true perversion is that the dialogue took place in a class on Literature and Cultural Diversity. On what basis does one determine whose speech was hateful?

Ostensibly, the Office of Civil Rights' ruling is ridiculous. The teacher's e-mail was neither anonymous (hence scary) nor face-to-face (required of "fighting words"). And of course, scathing speech by a (presumably) White teacher directed to a White student lacks the dimension of racial power and ability to hurt that gives ordinary hate speech (White on Black or brown) its sting (Delgado, 2005, personal correspondence).

Moreover, how can describing someone as "white, Christian, male, and privileged" be construed as hate speech (Claggett, 2005, personal correspondence)? Clearly, those are not epithets. Crystall described Mertes's homophobic comments as violent; she did not say he was violent. She did say he was privileged. That seems to be an observation, not an accusation worthy of being dubbed hate speech. How could a U.S. congressman suggest that if she had called him Black, Muslim, and homosexual, her academic appointment would be in jeopardy? She certainly would not be describing such a person as privileged. This is a good illustration of the latent functions of campus speech codes.

On the other hand, the teacher does wield vast power over the student. To be sure, the Office of Civil Rights felt she apparently abused it here by taking the student to task in an e-mail to her classmates.

This chapter addresses sexual orientation and hate speech. Hate speech can be expressed through homophobic messages, stereotypical characters, and subtle anti-gay or anti-lesbian indicators. In addition, a homophobic message includes the absence of positive gay and lesbian images in media. Gay and lesbian images, roles, and messages on television affect attitudes about gays and lesbians. Are homophobic television images and messages harmless entertainment or a harmful and hostile environment? Indeed, the media are very powerful agents of socialization. Should we restrict gay images and messages that are discriminatory or incite hatred or violence? The First Amendment guarantees free speech, but should anti-gay hate speech be allowed? This chapter investigates the history of the roles of gay and lesbian characters on television.

Gay and lesbian rights protests and demonstrations are also evaluated as a technique for securing equal rights and protection under the law. Hate speech in anti-gay and anti-lesbian demonstrations is looked at from a critical perspective, and we focus on positive responses to hatred, violence and discrimination against gays, lesbians, and transgendered people. Gay and lesbian rights demonstrations have been successful as a technique for obtaining equal rights. Perhaps the best solutions are education through public awareness and the enactment of gay rights and hate crimes legislation.

Other homophobic media messages—from Pope John Paul II to Florida Governor Jeb Bush to Nazi propaganda—are analyzed for hate speech. What harm is caused by expressions of contempt or hatred for gays and lesbians? Do gays and lesbians have the right to be protected against discriminatory statements, many of which intentionally incite hatred and lethal violence?

GAY AND LESBIAN CHARACTERS ON TELEVISION

Historically, countless male roles and images in films, television, and other media have consisted of men fighting or killing other men. Occasionally, there have been strong friendships between men. But traditionally, there have been no images of men romantically loving other men. These media images or their lack of reflect a culture where violence between men is casually accepted while love between men is entirely rebuffed.

Even though gay and lesbian characters have been a very small proportion of all male and female roles on television, there still is a long litany of them (see the appendix at the end of this book). This section examines gay and lesbian regular characters that have appeared on television series since

1961. The analysis focuses on the types of characters and how their relationships were portrayed. Finally, I build on that list by analyzing some of the very recent and current gay and lesbian roles on television—*Degrassi: The Next Generation, Ellen, Oz, Playmakers, Queer Eye, The Reagans,* and *Will & Grace.*

Gay and Lesbian Characters, 1961–2002

The appendix contains a list of television programs (network and widely syndicated entertainment shows in the English language) that have included gay, lesbian, or bisexual characters as a part of their regular (or recurring) casts. This does not include the many shows that have dealt with sexual orientation in a single episode or story line.

To be listed, a character must have appeared in at least three episodes and is explicitly gay, lesbian, bisexual, or transgendered. Effeminate (but not gay) male characters, mannish (but not lesbian) female characters, and gender-shifting science fiction characters are not listed. A character is described as "recurring" if he or she has appeared in at least three episodes.

The first documented gay or lesbian regular character on a television series was Daniel Sereno, who was played by actor Daniel Massey. Sereno appeared on the dramatic series *The Roads to Freedom,* which began on the BBC in 1970; it was also viewed on PBS in 1971. The show was set in Paris on the eve of World War II and was based on the novel trilogy of the same name by Jean-Paul Sartre. The first documented gay or lesbian character on an American television series was Jodie Dallas, played by actor/comedian Billy Crystal. Jodie was featured on the comedy series *Soap,* which began on ABC in 1977.

Since Daniel Sereno and Jodie Dallas, there has been a large growth in gay, lesbian, or bisexual recurring television characters over the decades. Some of the American series, both current as well as in the past, that have featured gay, lesbian, or bisexual characters include *All My Children, Beverly Hills 90210, Big Brother, The Bob Newhart Show, Boston Public, Buffy the Vampire Slayer, Cagney and Lacey, Chicago Hope, Dallas, Dawson's Creek, Days of Our Lives, Dynasty, Fame, Felicity, Friends, General Hospital, The Golden Girls, Hill Street Blues, Hollywood Squares, In Living Color, The John Laroquette Show, The Kids in the Hall, L.A. Law, The Larry Sanders Show, Mad About You, Mary Hartman, Mary Hartman, Melrose Place, Nash Bridges, Normal, Ohio, Northern Exposure, NYPD Blue, One Life to Live, Oz, Party of Five, The Practice, Profiler, Public Morals, Queer as Folk, The Real World, Roseanne, St. Elsewhere, Seinfeld, Sex and the City, The Simpsons, Sisters, Six Feet Under, South Park, Spin City, Star Trek: Deep Space Nine, Star Trek: The Next Generation, Suddenly Susan, Survivor, Thirtysomething, Three's Company,* and *The Tracey Ullman Show.*

The appendix is used as a database to examine gay and lesbian regular characters that have appeared on television series since 1961. Table 1 of the appendix shows the number of gay or lesbian characters that have been documented in English-language television series by decade. The pattern shows a large growth of gay or lesbian characters in the 1990s from the previous decade. The current decade continues to show growth.

The content analyses focus on the types of gay characters, whether they are lead or secondary, regular or occasional characters. Character substance and relationships are also examined. What is the character's personality, moral judgment, and occupation? How are their relationships characterized?

PREVALENCE, TYPE, AND SUBSTANCE OF GAY CHARACTERS

Gay characters on television have traditionally played minor or supporting roles. They were often friends of a central character. There have been very few gay lead characters in a television series (see below). There have been 35 minor, supporting, or occasional characters, and 23 gay characters were regular members of an ensemble cast.

Ellen Morgan, played by Ellen DeGeneres, became the first homosexual lead character on American primetime television. The history-making, mysteriously named "Puppy Episode" aired on *Ellen* (ABC) on the first day of the May ratings sweeps—April 30, 1997. The episode drew 42 million viewers, a 23.4 rating, and a 35 percent share of the TV audience in major cities. That was more than twice the show's normal audience.

Gay attorney Will Truman, played by Eric McCormack, has become the best-known and longest-running gay lead character on American primetime television. In 2005, *Will & Grace* (NBC) began its seventh season. The Emmy Award–winning comedy series has enjoyed both critical praise and ratings success. McCormack has won an Emmy for Outstanding Lead Actor in a Comedy Series; he has also been nominated for six Golden Globe awards.

Queer Eye (formerly *Queer Eye for the Straight Guy*) (Bravo) features an ensemble cast with five gay lead characters—Ted Allen, Kyan Douglas, Thom Felicia, Carson Kressley, and Jai Rodriguez. They call themselves the Fab Five. The show is a one-hour guide to "building a better straight man"—a "make better" series for men who would like to find romantic success, an efficacious job, or the latest fashion look. The makeover develops with lighthearted deconstruction of the subject's current lifestyle and continues as a humorous venue for the hottest styles and trends in fashion, home design, grooming, food and wine, and culture. The show received the 2004 Emmy Award for Outstanding Reality Program.

An openly gay couple, Reichen Lehmkuhl and Chip Arndt (the relationship has since crumbled), won the 2003–2004 season (the fourth competition) of *The Amazing Race* (CBS) and received $1 million and a measure of celebrity—especially for the former. For two consecutive years, *The Amazing Race* has been awarded the Primetime Emmy Award for Outstanding Reality/Competition Program. In 2004 it defeated two of its competitors from the previous year—CBS's *Survivor* (which an openly gay man won during the first season) and Fox's *American Idol*, along with two newcomers from NBC: *The Apprentice*, which was the pre-award favorite, and *Last Comic Standing*.

In short, openly gay and lesbian lead characters and couples have become more prevalent, both on scripted and reality television.

Analyses show prevalent stereotypical images, roles, and characters. For purposes of analysis, "stereotypically" gay includes flamboyant behavior, feminine tendencies, traditionally female occupations, and careers in various types of art, including but not limited to performing art. Throughout the period covered, there were six flamboyant "queens," four female impersonators/drag queens, five flight attendants, two nurses, a nursing assistant, a set designer, two secretaries, someone who always carries around a teddy bear, a dancer, an embroiderer, a dress designer, a painter, an art designer, eight actors, an art teacher, two hair stylists, a music teacher, a fashion designer, a violinist, a violin instructor, a dancer/singer, a drama teacher, a florist, a boutique manager, and an art teacher.

There is a wide range of gay characters, many of them nonstereotypical. These include a professional baseball player, three professional football players, a count, a Secret Service agent, a merchant marine, four police officers, three athletes, two of whom were Olympians, two in the military, including a sailor, two police detectives, two sportscasters, and two coaches, including a hockey coach.

There were also roles that depicted socially responsible characters such as a health care activist, a volunteer counselor, and a civilian member of Violent Crimes Task Force. Gay-related occupations or avocations include an AIDS hospice caregiver, an AIDS educator, three gay rights activists, and an AIDS Ball charity fundraiser.

There were also some very negative and disturbing portrayals of gays that are harmful and destructive in terms of expressions of hate against gays: a Nazi Lieutenant, a spy who betrayed his own lover, a jail enforcer working for the mob, a police informant who snitched on his own lover, someone who deserted his HIV-positive lover, a despicable character who broke up with his pregnant girlfriend in order to pursue her brother, and two drug addicts. A police detective became violent with a two-time victim of gay bashing after he refused to date him. Another man had an affair with a gay lover behind his wife's back and then framed his lover for her murder. Other harmful or negative roles include a bully, six inmates, and five promiscuous characters.

These negative portrayals are not specifically anti-gay; rather, they are just generally negative while happening to be gay. For example, if a woman is portrayed as a criminal ("negative"), it is not necessarily a misogynist portrayal; indeed, it could be a feminist portrayal. Likewise a lesbian character. It is not necessarily a homophobic depiction; it also could be feminist. However, when persons of marginal status are also criminalized or otherwise labeled deviant, they tend to be demonized by media, politicians, and public opinion. Consequently, I would like to suggest that it is this double whammy that often encourages destructive stereotypes, discrimination, hatred, and violence against gays and lesbians.

There were characters that were closeted and very uncomfortable with or in denial of their sexuality. Five characters were closeted; four others were in fraudulent marriages to maintain respectability, sometimes in business. At least three characters were explicitly in self-denial. One refused to cohabitate with his lover for fear of being outed. Two others were faced with blackmail by threat of outing, one of whom was a Team U.S.A. hockey coach who was blackmailed using pictures of him kissing his male lover. Another closeted character, a married but gay bar owner, was blackmailed; the blackmailer (who was an employee of the bar owner and who also was a closeted gay) threatened to expose the bar owner because of bitterness that the owner did not have sexual desire for him and also because of a loathing for his own sexual feelings.

Hate and Violence

Hate speech and other homophobic expressions against gays were prevalent. There were six homophobic gay bashings, one of which resulted in murder. Another gay man was killed by his ex-lover's father; one more commited suicide after his being outed on a live phone-in radio show. One gay character was fired from his job and, failing to find other work, commited suicide eventually after his lover was killed in a mining accident. An additional gay man murdered his lover. One gay man's lover was killed by terrorists.

There were a wide variety of occupations for gay characters on television, ranging from high status to moderate status to low status. Many gay characters were shown as upwardly mobile, professionally successful, and in high-status occupations. These included eight lawyers, five physicians, two public relations businessmen or executives, two accountants, a chef, an architect, a psychiatrist, a graphics designer, three professors, a press secretary, a chief of staff, two advertising executives, a clinic pharmacist, a writer, a banker, a police detective, a news magazine co-anchor, a weatherman, two movie writers, a funeral director, a physical therapist, a technical writer, a station stage manager, and five reporters.

In the middle range, there were two schoolteachers, two social workers, two café/restaurant owners, a photographer, a trainee lawyer, a relationship counselor, an owner/operator of a shoppers' weekly newspaper, an office manager, and a vice president of a talent agency.

There were also plenty of gay characters in low-status professions, many in the blue-collar or service professions. Some roles were socially marginal such as a religious cult leader and an unemployed actor. Three characters were identified as HIV-positive.

The low-status jobs included five waiters, a ticket scalper, a chauffeur, a camp assistant, a train steward, a social service worker, a coffee shop manager, a magazine editor's assistant, a struggling actor, an oil rigger, a roofer, a laboratory assistant, a motorcycle courier, two handymen, two personal assistants, two disc jockeys, four bartenders, a mail room worker, a boat ride operator, a security guard, a construction boss, a supermarket manager and an assistant manager, an aspiring writer, and a personal trainer. Sixteen gay characters were students, including 13 high school or college students, two medical students, and a law student.

Forty-five gay couples or relationships were documented, including an elderly pair; five of those displayed episodes of violence. One gay wedding was recorded. Twelve affairs or romantic episodes between gay men were documented. Two gay couples were shown with children. There was a single gay father. Finally, there were eight male-to-female transsexuals (including two models and a club owner) and one female to male transsexual.

Prevalence, Type, and Substance of Lesbian Characters

There have been only two lesbian characters that have played leading roles in a television series. There have been at least 30 minor or occasional lesbian characters, often the friend of a lead character. Six have been regular characters, including one regular in an ensemble cast.

Some characters have fit the archetypical stereotype for a lesbian. They often dress as a male. Some lesbian characters have displayed lesbian stereotypes: Two soccer players and a truck driver. Sometimes the negative stereotyping might be in the portrayal rather than the job description (e.g., the "butch" stereotype). On the other hand, the ultra-femme is a stereotype, too. There has been a wide range of negative roles for lesbian characters. These include seven prisoners (including a prostitute and another woman who commits a crime just so she can be jailed with her love interest), a jealous ex-girlfriend, a victim of a stalker. One lesbian character, after being outed, becomes disgusted and disassociates herself from her lover. Finally, three lesbian characters display confusion about their sexual orientation and attempt or appear to convert to heterosexuality. Some lesbian characters had less prestigious jobs: two receptionists, supermarket checker, nanny, landlady, salesperson, bartender, and bicycle courier.

In terms of relationships and family settings, 36 lesbian couples or relationships were observed, including a couple with a child and a single lesbian mother. One lesbian couple displayed an abusive and stereotypical dominant–submissive relationship. In addition there were nine romantic affairs.

There have also been positive and socially responsible roles for lesbian characters, including a reverend, a rapper-poet, and an AIDS hospice volunteer. Lesbian characters on television have had a wide array of non-stereotypical roles and professional occupations. There have been seven physicians (including a psychiatrist and a gynecologist), six lawyers (including an assistant district attorney, three police detectives and a police sergeant, two actors, and one of each of the following: nurse, nurse-practitioner, caterer, deputy editor of news program, interior designer, television producer, advertising copywriter, news anchorwoman, banker, stage designer, radio disc jockey, journalist, tutor, prison administrator, freelance video reviewer, and Web site manager. One young actor played a high school student who played in the band.

An extensive opportunity for queer reading of a televisual text was provided by the CBS police series *Cagney and Lacey*. This long-running (1982–1988), award-winning series about two women police detectives acquired a large and loyal following of lesbians who were able to read the women as lesbian despite the characters' explicit heterosexuality.

In October 1981, CBS broadcast the made-for-TV movie *Cagney and Lacey* starring *M*A*S*H* veteran Loretta Swit and newcomer Tyne Daly as a team of policewomen who become detectives. The movie was deliberately intended to present a contrast to the sexpot image of women in such TV hits as *Charlie's Angels*. It garnered the support of prominent feminists and was featured on the cover of *Ms.* magazine. After the TV movie became a ratings smash, CBS moved quickly to develop it into a series. In the series version of *Cagney and Lacey* that began in March 1982, the role of Chris Cagney was played by Meg Foster, while Tyne Daly continued as Mary Beth Lacey.

Cagney and Lacey was a critical success and achieved respectable ratings; still, CBS executives canceled the series. Producer Barney Rosenzweig was eventually informed that the price of renewal was to replace Meg Foster as Cagney. Media accounts began to reveal the reasons behind CBS's hesitation when network vice president Harvey Shepard was quoted as saying that "the characterizations of both Cagney and Lacey were too tough." An article in *TV Guide* made it easy for readers to connect the dots: an unnamed CBS programmer had said that the characters were "too tough, too hard, and not feminine. . . . They were too harshly women's lib. . . . We perceived them as dykes." The network, obviously uncomfortable with the feminist stance of the series, focused its objections on Meg Foster. Many felt that Foster was singled out because she had earlier played a lesbian character in the 1978 movie *A Different Story* (and not even a very positive portrayal: in the movie the lesbian and a gay man fall in love and get married).

When the show returned to the air in the fall of 1982, Chris Cagney was played by Sharon Gless, who was described by one reviewer as "blonde, single, and gorgeous." The character was also unquestionably heterosexual. The revised *Cagney and Lacey* continued to attract a faithful following among women viewers—including lesbians appreciative of the rare example of female solidarity—but CBS canceled it once again. This cancellation brought about a huge protest that, combined with the numerous Emmy nominations the series received, once again saved the program. Ultimately, *Cagney and Lacey* ran until 1988, receiving many awards along with high ratings and a large audience of lesbian viewers.

In a study utilizing the 1994 TV film *Cagney and Lacey: The Return*, Tanya Hands examined the interpretations and recollections of lesbian viewers, many of whom had recorded and kept the original series programs. These women had no problem reading the detectives as lesbians. As one respondent commented, "I always thought Cagney was a dyke, but they would have her with a guy once in a while. . . . I just didn't ever see her as a straight woman."

GAY REGULAR TELEVISION CHARACTERS, 1961–2002: HOMOPHOBIA, HATE CRIMES AND HATE SPEECH, AND STEREOTYPING

This section examines images of gays and lesbians in television, the nature of their relationships, character, and behavior. Homophobic behavior by heterosexuals as well as gay and lesbian characters is prevalent. There is also hate speech directed at gays and lesbians. Violent hate crimes, including assault and murder, were not uncommon. There were also plenty of stereotypical gay (e.g, drag queen, flamboyant, feminine) and lesbian (e.g., masculine, rough) characters. Gays were sometimes depicted as dishonest, manipulative, murderous, and betraying. Finally, there has been vigorous negative viewer reaction to gays' and lesbians' expressions of affection (e.g., holding hands, kissing) on television.

In a more positive light, there were many gay and lesbian characters that were affirmative, nonstereotypical, socially just, at the upper echelons of their profession, and well-adjusted and caring lovers. Highlights of hate speech and homophobic expressions and behavior in television series follow.

All in the Family (sitcom), CBS, 1971–1979

Archie Bunker performed mouth-to-mouth resuscitation on a woman who passed out in the back of his cab. The "woman" turned out to be a man—a female impersonator. She made two other visits to the Bunker household. The smash hit comedy series often made fun of Archie's bigotry—in this case, homophobia.

All My Children (daytime serial drama), ABC, 1970–present

After a woman realized an acquaintance was a lesbian, she naively concluded that she needed a relationship with a woman. The lesbian explained that women do not simply decide to become lesbians because their relationships with men are failures. After several months, the lesbian's character was written out of the series.

In 1995, producers introduced a full-time gay character whose sexual orientation was not revealed until several months after his addition to the series. A controversy developed about a gay teacher in the classroom. One of the gay teacher's students, who was the leading homophobe's younger brother, came out of the closet. The teacher and a gay orthopedic specialist began dating in September 1996 and moved in together in January 1997. During the summer of 1997, the gay high school student underwent "reparative therapy" by a conversion therapist sponsored by his homophobic parents.

The daughter of a central character slowly learned to come out of the closet with close friends. Her first love was anorexic.

And the Beat Goes On (drama), C4, 1996

This drama was set in 1960s Liverpool, England. A married but gay bar owner was blackmailed for sexual encounters with strangers in public restrooms. The blackmailer ended up being one of his employees, who was also gay and blackmailed his boss because he did not show romantic interest in him and also from a loathing and self-denial of his own sexual feelings.

The Box (serial drama), TEN, 1974–1977

This Australian series focused on the behind-the-scenes sexual activities and work at a TV station. It was another program of the *Number 96* genre. The show featured a TV station employee who was quite stereotypically gay.

The Crew (sitcom), FOX, 1995–1996

This series featured an ensemble cast of four flight attendants—two men and two women. One of the men was gay and out. Although a lead character, his principal role was one-dimensional—to frustrate the man-hungry, middle-aged woman supervisor. This same theme appears in the play *No Exit* by existentialist Jean-Paul Sartre. The plot involves three people stuck together for an eternity in hell—a lesbian, a gay man, and a nymphomaniac frustrated with the gay man's contempt and rejection.

Ellen (sitcom), ABC, 1994–1998

Ellen Morgan's self-acceptance and coming out as a lesbian on the 1996–1997 season finale induced more real-world press attention than any other gay or lesbian character in film or television before, as the first openly gay or lesbian lead/title character in U.S. commercial primetime programming. ABC/Disney cancelled *Ellen* a year later, apparently unhappy with the show's direction.

Fame (drama/musical), NBC, 1982–1983; syndicated, 1983–1986

The feature-length film, *Fame*, had one gay character who never appeared in the television series. This is another example of discrimination through character deletion.

Gems (daytime serial drama), U.K., 1984–1987

This British series was set in a Covent Garden fashion house. A 1985 episode in which gay men were shown holding hands resulted in a scandal and written protest from disgruntled viewers.

G.P. (medical drama), ABC, 1988–1996

The title is an abbreviation for "General Practitioner." The series garnered a positive reputation for its presentation of AIDS, gay/lesbian, and other social/medical issues. In 1992, a gay doctor joined the practice, but was twice graphically shown being gay-bashed and murdered in the second attack.

Heartbreak High (teen angst drama), TEN, 1994–1999

This drama focused on the lives and loves of disadvantaged high school students. A gay teacher wondered how parents would react if they knew he was gay in an episode about another teacher on the verge of an affair with a student. In the next installment, the teacher was falsely accused of fondling a male student, and his question was painfully answered.

Love, Sidney (sitcom), NBC, 1981–1982

The made-for-TV movie on which this short-lived series was based featured a lead gay character. However, by the time the series reached the air, NBC had forbidden the mention of the character's sexual orientation. Thus, this omission is a homophobic expression.

Melrose Place (serial drama), FOX, 1992–1999

A gay social worker operated a shelter for runaways. The character's sexual orientation was mentioned repeatedly in pre-premiere publicity, but was barely visible on the show for years. A navy lieutenant briefly dated the social worker. He later resigned from the navy, revealing that he is HIV-positive. A police detective investigated the social worker's second gay bashing, and became violent when the social worker refused his romantic advances. A married physician had a covert relationship with the social worker. The doctor framed the social worker for the murder of his wife. In 1996, a struggling actor moved in with the social worker. The actor entered a sham marriage with a lesbian actress co-worker. While in rehabilitation for a drug dependency in the fall of 1996, the social worker met a man with whom he had a relationship until he became physically abusive.

Neighbours (serial drama), TEN, 1985–present

After a high school student was rumored to be gay, parents mobilized to have the boy expelled from school. No gay or lesbian characters have lasted long on the program.

Northern Exposure (ensemble comedy/drama), CBS, 1990– 1995

The fictitious town of Cicely, Alaska, was founded by lesbian lovers after their automobile broke down in the wilderness. A gay couple managed a bed-and-breakfast in town. In 1994, their on-screen wedding made real-world headline news.

Number 96 (serial drama), TEN, 1972–1977

Number 96 created a sensation when it went on the air in 1972. The series was set in Sydney, Australia, and dealt graphically with homosexuality, drug and alcohol addictions, ambitious and promiscuous people, insanity, rape, and especially sex. A same-titled American version of the show (NBC, 1980–1981 and more of a sitcom) was much tamer and did not include any gay characters. This lack of gay characters in the American version is perhaps representative of American culture as being more homophobic than that of Australia.

One Life to Live (daytime serial drama), ABC, 1968–present

A 17-year-old high school student moved into town in the summer of 1992. He grappled with self-doubt and coming out to his homophobic parents. Paralleling the family turmoil, the town was bitterly divided over a rumor that the local minister was gay.

The Practice (lawyer drama), ABC, 1997–2004

A gay man was cleared of the stabbing murder of his lover, only to be charged with the stabbing murder of his new lover several months later.

Veronica's Closet (sitcom), NBC, 1997–2000

"Veronica's Closet" was a women's lingerie company. The company president's assistant insisted he was straight, but everyone else (including his own mother) told him he was gay. He finally accepted his sexual orientation at the end of the final season.

RECENT OR CURRENT SERIES WITH GAY OR LESBIAN CHARACTERS

Degrassi: The Next Generation (youth drama), CTV, 2001–present

This series boldly explores gay themes through a major teen character who comes out and falls in love with a classmate (Rowe, 2003). The gay teen character was introduced into a mainstream youth-oriented drama with a minimum of fanfare. If it were American television, it likely would have been a big deal. It is the third season of the revival of a classic television series that has recently begun to enjoy a generous fan base in the United States on the Nickelodeon-owned cable channel Noggin, which brings the show into 22 million American households. To be sure, people in the United States are viewing the series. In fact, *Degrassi* was a finalist for the GLAAD Media Awards in the Outstanding Drama Series category, against such high-profile shows as *Nip/Tuck*, *Playmakers*, *Queer as Folk*, and *Six Feet Under*.

Set in a downtown Toronto high school, the show brings the character of tenth-grader Marco out of his closet and into the jungle of secondary school society. In the 2003 season he's met Dylan, who until recently existed in the series only as the spoken-of-but-never-seen openly gay older brother of Marco's friend Paige.

The show received enthusiastic marks from its young stars for being true enough to life that the actors do not feel dishonest playing their characters as written. There is a fine line to walk regarding the development of the television relationship. In general, coming out is less shocking to today's youth than to previous generations. However, homophobia is still a major force in society that cannot be ignored.

People are now learning at a much earlier age about the idea of coming out. Accordingly, it is not such a surprise anymore when they do. Today's teenagers are growing up with it. They are seeing their siblings, friends, relatives, and classmates come out.

Degrassi is set in an urban school, and urban settings have traditionally been more tolerant of diversity than rural or small town ones. Of course, there is a danger of making the coming-out experience seem too candy-coated or unrealistically pleasant on television.

The Ellen DeGeneres Show (talk variety), syndicated, 2003–present

This show is viewed as a fresh, fun, and unpredictable alternative in daytime television (*Advocate*, 2003b). Emmy Award–winning comedian and actress Ellen DeGeneres is now into the syndicated daytime talk arena, showcasing her unique brand of comedy and accessible point of view. The hour-long, five-days-a-week, talk-variety show highlights the comedic skills that Ellen has honed as a stand-up comedian.

Whether she's opening the show with her fresh take on real life, in the studio chatting with a celebrity guest or trendy newsmaker, or interviewing an "ordinary" person with an extraordinary talent, Ellen effortlessly brings her incomparable style to the show. Her intelligence, observational humor style, and openness break barriers of stereotypical lesbian images and attitudes. The show also regularly incorporates audience and everyday life-on-the-street segments, showcasing Ellen's approachability and empathy, further breaking down any communication barriers.

With over two decades of experience as a stand-up comic, actress, and host of major award shows including the Emmys and the Grammys, Ellen has the proven comedic skills to connect with viewers with her "everywoman" approach to everyday situations. The series airs on NBC and also is cable broadcast on the Oxygen network.

Oz (prison drama), HBO, 1997–2003

Oz was an experimental prison where both inmates and correctional officers competed for favors and fought to survive in the midst of rival groups and volatile acts of revenge. The series captured the moral relativism, manipulation, and brutality of prison life in addition to the all-too-rare acts of redemption and forgiveness.

This gritty, critically acclaimed series contained a great deal of situational, often predatory homosexual behavior. In the context of prison as a total institution, such behavior is often a survival technique to prevent extortion and rape by violent inmates. A minor character, self-identified as gay, represented gay inmates on the local city council and was framed for a prison murder. After an appeal overturned a death sentence, he returned to prison only to be promptly murdered.

Two other inmates, both in the closet, went through a brutal, vengeful, deceitful "courtship" but eventually admitted to being lovers by the 2000 season. Another inmate was imprisoned for murdering his lover.

Playmakers (drama), FOX, 2003

There has been a range of gay and lesbian characters and relationships on television. During the summer of 2003, there were the macho infantrymen surrounded by drag queens in Showtime's innovative film *Soldier's Girl*. Also in 2003 was outed gay professional football player Thad Guerwitcz on ESPN's first dramatic series, *Playmakers*. The briefly aired show explored the off-the-field lives and relationships of players on a fictitious professional football team.

The character of Guerwitcz, played by Daniel Petronijevic, evolved from a devout Christian with no hint of a gay sexual orientation. After being approached by the show's producers, the rugged 22-year-old Petronijevic said, "I wanted to play a guy who wasn't stereotypical. I wanted to play a guy who is a football player and who is gay" (Rowe, 2003).

Since football continues to be a temple of traditional machismo, perhaps the gay story line did not calibrate well with heterosexual males—the station's primary audience. Knowing that, and knowing it could be a devastating problem, the network still decided to take on the topic—at least for a single season. The network decision seems less bold and more opportunistic considering significant changes in sexual attitudes among young adults from previous generations. Although the series attracted a large share of the viewing audience, ESPN bowed to pressure and criticism from the National Football League for depicting professional football players as crack addicts, narcissistic, wife-beaters, gay and confused, womanizers, and enthusiastic strip-bar patrons.

Queer Eye (reality), Bravo, 2003–present

> *Five gay men, out to make over the world—one straight guy at a time.*
> —*Queer Eye* tagline

Clearly, casting for *Queer Eye*, formerly *Queer Eye for the Straight Guy*, was based on stereotypical characteristics for gay men. Five gay men who specialize in fashion, food and wine, grooming, culture, and interior design go to the rescue of helpless straight men with no sense of fashion and only basic grooming skills and do a complete makeover. This elite team has dedicated itself to worshiping the simple virtues of style, taste, and class. At the beginning of each episode they show the chaotic house of the straight guy with his closet full of tasteless clothes and trash all over. In one episode, the heterosexual has dry-looking long hair. Each week their mission is to transform a style-defective and culturally deprived straight man from dull to amazing in each of their respective categories: basically a man who cannot cook, who is not very sophisticated culturally, and is clueless about using the space he lives in. These five gay guys show the man their perceptions of how to fix all the problems pertaining to the correspondent specialties. It represents a total lifestyle makeover. At the conclusion of each episode, the transition is complete. A freshly polished, newly enlightened, ultra-hip man surfaces. The series was created by David Collins, a gay man, and developed by David Metzler, a heterosexual—a union of sensibilities that gives the show its depth, humor, and edge. In June 2004, the series began its second season, moving from New York to Texas.

The Reagans (miniseries), Showtime, 2003

> *We urge everyone to read the script . . . and watch . . . this movie to see . . . the political agenda of the Hollywood Left. This is the movie even CBS president Leslie Moonves had to admit was slanted and an unfair portrait of the Reagans.*
>
> *It's time to stand up America, and let these people know that it's not "ugly" to be a patriotic American and we . . . will refuse to watch their liberal propaganda disguised as an historical portrait.*
>
> *Help us today . . . and let's continue the fight for morality, honesty, and truth from Hollywood.*
>
> *Mission Accomplished! CBS has pulled "The Reagans" from the schedule! It's unclear whether or not they will attempt to air the movie on Showtime, so for the time being let's keep the letter campaign going.*
> —Defend Reagan Committee, defendreagan.org

A flood of right-wing protest convinced CBS to demote its sweeps miniseries to its cable network, Showtime, which assembled several cast members, the movie's director, and executive producers to decry the "eye" network's censorship. The filmmakers spoke out, denying any political agenda.

The Reagans aired November 30, 2003, on Showtime, which is seen in approximately 13 million homes compared to CBS's 100 million homes. Despite the hype surrounding the controversial movie, only a small stream of viewers tuned in to its premiere. Sold by CBS to its cable sibling amid criticism of its depiction of the former first couple, Ronald and Nancy Reagan, the three-hour movie drew just 1.2 million total viewers (Showbizdata, 2003).

Originally scheduled to air in March 2004, the film was rushed to air in order to capitalize on the controversy. Despite a meager national audience, *The Reagans* more than doubled its prime-time average and was the premier channel's highest-rated original film in two years. (*The Reagans* tied another Reagan-themed movie, *The Day Reagan Was Shot*, which aired in December 2001.) CBS appeared to cave in to disapproval so quickly. Apparently, a relatively small exclusive group of individuals persuaded a major network to not broadcast the controversial film—a film that they had not even seen.

Robert Greenblatt, Showtime's president of entertainment, who is gay, joined in the attack on CBS and its chairman, Les Moonves, for pulling the movie (Collins and Littleton, 2003). He commented:

> The script, the casting, every single day of dailies was available to him, and he in fact commissioned it and paid for it. If he didn't know what movie he was getting, that's not the fault of the producers, the director, or anyone associated with the film.

Moreover, director Robert Allan Ackerman maintained, CBS execs "were very happy with the movie when they saw it in a rough cut" before it was attacked by Reagan supporters. After that, Ackerman said, CBS wound up "artistically butchering" the film in an effort to appease conservatives. The editing process left an incoherent and unmarketable glimpse at the fortieth president and his family.

CBS chief Leslie Moonves claimed that the film was unfair to the Reagans and that even extensive edits had not produced an acceptably balanced portrayal. Critics have vehemently attacked *The Reagans*, complaining that early drafts of scripts leaked to the press have included scenes with little or no basis in historical fact. At least one version of the script reportedly included material suggesting that President Reagan suffered from Alzheimer's disease as early as 1984 and refused to help AIDS victims because of their "sins."

Ackerman eventually quit the production over creative differences with CBS executives who had insisted on numerous last-minute alterations to the miniseries. Ackerman even considered requesting that the Directors Guild of America remove his name from the movie in protest.

Singer, actor, director, producer, mother, and activist Barbra Streisand publicly distanced herself from any involvement in the controversial film, although the film starred her husband and was produced by Streisand frequent collaborators, Craig Zadan and Neil Meron. Streisand declared on her Web site's Truth Alert that she had not even read the script.

The Republican National Committee (RNC) insisted that a historical panel and people who actually knew President and Mrs. Reagan review the film for accuracy. If these conditions were not met, the RNC demanded a disclaimer for any content that was inaccurate and not factual.

The project was widely condemned by supporters of the former president and his wife. Critics maintained that the film takes the perspective of political liberals, something the film's producers admit. The protests were sparked by published reports that the miniseries portrays President Reagan as a doddering old fool callously unconcerned with AIDS as it became an epidemic. The miniseries quotes him as saying of the primarily gay AIDS victims at the time, "They that live in sin shall die in sin," a statement the miniseries' screenwriter, Elizabeth Egloff, acknowledged he never said.

Moreover, Reagan insiders say he did not, and never would have, spoken like that. This opens the liberal filmmakers to criticism that what they cannot accomplish in real life, they will simply make up. Nancy Reagan, played by Judy Davis, is reported to come across as aggressive, harpy-like, and as a pill-popping control freak. CBS agreed and began unsuccessful edits to try to present a more fair picture of the Reagans.

The negative publicity CBS meted out on itself when it buckled under pressure, canceled *The Reagans*, and shifted the miniseries to Showtime certainly has disappeared by now. However, there may be serious repercussions for television for a very long time. It is similar to the firestorm over another television program that was handled very differently.

In 1980, PBS scheduled *Death of a Princess*, a portrayal of the public execution of a young Saudi princess who had been accused of adultery, to run on World, the network's news and public affairs series (Grossman and Minow, 2003). The government of Saudi Arabia and Mobil Oil, PBS's major underwriter, publicly urged the channel not to broadcast the program because it reflected badly on Saudi life. The secretary of state wrote a letter, released simultaneously to the press, urging PBS to reevaluate its decision to broadcast the program, given the subject's potential damage to U.S. relations with an important ally. Members of Congress from both parties decried *Death of a Princess*, fearing the Saudis would shut off the nation's oil supply and cause a severe economic recession. The protests against the program made headlines nationwide before anyone even had a chance to see it.

Much as CBS president Les Moonves had reservations about *The Reagans*, PBS executives also had some doubts about *Death of a Princess*, which unlike all other documentaries on World, was a docudrama rather than a purely factual presentation. Because no footage or interviews could be obtained from Saudi Arabia, the program used actors to recreate actual events, a fact that was made clear at the beginning of the show. Despite their misgivings about docudramas, PBS executives believed that the integrity and independence of PBS was at stake. This is exactly the dilemma CBS faced with *The Reagans*. PBS decided that despite polls showing public opinion strongly against running the program, the nation's viewers should have the chance to see it for themselves and make their own judgment. In view of the huge controversy, PBS executives required (over the bitter protests of the producer) that the broadcast be followed immediately by a special live program that featured representatives of all sides discussing the issues.

However negative public opinion may have been before the broadcast, after *Death of a Princess* aired, the public turned supportive. What started out as the most unpopular program in PBS's history ended up as its highest-rated broadcast. Critics commented after seeing *The Reagans* on cable that it was hard to figure out what all the fuss was about. Viewers of *Death of a Princess* had the same reaction. PBS received applause and awards for standing up to the pressures and preserving its independence against threats from the U.S. government, the Saudis, its own underwriters, and even its own audience.

If you ask Americans whether broadcasting a single television program is worth the cost of a gasoline shortage their answer, sensibly, would most likely be, "Absolutely not. Cancel the show." However, if you ask Americans whether a network should buckle under pressure, threats, and boycotts, their response would probably be exactly the opposite: "Absolutely not. Run it."

CBS made three mistakes in its handling of *The Reagans*. First, it produced an entertainment series that focused on President Reagan's personal life, at a time when he was on his deathbed, suffering from serious illness and being cared for by his wife. That was exploitative and crass. Second, it bowed to outside pressure by abruptly canceling the series and putting it on Showtime, its more restricted cable network. Finally, CBS denied that it had caved in to outside pressure. Instead, it claimed it was a "moral call." This was misleading.

By canceling *The Reagans*, CBS set a dangerous precedent for dealing with the pressures that invariably arise to kill controversial programs before they can be seen. The network's weakness will only encourage future protesters from both the political left and right to demand that programs of which they do not approve be pulled. Such programs, especially news documentaries on tough issues, are already network television's most endangered species. If *The Reagans* had not been a drama but a legitimate CBS News documentary, would CBS still have canceled it? Instead of running for cover and palming it on Showtime, CBS should have run it, made television time available to give critics and supporters their say, and let the people decide for themselves. In the end, perhaps the source of information is less important than the fact that hateful speech against gays was aired for public consumption.

Will & Grace (sitcom), NBC, 1998–present

Today there are several major positive and path-breaking gay roles on television. For example, the unique relationship between Will and Grace continues to evolve in an adult comedy about two best friends and roommates. Will is gay—the first American post-*Ellen* lead gay character—and Grace is heterosexual. The odd couple tangle as less-than-perfect companions with mutual respect for each other. Each looks for the just-right romantic lover.

In its 2004 season, *Will & Grace* was prime time's number-three show among adults 18 to 49 and number-two comedy in that category. The comedy led its time period last season among adults 18 to 49, defeating *CSI: Crime Scene Investigation*. The show garnered three Emmys in 2000, including Outstanding Comedy Series, Outstanding Supporting Actress, and Outstanding Supporting Actor. In November 2001, Eric McCormack received an Emmy for Outstanding Lead Actor in a Comedy Series. In 2002, *Will & Grace* received more Emmy nominations than any other comedy series, leading the group with 13 nominations.

The show also has won a People's Choice Award as Favorite New Comedy Series, 14 Golden Globe nominations for Best Comedy Series, an American Comedy Award nomination for Funniest Television Series, three GLAAD Media Awards for Outstanding TV Comedy Series, and a Founders Award from the Viewers for Quality Television.

On the show, Will is a successful lawyer in Manhattan—friendly, good-looking, and charming. He recently ended a long-term relationship. Likewise, Grace is a gorgeous, self-employed interior decorator. They both have a flair for fine wine, fashion, and shopping. Will and Grace have been pals for a long time, and although they are both in search of love, much earlier in their history, they jointly came to the realization that there will never be any romance between them. Consequently, they cope with the positive and negative situations together, aware they will always have each other to depend on. Will has another good friend—the offensive Jack McFarland, who has good intentions but is a self-centered young man with a lot of stereotypically gay emotional baggage.

HOMOPHOBIC MEDIA MESSAGES AND HATE SPEECH

Growing up as a gay kid in America, I remember hearing antigay slurs as early as kindergarten—before I even knew what gay really meant. By the time I was a teen I had already lived abroad, and my experience showed me that my beloved USA was the most violent and homophobic culture in the West.

—Taro Gold, 2003

This section addresses the rights of people—from the late Pope John Paul II to Florida Governor Jeb Bush—to publicly express their highly valued disapproval, contempt, or hatred for gays and lesbians. Do gays and lesbians have the right to be protected against discriminatory statements expressed in the public domain, many of which intentionally incite hatred and lethal violence against them?

Gays in Law Enforcement and Hate Speech

Joseph L. Ciccone was the first openly gay sheriff in the nation (Bergen County, New Jersey), in fact, one of the nation's first openly gay elected law enforcement officials. He notes a high level of hate speech, prejudice, and discrimination facing law enforcement or political officials who are gay, lesbian, bisexual, or transgender. There does not appear to be equal treatment. Ciccone's openness about his sexual orientation was met with ignorance, hate, and homophobia in the political, government, and law enforcement arenas.

Ciccone documented various types of written messages containing hate speech that he received or were made public about him:

1. Hate poems about Sheriff Ciccone
2. Newspaper articles on the "Gay" Sheriff
3. Attorney General investigation documentation

Ciccone had dedicated the past 20 years of his life to public service—primarily as a police officer and later as an educator. Before anti-discrimination laws protected gays and lesbians in New Jersey, as a rookie officer, Ciccone was repeatedly the victim of inappropriate comments and jokes behind his back, the placement of obscene photos on his locker, and other forms of behavior perceived as cruel.

But no matter how cruel and uncomfortable his early experience in law enforcement was, the hatred Ciccone faced as newly elected, openly gay Sheriff of Bergen County, New Jersey, was different and much more frightening. The resistance, ignorance, and hatred were immediate and almost as surprising as the election victory itself. The officer's union initiated both a public and underground campaign of anti-gay hate speech. Most of the anti-gay hate speech came from union members under the cloak of anonymity: underground newsletters, anonymous phone messages, anonymous e-mail messages, and even a "white bed sheet" with a hateful message in red paint hanging from the building.

Ciccone trimmed the office's overtime budget by $1.3 billion because he considered it to be wasted tax dollars. It is not difficult to imagine a vigorous negative response from the union. He recruited women and Latinos into the police academy who eventually became officers. It was obvious that the Ciccone administration was not business as usual. Political and religious conservatives began a fierce and unprecedented public attack on Ciccone's policies and management. His administration soon became the focus of a statewide investigation.

The political attacks and investigations began with Ciccone's family, and became more intense as the months continued. Operatives or undercover officers were placed within the Sheriff's Department and began to secretly infiltrate the agency staff. Sherrif Ciccone's first term was marred by political conflict, ideological wars, and volatile tensions. As the investigation of Ciccone continued, he began his reelection campaign.

There were fears that the investigation would be used to terrorize Ciccone and his supporters and family. Investigators detained Ciccone's closest confidant and life-long friend, a veteran law enforcement officer whom Ciccone had trained as a rookie cop a decade earlier. Then they pressured him in hopes that he would provide information damaging to Ciccone. There were rumors that Ciccone or his mother and campaign treasurer would be arrested.

As the investigation spread to include campaign issues, Ciccone hired private attorneys who were cooperating with authorities. For Ciccone and his supporters, the fear, torment, and the legal bills grew and grew. The innuendo through the media was that Ciccone and his associates were dishonest and corrupt.

One morning at 6:00 A.M., Ciccone received a phone call from the supervisor of internal affairs. It was a somber greeting, one he had heard before: "Good morning, boss, we got another poem this morning; it's a bad one." The poem was published in an underground newsletter that was being circulated throughout the courthouse, the jail, and even being faxed to elected officials, in addition to statewide police departments and local newspapers. The poem was written with the rhythm to "The Night before Christmas," and began with graphic and hateful references to gay life. In the end, Ciccone resigned to escape the seemingly endless pressures of being an openly gay sheriff.

In November 2004, a lesbian Latina was elected sheriff of Dallas County. In the Republican stronghold, no Democrat had held the post since the 1970s. One-time migrant farm worker Lupe Valdez made history when she became the first woman, first Latina, and first openly gay or lesbian to be elected Dallas sheriff. The Gay and Lesbian Victory Fund, a political action committee that endorsed Valdez and trained her on answering questions related to her sexual orientation, hailed her as the "first-ever Latina lesbian sheriff."

"I can imagine my mom crying for joy last night as this happened," Valdez said, the day after she defeated Republican Danny Chandler. In Valdez's vision, her dead mother looked down from heaven and watched her daughter go from picking beans in a field to leading a 1,900-employee law enforcement agency with a $90 million budget.

The journey to the sheriff's office had started years before when Valdez's mother encouraged her to better herself through education. After working two or three jobs simultaneously to pay for college, Valdez became a federal agent. She worked undercover on drug, organized crime, and fraud cases for U.S. Customs. Now, she is in charge of a department plagued by scandal.

Questionable business dealings by 21-year incumbent Sheriff Jim Bowles—whose father had been a leader in the resurgent Dallas Ku Klux Klan in the early 1920s (Alexander, 1962)—resulted in a grand jury investigation and an indictment that was eventually thrown out. A life-long resident of Dallas County, Sheriff Bowles had followed his father and grandfather in law enforcement. The sheriff had been a member of the Dallas Police Department for 30 years before entering county service in 1981.

Chandler, a 29-year sheriff's department veteran, ousted Bowles in the Republican primary. Chandler, who was 53 years old at the time of the election, attacked his former boss during the campaign, hoping to distance himself from Bowles. But that strategy failed. The election campaign was generally cordial until the end, when Chandler took issue with Valdez's endorsement by the Gay and Lesbian Victory Fund, based in Washington, DC. Chandler issued a statement the day after the election expressing his confidence in Valdez's ability to restore trust to the office and saying she "will have the privilege of leading the finest crime fighters in the country."

Margo Frasier, who directs the 1,350-employee Travis County Sheriff's Department in Austin, expressed her delight with Valdez's election but said a woman serving as sheriff faces hurdles. "The reality of it is, when you make mistakes that anybody makes, they decide you made that mistake because you're a woman," Frasier said. But once the "good ol' boys in Dallas County" understand Valdez is competent, Frasier said, she will earn their respect and her gender, race, and sexual orientation will no longer matter.

Anti-Gay Speech from the Vatican

Rome at the turn of the millennium: a Jubilee Year and a celebration for the Vatican and the Catholic Church. But there's another celebration being organized in the Holy City: Gay Pride 2000. The Catholic Church regards the homosexual lifestyle as sinful, and asked the Roman and Italian authorities to ban the Gay Parade. According to Pope John Paul II, outward expressions of homosexuality are contrary to human nature and to church doctrine. This speech received worldwide attention.

In November 2003, Episcopal bishops in Massachusetts warned that anti-gay comments from the Vatican could lead to hatred and violent crimes in the United States. The bishops criticized the Catholic Church's linking homosexuality with pedophilia. As the Vatican drafts new guidelines for accepting candidates for the priesthood, the Roman Catholic Church is expected to tackle whether gays should be barred from becoming priests.

In formal church documents, Cardinal Jorge Arturo Medina Estevez, a recently retired top Vatican official, said the ordination of gays would be imprudent and risky. His stance seems to be the Vatican's emerging public position on the issue. The bishops felt compelled to speak out despite reluctance about struggling with another denomination's controversy. The issue also affects people outside the Catholic Church. Such policy invites discriminatory, hateful, or violent behavior with the Church's blessing.

Eighty-year-old Belgian cardinal Gustaaf Joos, a close friend of Pope John Paul II, told the Belgian weekly *P-Magazine* that only 5 percent to 10 percent of homosexuals are actually gay and the rest are "sexual perverts" (Expatica, 2004). "True homosexuals don't run in the streets dressed in an extrovert way. True gays have a serious problem. We must help these people. They're either perverts, or they're sick."

Subtle Homophobic Hate Speech by a State Governor

Hate speech can sometimes be subtle or unintentional. If a statement is offensive to its target population—even if the target is implicit, it is discriminatory in its consequences. Florida Governor Jeb Bush joked during a November 2003 cabinet meeting that the people of San Francisco may be endangered and "that's probably good news for the country" (*Advocate*, 2003f). The cabinet had been talking about environmental protection.

Bush was viewing a map displaying sites having many different types of wildlife when he made his off-the-cuff comment. "It looks like the people of San Francisco are an endangered species, *which may not be a bad thing. That's probably good news* for the country" (italics added). People in the room burst into laughter. "Did I just say that out loud?" the governor added to excuse his quirky report.

San Francisco Mayor Willie Brown reportedly was amused with what he considered to be a tongue-in-cheek remark. However, Matt Foreman, director of the National Gay and Lesbian Task Force, was offended and considered it an anti-gay remark because of San Francisco's sizeable gay population. "It's extremely insulting," Foreman said.

Bush informed reporters he was joking, then added, "Don't call Willie Brown." Bush spokesman Jacob DiPietre later attempted to justify and further excuse the governor's statements: "The cabinet was talking about endangered species, and everyone knows that Republicans are an endangered species in California."

In conclusion, these statements meet the criteria of hate speech. They characterize an individual's negative beliefs and especially feelings about the members of some other category of people based on their ethnicity, race, gender, sexual orientation, religion, age, or physical or mental disability. In this case, Bush expressed his negative feelings about gay and lesbian people. Bush was implicitly saying that if gays and lesbians were dying out, it would be good news!

Furthermore, Bush knew it was insulting because he tried to excuse his behavior by saying, "Did I just say that out loud?" He also tried to conceal his behavior when he said, "Don't call [San Francisco Mayor] Willie Brown." Kidding or not, Bush said what he was thinking. Had his comment been targeted toward women instead of gays, it would have been considered sexual harassment.

Finally, Bush tried to deny (through his spokesman) that he was even talking about gays and lesbians: "The cabinet was talking about endangered species, and everyone knows that Republicans are an endangered species in California." Clearly, this is a lie for two reasons. First, Bush tried to excuse his comments as a joke. Second, Bush, a loyal Republican, would not consider the threat of extinction of Republicans in California as good news.

A GOD OF HATRED: HOMOPHOBIC HATE SPEECH FROM THE RELIGIOUS RIGHT

> *Matthew Shepard entered hell October 12, 1998.*
> —Reverend Fred Phelps's proposed (and
> rejected) display of a bronze placard with
> Matthew Shepard's portrait

This section shows how hate speech is used in anti-gay demonstrations. Hate speech against gays and lesbians is surging with deadly consequences. It provides support and justification for hate crimes against gays, most notably, the 1998 shocking torture-murder of Matthew Shepard in Laramie, Wyoming. Such hate speech emanates not only from racist skinheads and other violent outcasts, but from mainstream society as well. As explained above, it comes from the lyrics of Eminem's rap music as well as some of the homophobic and misogynist *gangsta* rap artists.

It comes also from the religious right as an extension of fundamental Christianity's strong opposition to homosexuality. For example, at Matthew's funeral, Fred Phelps, a minister of the Westboro Baptist church of Topeka, Kansas, held a cruel demonstration. He and his followers (almost exclusively relatives by blood or marriage) picketed fervently against homosexuality, shouting hate speech and carrying signs with the words "Matthew burns in hell" and "AIDS cures faggots."

Hate speech not only includes the spoken word, but public displays as well. In October 2003, the Casper, Wyoming, city council voted to move a Ten Commandments monument out of a public park because Reverend

Phelps wanted to erect his own monument condemning slain gay college student Matthew Shepard (*Advocate*, 2003a). Phelps chose Casper as the site for the 6-foot-tall granite display because it is where the University of Wyoming student learned that it is "OK to be gay." The Ten Commandments monument was a precedent for legally opening the park's public spaces as a forum for free speech, despite how offensive it might be. The town could not discriminate.

Phelps's proposal was unanimously rejected by the city council, which then voted 5–4 to move the Ten Commandments monument into a plaza that will honor a variety of historic documents. But the proposed move did not discourage Phelps's plan or satisfy a separate complaint from the Freedom from Religion Foundation, which threatened to sue if the Ten Commandments monument was not removed from City Park, where it had been for 38 years. The monument was later taken to the Casper Service Center, where workers would remove the uneven concrete foundation from the base in preparation for its eventual placement at the plaza (*Advocate*, 2003a).

In a ruling in 2002, the Tenth U.S. Circuit Court of Appeals decided that any city displaying a Ten Commandments monument on city property must also allow monuments of other religious or political groups. Phelps used that decision to back his case. His $15,000 display would show a bronze placard with Shepard's portrait and an inscription reading, "Matthew Shepard entered hell October 12, 1998, at age 21 in defiance of God's warning: 'Thou shalt not lie with mankind as with womankind; it is abomination.' Leviticus 18:22." Phelps's proposal coincided with the five-year anniversary of Shepard's brutal murder.

In the wake of another threatened lawsuit by Phelps, who wanted to erect an anti-gay monument in Boise, Idaho, the Ten Commandments monument that has stood in Boise's Julia Davis Park since 1965 will be moved (*Advocate*, 2003g). The Boise city council voted 4–2 in November 2003 to return the monument to its original donor, the Fraternal Order of Eagles, which will display it at the entrance to its building in Boise. The Eagle Lodge supported the city's action. The city feared possible lawsuits from Phelps, who was denied his request to place an anti-gay monument in Julia Davis Park. Phelps approached the Boise Parks and Recreation Department, requesting to erect a granite monument condemning Matthew Shepard. The department rejected his request, but he appealed.

Phelps cited the above-mentioned Tenth U.S. Circuit Court of Appeals ruling that any city displaying a Ten Commandments monument must also allow the display of monuments espousing other beliefs. Phelps also petitioned Minidoka County, Idaho, commissioners after American Legion Post 10 asked to buy a 2-by-3-foot section plot for a Ten Commandments monument. He also petitioned Twin Falls, Idaho, for another monument after *The Times-News* ran an article about the county Parks and Waterways

Board's program allowing people to memorialize loved ones in city parks by buying trees, park benches, and picnic tables.

TAKING IT TO THE STREETS: THE FRUITS OF PROTEST

This section examines gay and lesbian protests as social movements for opposing homophobic hate speech and securing equal rights for gays and lesbians. The year 2003 was marked by a series of advances for gay and lesbian rights. First, the U.S. Supreme Court struck down anti-sodomy laws. The ordination of an openly gay bishop in the Episcopal Church was also a major achievement. In addition, a Canadian appeals court ruled that it was unconstitutional to deny gay couples the same marriage rights as heterosexual couples. Belgium and the Netherlands also have legalized gay marriage.

We focus on positive responses to hatred, violence, and discrimination against gays, lesbians, and transgendered people. Gay and lesbian rights demonstrations have been successful as a technique for obtaining equal rights. Perhaps the best solutions are education through public awareness and the enactment of gay rights and hate crimes legislation.

Student Challenges Ban on Same-Sex Partners at High School Dances

A heterosexual teenager challenged a Wyoming school district policy that bars students from bringing same-sex dates to school dances. In September 2003, Amanda Blair tried to defy the rule by taking another young woman to the homecoming dance at Big Piney High School in Big Piney, Wyoming. At the request of school officials, sheriff's deputies prevented the two women from entering the dance.

Blair, a senior at Big Piney, then enlisted the help of the American Civil Liberties Union in formally calling on Sublette County School District No. 9 to lift the same-sex date ban. The ACLU stated that the policy violates a 1980 federal court ruling out of Rhode Island. The decision handed down in *Frick v. Lynch* found that students who bring same-sex dates to school dances are not only protected by the Constitution but that schools must take steps to ensure their safety when they attend the dances (Associated Press, 2005).

The ACLU maintains that the ban violates students' constitutional rights of freedom of expression and equal treatment under the law. Testing the policy is meant to help and support gay or lesbian students. Blair and her mother went to the school board after the homecoming dance, requesting that the rule be changed. Kris Blair said she and her daughter contacted the ACLU after receiving no indication from board members that the ban was going to be lifted. A scheduled Sadie Hawkins event was called off after school officials said there could be no dances in the district.

Kissing as Protest

In two separate and unrelated demonstrations, gay rights campaigners used the provocative technique of gay men and lesbians kissing in public to support gay rights. Gay rights activists in Greece called for gay men and lesbians to gather in Athens and kiss in public to protest a $117,000 fine imposed on a local television station for showing a male couple kissing (*Advocate*, 2003d). The protest was held at the National Audiovisual Council, Greece's media watchdog.

The council fined Greece's second-biggest channel for broadcasting two young men kissing in the popular late-night series *Close Your Eyes*. According to media viewers, it was the first time that men were broadcast kissing on a well-liked Greek television show. The council charged that the program also contained "obscene atmosphere" and "unacceptable dialogue."

In Edmonton, Alberta, six gay and lesbian couples hurried onto the stage where Alberta Premier Ralph Klein was giving a speech promoting the western Canadian province, and began hugging and kissing (Peters, 2003). Klein had just begun his speech to a crowd of about 6,000 at the Edmonton's Klondike Days festival when the same-sex couples stormed the stage.

The group was protesting Klein's resistance to same-sex marriage. The premier had previously promised that the province of Alberta would pay no attention to any federal law that legalizes gay marriage. Soon after the federal government announced it would legalize gay marriage, Klein declared that Alberta would not permit gay marriages to be catalogued in the province. As the couples kissed, Klein continued his speech undaunted and sarcastically thanked the protestors at the conclusion of the talk.

In both cases, peaceful demonstration was used to voice minority views regarding equal protection under the law. Both protests represent the use of free expression guaranteed by the First Amendment to address discrimination against sexual orientation.

GAY MARRIAGE

Whether and whom to marry, how to express sexual intimacy, and whether and how to establish a family—these are among the most basic of every individual's liberty and due process rights . . . And central to personal freedom and security is the assurance that the laws will apply equally to persons in similar situations.
—Massachusetts Supreme Court majority opinion in
November 2003 gay marriage ruling

On November 18, 2003, the Massachusetts Supreme Court ruled 4–3 that the state's ban on same-sex marriage is unconstitutional. The majority opinion argued,

> Barred access to the protections, benefits and obligations of civil marriage, a person who enters into an intimate, exclusive union with another of the same sex is arbitrarily deprived of membership in one of our community's most rewarding and cherished institutions.

The state's highest court gave lawmakers six months to develop a solution that would permit gay and lesbian couples to marry. The court, however, did not issue marriage licenses to the seven couples that took legal action, leaving the particulars to the legislature (Peter, 2003).

The plaintiffs in the Massachusetts case maintained that barring them from marrying a partner of the same sex denied them access to an intrinsic human experience and violated basic constitutional rights. The decision means that gay couples are entitled to all the rights of marriage and that establishing a separate type of marriage—such as civil unions—would not be acceptable. The ruling may draw a hostile reaction from the Massachusetts legislature, which has been considering a constitutional amendment that would legally define a marriage as a union between one man and one woman. However, such a constitutional amendment could not be passed until 2006 at the earliest, well past the high court's deadline.

The decision exceeds a 1999 Vermont Supreme Court ruling, which resulted in its legislature's authorization in 2000 of *civil unions*, which give same-sex couples in that state separate-but-equal status. Even those who feel that marriage is a special institution reserved for a man and a woman concede that the state must provide basic civil rights and appropriate benefits to nontraditional couples. Courts in Vermont, Hawaii, and Alaska have previously ruled that the states did not have a right to deny marriage to gay couples. In Hawaii and Alaska, the decisions were followed by the adoption of constitutional amendments limiting marriage to heterosexual couples. No American court has ordered the issuance of a marriage license—a privilege reserved for heterosexual couples.

In its momentous decision, the Massachusetts Supreme Court maintained,

> The exclusive commitment of two individuals to each other nurtures love and mutual support. It brings stability to our society. For those who choose to marry, and for their children, marriage provides an abundance of legal, financial, and social benefits. In return, it imposes weighty legal, financial, and social obligations.

In 2004, The U.S. House rejected a constitutional amendment that would have banned gay marriages. In November 2004, all 11 states that had referendums on their ballots easily rejected the legalization of gay marriages.

Hate Crime Legislation

Hate speech presupposes a system of domination between groups in which violence is encouraged, justified, and, in fact, sometimes even necessary to maintain the status quo. It follows then that hate speech is a necessary and contributory factor in hate crime. To help call attention to the numerous and deadly cases of anti-transgender violence around the world, transgender activists organized a Day of Remembrance to honor those lost since the death of Gwen Araujo, a 17-year-old transgendered woman who was brutally murdered on October 3, 2002 (*Advocate*, 2003h). While Araujo's murder gave national attention to the issue of anti-transgender violence, deaths similar to hers are happening at a rate of about three per month worldwide. Araujo's tragic murder was not an isolated incident. Since her death, there have been 35 other reported cases of anti-transgender violence leading to death—16 of those cases have been in the United States.

There is bipartisan support for proposed hate crime legislation. Republican senator Orrin G. Hatch of Utah, who has disagreed with Massachusetts senator Edward Kennedy's hate crime legislation in recent years, has astonished many by uniting with Kennedy in sponsoring a new proposal to pass the law (*Advocate*, 2003e). The proposal, supported by Democrats and several key Senate Republicans, would greatly enhance the federal government's ability to prosecute hate crimes committed in the United States, including those based on sexual orientation. In a striking turnaround of his previous stance on hate crimes, Hatch has recently stated that those lawmakers who oppose the inclusion of sexual orientation as a protected category "have got to grow up."

Kennedy-sponsored hate crimes legislation has been introduced many times in the past but has always been defeated, usually through parliamentary procedures or in conference committees after being ratified by the Senate. In recent years, Hatch, in his capacity as chairman of the Judiciary Committee, has personally stalled the legislation. Now he has linked with Kennedy to back it. At the time of this writing, it is believed that the measure would pass in the Senate where there is virtually full support from Democrats as well as support from at least eight key Republicans.

Homosexuality continues to be condemned in demonstrations not only by the Christian right but also by Muslims. In November 2003, a gay tour group from the United States had their arrival in Tanzania marked with a large anti-gay protest (uk.gay.com, 2003). A group of approximately 100 gay tourists came to spend a month on safari in the country. Security around Dar es Salaam airport was strict; officials did not verify the group's arrival. Tanzania is primarily a Muslim society. Homosexuality is considered immoral and against the teachings of Islam outlined in the Holy Koran.

Nazi Homophobic Hate Speech and the Persecution of Gays and Lesbians

Germany will construct a national memorial to gay men and lesbians persecuted or killed under the Nazis, accompanying the proposed German memorial to the 6 million Jews who died in the Holocaust (*Advocate*, 2003c). Nazi Germany used homophobic hate speech, declaring homosexuality an aberration that endangered the German race, and convicted some 50,000 gay men and lesbians as criminals. An estimated 10,000 to 15,000 gay men were deported to concentration camps, where few survived.

A bill to build a memorial in Berlin passed the lower house's culture committee with the support of the governing Social Democrats and Greens, who also have the majority on the house floor. It was not surprising that the conservative opposition Christian Democrats opposed the measure.

Few gays convicted by the Nazis came forward after World War II because of the continuing stigma and criminalization of homosexual behavior in West Germany until 1969. In 2002, the German parliament issued a formal pardon for gays convicted under the Nazis. One reason the pardon was postponed for so long was because supporters linked it to a blanket treatment of 22,000 Wehrmacht deserters, a step many conservatives opposed.

CONCLUSION

This chapter has examined sexual orientation and hate speech. There has been a trend among American colleges and universities to attempt to protect minorities from hostile environments on campuses by establishing speech codes that restrict hate speech against gays and lesbians, racial, ethnic, and religious minorities, and women. Although well intended, the enforcement of these speech codes has proven to be problematic as evidenced in the case at the University of North Carolina at Chapel Hill. It is clear that speech codes on college and university campuses created to restrict hate speech and provide egalitarian and safe environments for women, gays and lesbians, and racial and ethnic minorities can be used as a Trojan horse to subvert the rights they were intended to protect.

This chapter has paid special attention to the history of the roles of gay and lesbian characters on television over the past four decades. We have seen that hate speech can be expressed through homophobic messages, stereotypical characters, and subtle anti-gay or anti-lesbian indicators. Indirect homophobic messages included a sharp underrepresentation of positive gay and lesbian images in media. Gay and lesbian images, roles, and messages on television affect attitudes about gays and lesbians regardless of their validity as accurate and realistic portrayals. Regarding the model of hate-speech severity, televised gay and lesbian images, roles, and messages represent the entire range of stages, from unintentional to deliberate discrimination, to inciting hatred and violence.

In general, gays and lesbians on television have been portrayed positively, as multidimensional human characters with not so untypical goals, feelings, and flaws. To be sure, stereotypes of and micro-transgressions against gays and lesbians persist—both in scripted and well as in "reality" television. Yet, through television, large numbers of children, adolescents, and young adults especially can view some realistic portrayals and images. Consequently, they develop critical reasoning ability and are able to realize the irrationality of homophobia and reject it.

Indeed the media are very powerful agents of socialization. Nevertheless, the family and network of support, including spiritual and religious leaders, can, through early moral education and development, prevent the development of homophobia and hate speech about or toward gays and lesbians.

We should restrict gay images and messages that are discriminatory or incite hatred or violence. There is no room in a democracy for unfair treatment of minority groups or individuals who are members of such groups. The First Amendment guarantees free speech, but mass media, including television, should take the responsibility to restrict anti-gay hate speech. Gays who are the victims of hate speech are also more likely to be victims of violence than other groups who are merely victims of hate speech.

6

The Future of Democracy: Beyond Legal Realism

Democracy must be something more than two wolves and a sheep voting on what to have for dinner.
> —James Bovard, libertarian social commentator and
> policy analyst for the Future of Freedom Foundation
> (Hamlin, 1980)

Bovard's quote aptly and lucidly demonstrates that democratic process extends beyond mere majority rule. Minority rights must also be protected. Our country's founders recognized this, accommodating and applying this important principle by creating a bicameral Congress: the Senate and House of Representatives. The number of representatives that a particular state has is based on its population, thus reflecting majority rule. However, in the more constitutionally powerful Senate, every state has two member senators, reflecting minority rights and a guard against discrimination. Hate speech disparages those who do not conform to the culturally hegemonic paradigm.

When hate speech is antithetical to the underlying democratic principles that inform both the First Amendment and the equal protection clause of the Fourteenth Amendment, it should be restricted. The strong link between hate speech and hate crime, and the harm experienced by victims of hate speech, makes evident the contradiction between First Amendment absolutism and the democratic goals of liberty and equality. There is a critical distinction between dissent—the right to criticize the powerful institutions that govern our lives—and hate speech, which is directed against the relatively powerless segments of our society (Matsuda et al., 1993).

In spite of a history of ethnic and racial discrimination, the court system and legislative processes in the United States have appeared to be dragging their feet in terms of acknowledging the damage of hate speech and its ability to instigate violent hate crime. It is difficult for hate-speech victims to attain judicial restitution even when their injuries are severe, straightforward, and extraordinary. The hate speech must also seemingly breach the boundaries of decency.

The political and voting power of ethnic minorities in the United States is increasing as their numbers swell. For social harmony, this necessitates an increase in ethnic and racial tolerance. The new millennium has also brought the advent of First Amendment legal realism—a school of legal thought that rejects perfunctory or standardized jurisprudence in partiality to social science theory, methods, and research findings; social policy decisions; and common sense.

Instead of using a standard formula, hate-speech court cases will closely examine the messenger, the harm to and the social status of the victim, the tenacity of the message, the speech mode (e.g., Internet Web site, graffiti, face-to-face, e-mail, telephone call, etc.); whether the message was recurring, threatening, or incited violence; and whether the victim had opportunity to reply to the message. The First Amendment essentially is becoming more nuanced. The social science literature has provided and continues to provide very specific and theoretically useful evidence on the severity and harm of hate speech (e.g., Boeckmann and Turpin-Petrosino, 2002; Cowan et al., 2002; Leets, 2002; Leets and Giles, 1997; Nielsen, 2002).

Hate speech demonstrates contempt for the constitutional values of social equality and fairness for all citizens. It often supports violence against ethnic, racial, and religious minorities, women, and gays and lesbians. Consequently, given the basic tenets of American society and culture, hate speech goes beyond acceptable civil treatment.

First Amendment absolutists mistakenly believe that the playing field is even. This erroneous notion assumes that there is an open marketplace for ideas in which everyone participates equally. Ideological arguments like this end up reinforcing the very inequality that hate-speech controls and international conventions are aimed at redressing (Delgado, 2004b).

This chapter begins with a legal response to hate speech. Regarding social equality and free speech issues, we show support for a transition from an abstract mechanical notion of justice to one based on the context of the message, intent to harm, as well as the severity of harm cause.

Next we look at the special case of children concerning hate speech and the First Amendment. The courts have shown examples of protecting children from possible harm—even at the expense of restricting adult free speech.

Then the case is made to go beyond the emerging First Amendment realist paradigm. Legal solutions to hate speech are too cumbersome and impractical. There is a push to move hate speech partially away from the legal, political, and court systems—where absolutist views of the First Amendment are still dominant—to looking at the processes of group identification, cultural transmission, and moral education.

This chapter ends with a practical guide to what individuals can do to oppose hate speech on their own.

A LEGAL RESPONSE TO HATE SPEECH

Learning how law really works is an important step toward social reform.

—Richard Delgado, 2004b: 223

Speech and equality stand in reciprocal relation; neither can thrive without the other.

—Richard Delgado, 2004b: 217

Legal realism (Delgado, 2000) proposes that the courts assess any injurious intentions of the speaker or harmful consequences of the message communicated. The thread of subordination weaves through analyses of hate speech, legal history, affirmative action, desegregation, religious freedom, civil rights, and reparations. Not surprisingly, there has been a vigorous backlash to affirmative action. Traditional interpretations of the First Amendment arm conscious and unconscious racists—from members of the Ku Klux Klan to political liberals—with the right to be racist. Accordingly, racism is merely another idea that deserves to be protected by the Constitution. The First Amendment is misused to nullify the only substantive meaning of the equal protection clause of the Fourteenth Amendment, that the Constitution requires the unstructuring of racist ideology.

Freedom is a basic right supported by the Constitution. Freedom connotes freedom from degradation, humiliation, battering, and other forms of violence to a person that denies one's full humanity. The danger of White supremacist groups surpasses their violent hate crimes. Their mere existence and the active distribution of racist propaganda result in the nullification of personal security and liberty for targeted victims in their everyday life. Consequently, formal criminal and administrative censure is an appropriate reply to hate speech.

This push for a formal response to hate speech is to reinforce our commitment to tolerance as a value. When hate speech is antithetical to the underlying democratic principles that inform both the First Amendment and the equal protection clause of the Fourteenth Amendment, it should be restricted. The strong link between hate speech and hate crime, and loss of liberty experienced by victims of hate speech, makes evident the contradiction between First Amendment absolutism and the democratic goals of liberty and equality. There is a critical distinction between dissent—the right to criticize the powerful institutions that govern our lives—and hate speech, which is directed against the relatively powerless segments of our society.

We should recognize the grave injuries inflicted by hate speech and the potential tensions between legal solutions to those injuries and the First Amendment. Values central to the First Amendment itself are subverted by hate speech. Racism, sexism, xenophobia, and homophobia are the causes of this selective disregard. "Commonly shared justifications for preserving the status quo [have] become more questionable in the wake of exploding contradictions" (Cortese, 1990: 158).

Hate speech—disguised as free speech—can create, maintain, and justify social inequality. Not everyone has equal access to the creation of culture or the marketplace of free ideas. Some voices go unheard, having been silenced and marginalized. Stereotypical attitudes and bigotry preclude a fair assessment of all types of speakers, proposed policy, or ideas. Messages, ideas, manifestos, or communications that do not abide by the hegemonic paradigm are shunted off to the side. Economic inequality prevents equal ability to speak—to be heard—and get ideas out to a public audience. Clearly, the dominant paradigm renders minority viewpoints obsolete, untrustworthy, and pointless. Perhaps we are unconsciously barring equally valuable messages, speakers, and ideas.

The wisdom of legal realism over the inflexibility of First Amendment absolutism parallels the wisdom of the U.S. Constitution's use of equity as fairness over the contextually blind, rigid, naive, and obtuse application of equality as "one size fits all." Usually, laws and social norms should be obeyed. However, when a law conflicts with a basic human principle, the Constitution calls for us to maintain the higher principle and eliminate or change the law. For example, even though it was the law to publicly segregate the races in the South until *Brown v. Board of Education*, civil disobedience served as a means to produce a greater good for society—namely, respect for the human dignity of all persons, the restriction of discrimination, and a roadmap for equal social relations. Although *Brown v. Board of Education* outlawed racial segregation in government-owned facilities beginning in 1954, it was not until the passage of the Civil Rights Act of 1964 that *Brown* was extended to privately owned places of public accommodation.

The four-stage theory of hate-speech severity presented in Chapter 1 and applied throughout this book can be gainfully applied to laws restricting hate speech and sentencing for convicted offenders.

GROUP IDENTIFICATION, CULTURAL TRANSMISSION, AND MORAL EDUCATION

We have to empower ourselves and our children with the awareness that racism, religious intolerance, xenophobia, and homophobia are embedded in our culture, language, and speech. All forms of bigotry are immoral, having no legitimate place in a democratic society based on equal treatment, fairness, and freedom from discrimination. Yet these cultural ideologies unconsciously have an effect on our systems of cognitive and moral development and communication.

Hateful attitudes are rooted in our vocabulary, stories, and unspoken understandings, thus tainting our social relations and worldview. These bigoted and sometimes implicit attitudes have become institutionalized. They are so powerful that if you oppose them, you appear inconsistent or incoherent (Delgado and Stefancic, 1992).

Group-identification and cultural transmission theories claim that dominant groups use language as a means to socially control members of subordinate groups. For example, continuous portrayal of a particular ethnic minority as unintelligent or dishonest can construct social reality in a manner that results in suffering, discrimination, and oppression for members of that minority group. If members of a dominant group incessantly use pejorative images, hate speech, and other forms of language to label, prejudge, and put down a minority group, they are internalized. Minority group members actually appear to take on the thinking and behavior that are attributed to them. For example, those from schools whose students are mostly under privileged tend to label students as "slow learners." This perpetuates a self-fulfilling prophecy (see Rosenthal and Jacobson, 1968).

At the same time, speech that challenges or jeopardizes the chosen pursuits of the dominant group will be sharply criticized, reined in, or censored by edict. For example, let us consider the Reverend Al Sharpton's address at the Democratic National Convention in Boston in July 2004. His comments were sharply criticized by the media as counterproductive to the Democratic cause. Yet his supporters called it brilliant—the best speech at the Convention. Clearly, Sharpton was inspiring to the those in attendance. Yet he was berated for veering away from his scripted speech because his ideas were basically different from those representing cultural hegemony.

A second example is the August 2004 termination of singer Linda Ronstadt by the Aladdin Hotel-Casino in Las Vegas—where she was performing—for supporting director Michael Moore's controversial film, *Fahrenheit 9/11* (Associated Press, 2004). The documentary film is severely critical of President George W. Bush and his administration's foreign policy in the aftermath of the terrorist attacks on September 11, 2001. Some of the concerts on Ronstadt's planned tour, including two in Dallas, Texas—home state of President Bush—have been cancelled due to her outspokenness against dominant political ideas and foreign policy during wartime.

Before singing her famous "Desperado" for an encore performance, the 58-year-old Latina called Moore a "great American patriot" and "someone who is spreading the truth." She also encouraged the audience to see Moore's film. Some of the audience vigorously and loudly booed her for her political statements; others among the 4,500 people in attendance left the theater simultaneously in anger. People also ripped up concert posters and tossed their drinks into the air on their way out.

Aladdin President Bill Timmins, a Briton, was in the audience and immediately decided to permanently terminate Ronstadt on the spot. Ronstadt was not permitted to return to her luxury suite and was briskly escorted off the property. Afterwards, Timmons justified his decision by, first, blaming the veteran singer for ruining a wonderful evening for the guests and, second, by appealing to the necessity for instant and irrevocable punishment: "We had to do something about it . . . As long as I'm here, she's not going to play."

Since Ronstadt had been booked to play the Aladdin for only one show, her firing was meaningless. It was done for posturing, for fronting, for appearances. Symbolically, the termination was punishment of a subordinate by a boss. In an interview with the *Las Vegas Review-Journal* before the show, Ronstadt hinted at a possible schism: "I keep hoping that if I'm annoying enough to them, they won't hire me back." It appears that Linda Ronstadt's wish was granted.

The dominant group looks for ways to restrict countercultural—or simply, just different—free expression by making exceptions to the right of free speech by categorizing it as "fighting words," national security, false advertising, threats to attack or kill, obscene, and so on. In this case, Timmons, a member of the politically dominant group, "punished" Ronstadt, a self-professed member of the political minority group, for dissent—a basic right guaranteed by our First Amendment. However, if a humanist or civil rights advocate requests an additional exemption to the First Amendment in order to protect a disadvantaged or vulnerable person, such as a female Asian undergraduate harassed because of her race and gender, a gay man threatened because of his sexual orientation, a desperate woman working in pornography, or an ethnic minority student in a White institution of higher education, the response, of course, is a cringe.

INTERNATIONAL MODELS FOR OPPOSING HATE SPEECH IN AMERICA

When the Nazis attacked the Jews, I didn't object, for I wasn't a Jew. Then they attacked the socialists, and I didn't object, for I wasn't a socialist. Then they attacked the Catholics, and I didn't object, for I wasn't a Catholic. Then they attacked the unions, and I didn't object, for I wasn't a member of the unions. Then they attacked me—and there was no one left to object.

—Martin Niemöller, Jerusalem, Yad Vashem
Holocaust Memorial (engraved)

Western first-world postindustrial societies such as the Netherlands, Germany, and Canada have laws against numerous types of hate speech, yet they have not suffered a corrosion of free speech, expression, or inquiry. In fact, mass media in those countries are quite vocal, autonomous, and aggressive at least as independent as those in the United States. Hate speech silences its victims (Delgado, 2004b), triggering them to retreat from basic interaction with others.

Instead of encouraging a free exchange of ideas, it results in less speech and conversation. Absolute interpretations of the First Amendment seem to be the dominant paradigm in legal analysis. However, legal and social tolerance of hate speech is a "contract of indifference" similar to the social atmosphere just before the Holocaust and American slavery (Taslitz, 2000). In adopting the Fourteenth Amendment, American society transformed the First Amendment from a heartless mechanical proviso to a manifesto of goodwill.

CHILDREN: THE SPECIAL HARMS OF HATE SPEECH

Children are often the victims of cruel, intimidating, and emotionally distressing hate speech. Because of the potential for emotional damage, extra care should be taken not to expose them to it or teach it to them. This includes passing on values of fairness and equal treatment, teaching acceptance of other groups (not ethnocentrism and xenophobia), and moral education. Hate speech that targets children is even more harmful than talk that targets adults. Accordingly, there is also a strong case to restrict it (Delgado, 2004b; Saunders, 2003).

There are also other reasons for protecting children from certain types of speech. The mass media are major players in exploiting children. Consider, for example, how and what unscrupulous advertisers and entrepreneurs market to children. When children are involved, the potential costs are greater. For example, their psychological development may be arrested or otherwise adversely affected by a stimulus, ad, product, or service that would be perhaps only slightly annoying to an adult (Saunders, 2003).

Differences in emotional maturity and intellectual levels between children and adults make those costs less bearable. In short, a dual approach to the First Amendment would protect children not only against obscenity and sexually explicit materials permissible for adults but would also protect them against other types of speech such as violence-inciting hate speech; misogynist or racist video games; and false, misleading, or exploitative advertising.

If we are to prevent children from learning and repeating hate speech, the case for protecting them from hateful tirades takes on a special meaning. Children are especially vulnerable to the painful harm of hate speech. Simultaneously, the traditional lines of reasoning against restricting hate speech lack teeth where children are concerned. Children generally are not on the same authority, physical, psychological, and intellectual level as adults. As a consequence, they typically are not able to talk back to those who subject them to hatred (Delgado, 2004b).

On account of these special circumstances, it is not surprising that the legislatures and the courts have advocated children's rights, protecting them from the adverse consequences of hate speech. Because children are especially vulnerable, they deserve special shelter from hate-mongers. In particular, hate speech damages the socioemotional development of the child.

What children are especially vulnerable to hate speech? What are the types of hate speech that target children? What are the roles of technology and mass media in exposing children to hate speech? The next section will address these questions. In order to evaluate the emotional harm of hate speech to children, we start with an examination of Jean Piaget's theory of cognitive development. Then analysis is expanded to Lawrence Kohlberg's six-stage theory of moral reasoning, based on Piaget's theory.

Child Cognitive and Moral Development

The writings of Immanuel Kant (e.g., *The Critique of Pure Reason*) are considered to be the foundation of Western ethical thought. Piaget borrowed from Kant the key notion that individuals actively construct a social reality and constructed the fundamental assumptions of cognitive-developmental theory (Piaget, [1932] 1965).

Piaget's theory of cognitive development represented a paradigm shift regarding our understanding of how children think and learn. Prior to Piaget, it was assumed that children and adults thought exactly alike and the only difference was that children simply knew less than adults. This was based on social learning theory in which children's notions of, for example, race, justice, or morality are merely imitations of adult ideas. Although the idea that thinking develops through a series of stages for individuals is now widely accepted, it was quite revolutionary when Piaget first proposed it.

According to Piaget (1952, 1954), cognitive development is a series of universal stages. These stages form an invariant sequence in development. "While cultural factors may speed up, slow down, or stop development, they do not change its sequence" (1960: 15). Stages imply distinct or qualitative differences in children's styles of thinking and problem solving (Cortese, 1990).

Piaget viewed cultural transmission—especially through the family—as an important source in the rate of a child's development (Cortese, 1985; Cortese and Mestrovic, 1990). He suggested that intellectual development in children is largely the consequence of social factors, such as language (Piaget, 1926). That is why hate speech and First Amendment issues are so crucial to the emotional growth and self-identification of children.

Parental and peer support and constraint are also important sources for a child's development (Piaget, [1932] 1965). Piaget proposed that social experience stimulates development through the stages by encouraging processes of role-taking—the coordination of perspectives of self and others as a basis for choosing (Cortese, 1990: 20). Piaget distinguishes two levels of moral development—heteronomy (based on constraint) and autonomy (based on cooperation). "Piaget's theory remains a dominant force in developmental psychology, despite the fact that much of it was formulated half a century ago" (Van Ausdale and Feagin, 2002: 5). Cognitive-developmental theory has long-lasting appeal to scholars and parents alike because of the important achievements it illustrates, the wide range of childhood experience it includes, and the reliability and draw of many of its interpretations.

Piaget's ([1932] 1965) cognitive-developmental theory provides the infrastructure for Kohlberg's (1981, 1984) six-stage theory of moral reasoning and school of moral education. Kohlberg is credited with expanding Piaget's pioneering study of moral development in children. Kohlberg (1984) bases his highest level of moral reasoning (Stage 6) on principles of respect for persons that are compatible with engaging in actual dialogue. This has implications for how we, as a culture, handle hate speech.

Mutual respect for human dignity would permit meaningful dialogue— even opposing ideas could provide telling and consensus-building discourse without the use of hate speech. In short, children know more about group identification, stereotyping, prejudice, and the so-called "adult world" than parents realize or wish to admit. For that reason, we should adapt, prevent the learning and expression of hate speech, and create an atmosphere that celebrates cultural and ideological diversity.

Child Development of Racial Awareness and Racial Prejudice

Segregation affected the hearts and minds of Negro children in a way unlikely ever to be undone . . . The message of segregation was stigmatizing to black children. To be labeled unfit to attend school with white children injured the reputation of Black children, thereby foreclosing employment opportunities and the right to be regarded respectable members of the body politic.
—Brown v. Board of Education, 1954: 494–495 n.11

The *Brown* decision speaks directly to the severe psychic injury inflicted by racist hate speech (Lawrence, 1990; Matsuda et al., 1993). Given the robust support for Piaget's cognitive-developmental theory through extensive research, it is not surprising that children as young as age three have developed, through their own experience and cognitive map, the meaning of race and, unfortunately, racist hate speech as well. For example, Carla, a White 3-year-old preschooler, moves her nap-time cot away from a Black classmate and casually states, "I can't sleep next to a nigger . . . niggers are stinky" (Van Ausdale and Feagin, 2001).

As Chapter 1 indicated, underlying the *Brown* decision was the Supreme Court's lucid awareness of the adverse effects of compulsory segregation on the psyches of its victims. In essence, the case focused on the severe nature of the emotional harm caused by hateful expression in the form of public educational segregation. Young minority children often develop a negative self-image. They are unconsciously taught to hate themselves, as evidenced by tales of children trying to scrub the dark color out of their skin, favoring light- over dark-colored clay when asked to make a model of a person (Delgado, 1995b), and Black children preferring to play with White dolls instead of Black ones (Clark and Clark, 1947).

The latter study was gainfully applied by the plaintiff's attorneys in *Brown* in their arguments on the harmful effects of educational segregation. Although subsequent doll studies have sometimes shown Black children's preference for White dolls, other social scientists (Bloom,1971; Powell-Hopson and Hopson, 1988) argue that this demonstrates a realization of what most commercially sold dolls look like rather than documenting low self-esteem.

Just because Black children know that Whites have more power and resources and, therefore, rate Whites higher than Blacks does not necessarily mean that the latter have low self-esteem. In fact, "decent" culture vis-à-vis the code of the streets provides strong emotional support to deflect social labels of inferiority (Anderson, 1999). Moreover, when the self-images of middle-class or affluent African Americans are measured, their feelings of self-esteem are more positive than those of comparable Whites (Gray-Little and Hafdahl, 2000).

Nevertheless, institutional racism taints linguistic development. With unconscious hints of inferiority to Whites, some minority children resort to denial or lying to avoid what they have been made to feel is the truth about themselves. Given this backdrop, what then happens if minority children are the deliberate target of hate speech? Since children have fewer coping mechanisms than adults, hateful words can cut them much more deeply than others. A child who reacts with anger, undoubtedly, will be punished and likely alienated; internalizing the hurt only undercuts the young person's confidence and motivation (Delgado, 1995b).

Hate Speech Targeting Children

If we are going to teach the world to stop hating, we have to start with the children.

—Mary Travers, Peter, Paul and Mary

Children are sometimes the targets of hate speech by other children, teachers, neighbors, coaches, and adults in public settings, such as transportation workers, social workers, and religious authorities. Hateful words can inflict irrevocable emotional harm on children, shaping their self-esteem, relationships with others, and worldview.

In *Rogers v. Elliot*, two Black parents brought suit on behalf of their children against a Georgia Wal-Mart and some of its employees. After her candy had been scanned by the checker, Mrs. Rogers opened it and gave some of it to her children. As her children walked away from their mother, another checker from another line exclaimed, "Hey, get over here, boy, and pay for this candy." Think of how demeaning this must have been to Mrs. Rogers to explain that the candy had already been paid for. Now the checker pursued her in the parking lot, confronting her again—in front of her children, and insulted and slapped her. The court relied on the unfeeling, mechanical view that when the attack took place they were no longer "shopping at Wal-Mart." Hence, the court dismissed the case, leaving a civil suit the only remaining choice for the plaintiffs.

Litigation in civil court was not possible for the Black family who shockingly witnessed a cross burned on their front lawn in St. Paul, Minnesota, in 1990 (see Chapter 1). After being convicted of violating the city's ordinance banning racially hostile symbols and artifacts on public or private property, the White teen challenged the constitutionality of the ordinance. The case gained national attention, especially after the Supreme Court ruled the statute was an unconstitutional intrusion into the protection of freedom of speech and expression as guaranteed by the First Amendment. The high court did not consider the traumatic effect of such a provocative symbol on the minds of young children. The children were punched in the stomach with racism. Additionally, the Joneses have indicated that now the children are much more aware of racism, with one child extra sensitive to name-calling.

In *Quinn v. National Railroad Passenger Corporation* (1999), a woman sued Amtrak for the mistreatment she and her two young children were subjected to on an aborted train trip across the country. The family was not given seats and was twice forced to de-board. The worst was yet to come. While the children played on a blanket with two other Black children, a White passenger threatened them. When the conductor arrived, he immediately sided with the White woman in the quarrel.

Hate Speech at School

A major point of contention in schools is whether individual style—clothing, accessories, or symbols are sometimes hateful and harmful expressions or propaganda and should be prohibited. When these types of cases have been litigated, there have been mixed results. Sometimes the free expression guaranteed by the First Amendment is favored; other times the courts recognize the harmful effects of hate speech or other symbols of hateful expression.

The confederate flag is a prime example. In *Castorina v. Madison County School Board* (2001), the Sixth Circuit Court of Appeals ruled that school districts could not selectively ban racially sensitive symbols in clothing. For example, a school could not permit some students to wear Malcolm X t-shirts but simultaneously ban Confederate flags (Delgado, 2004b).

This ruling is based on the same logic as in the case involving Reverend Fred Phelps's petition to put up a homophobic monument disparaging hate crime murder victim Matthew Sheppard (see Chapter 5). In that 2002 case, the Tenth U.S. Circuit Court of Appeals decided that any city displaying a Ten Commandments monument on city property must also allow monuments of other religious or political groups. The city council voted to remove the Ten Commandments rather than be forced to allow Phelps's monument of hate.

In *West v. Derby Unified School District No. 260* (2000), the Tenth Circuit Court supported a school district's anti-harassment policy and affirmed its punishment—a suspension—of a student who sketched a Confederate flag on a piece of paper.

In *Denno v. School Board of Volusia County, Florida* (2000), the Eleventh Circuit refused to support a student suspended for exhibiting a Confederate flag, despite the fact that there was no evidence presented that he had acted with racist intentions. This puts the onus on the content of the symbol or message.

All three cases cited *Tinker v. Des Moines Independent School District* (1969). Each, however, came to a different conclusion. In the *Tinker* case, the Supreme Court ruled that students do not lose their constitutional rights to free speech and expression once they set foot on campus. The ruling permitted students to wear black armbands to symbolize their protest of the Vietnam War.

The school district's policy resulted from previous racial violence in two of the cases—*Castorina* and *West*. In *West* (2000), this appears to have played a major role in the decision. However, in *Castorina* (2001: 544), the Sixth Circuit indicated that "even if [a history of] racial violence . . . necessitates a ban on racially divisive symbols" the school district cannot selectively single out which ones to accept and which to prohibit.

Hence, the distinction between the two is the selective enforcement of a prohibition in *Castorina* (2001: 541) where White students were not able to exhibit racist material, but Black students were able to publicly display their political views about race. In short, each court appears to support a prohibition on racially offensive material, regardless of its content and its intentions, so long as it is applied evenly to all students (Delgado, 2004b).

In *Graham v. Guiderland Central School District* (1998), a Black high school student took legal action against a school district for being called "nigger" by her teacher. In reply to another student's expressed issue with why gays should not be called "faggots," the teacher gestured to the only African American student in the room and declared, "Why not call Liz a 'nigger' because that's what she is? Liz, why not tell us what it feels like to be called a 'nigger'?" (*Graham v. Guiderland Central School District*, 1998: 863).

The lawsuit was thrown out since the teacher's comments did not satisfy the criterion of "extreme and outrageous conduct" (*Graham v. Guiderland Central School District*, 1998: 863) as required by the tort law. This ruling is suspect considering that the girl's young age and isolation as the only Black in class made her especially vulnerable to the harmful effects of hate speech. Judge Cardona penned the minority decision and argued that the case should proceed because the victim "was not an adult, but rather an adolescent" (*Graham v. Guiderland Central School District*, 1998: 865, Cardona, P. J., dissenting).

The pattern of dismissals against hate-speech suits—even such a particularly malicious case, the requirement that the hate speech be intentional, extreme, and outrageous, and the great difficulty of proving that the aforementioned conduct directly causes an exceptionally severe emotional distress support a push for going beyond a legalistic approach to restrict hate speech.

Sexual harassment at the elementary school level is a major problem (Pitchal, 1996). A study by the Minnesota Attorney General's office reported that in the 1992–1993 academic year, there were over 2,200 reports of sexual harassment in 720 elementary schools. There were an additional 377 reports of sexual violence.

In *Saxe v. State College Area School District* (2001), a guardian went to court on behalf of his children, claiming that his students were denied their right to free speech—to speak out against homosexuality. The school's anti-harassment policy kept these students from sharing their views regarding the sinfulness of homosexuality and its dangerous consequences. The Third Circuit ruled the policy unconstitutional, overturning the district court's verdict to support student protection from harassment. In conclusion, we again focus on the legal and moral conflict between two sacred rights: free speech and equality or protection from discrimination.

In *Davis v. Monroe County Board of Education* (1999), two parents went to court against their daughter's school district under Title IX's anti-harassment protection. The student, a fifth-grader named LaShonda Davis (also called Shonda) and several classmates were exposed to repeated sexual harassment by one of their cohorts. The boy's behavior ultimately increased to a criminal level resulting in a charge of and guilty plea to sexual battery in a Georgia court. LaShonda's principal knew of the pattern of harassment against her but, amazingly, the school took no disciplinary action against the boy.

LaShonda suffered for months. The boy who sat next to her kept trying to touch her breasts and vaginal area. He told her, "I want to get in bed with you," and "I want to touch your boobs" (Pitchal, 1996). He trapped her in hallways and rubbed up against her in an erotic manner. LaShonda regularly complained to her teachers, but they did nothing. It took three months of daily requests before her teacher finally agreed to reassign the boy to another desk. The principal's efforts were limited to unsuccessful threats and he could not seem to get past his belief that 'Shonda was the only student who was complaining.

LaShonda suffered from depression and her grades slipped. The harassment had such a devastating effect on her that she penned a suicide note. If she had been an adult—not a fifth-grader—and her harassment had occurred in the workplace, her employer would have been liable. Under Title VII, a federal law prohibiting sex- and race-based discrimination on the job, businesses are responsible for ensuring that their employees work in an environment free from sexual hostility. Employers are liable whether the source of sexual harassment is a supervisor or a co-worker.

But LaShonda was only 10 years old, and because her emotional trauma occurred at school, it seemed as though she lacked protection. The school's lawyers maintained that her teacher and the school principal were under no legal duty to listen to her pleas and notice the constant barrage of humiliation and sexually inspired torture she faced every day. The court held the district "liable for their deliberate indifference to known acts of peer sexual harassment" (*Davis v. Monroe County Board of Education*, 1999: 648).

The court's decision shows that the school should have intervened on behalf of the victim. The psychological ramifications could not have been any worse if the principal had been the harasser, as opposed to the one who made allowances for it.

Eve Bruneau, a sixth-grader in upstate New York, was also the victim of spiteful student-to-student sexual harassment. She and other girls in her class were cruelly referred to by some boys as lesbian, prostitute, whore, and "ugly dog face bitch." Boys also snapped the girls' bra straps, crammed paper down their blouses, and cut their hair.

In a landmark 1992 decision, the Supreme Court ruled that sexual harassment of students by teachers violates Title IX, the federal law which mandates equal educational opportunities for boys and girls. However, whereas Title VII covers worker-to-worker harassment, courts currently disagree about whether Title IX should be interpreted to prohibit student-to-student harassment when teachers and principals stand by and do nothing.

This is the setting for the case of Jonathan Prevette, the 6-year-old North

Carolina boy who was suspended from first grade for kissing a female class-mate on the cheek. School officials originally said that Jonathan had vio-lated the school's sexual harassment policy. The outrage in response to this story was international. The consensus was that political correctness had gone out of control. After all, "What's wrong with an innocent peck on the cheek?" Had the pendulum swung too far the other way? Or had the girl been chased on the playground, frightened, and kissed without her ap-proval?

The sexual harassment policy at Jonathan's school was instituted in di-rect response to LaShonda's case and others similar to it. These policies are a persistent reminder to teachers and administrators to take students' com-plaints of sexual harassment very seriously.

Perhaps the officials at Jonathan's school reacted excessively when they applied their policy to his behavior. This 6-year-old undoubtedly did not intend any harm to his classmate—according to his parents, he is a very affectionate boy. Kissing in class is probably inappropriate, and this should have been explained to him the same way most first-grade rule violations are. The Prevette case pales in comparison to the miserable pattern of ha-rassment suffered by LaShonda Davis and Eve Bruneau. One must be able to use common sense, context, and discernment to distinguish flirting from hurting.

It is possible that strong backlash to the Prevette case will push the pen-dulum back the other way—toward the erosion of strong policies to elim-inate sexual harassment among students. Media exposure (e.g., Camille Paglia and Rush Limbaugh) has enhanced a coordinated backlash cam-paign. In the meantime, the U.S. Department of Education's Office of Civil Rights has official guidelines on peer harassment. The timing of the Pre-vette story is amazing. The story became news only five days before the end of the public commenting period on the Education Department's draft guidelines.

What happened in the Prevette case was unfortunate. School officials have since acknowledged their mistakes and have expressed regret. Never-theless, intentionally disregarding an oppressive pattern of student-on-student sexual harassment is a serious injustice. What happened to LaShonda Davis was not a little kiss—it was harmful and degrading.

In *Montiero v. Tempe Union High School District* (1998), the main issue was whether particular books should be prohibited from the curriculum because of racist content. The court recognized the conflict between the First Amendment—instructors' rights to academic freedom as well as stu-dents' rights to be exposed to new ideas and information versus the Four-teenth Amendment—students' rights to be educated in an atmosphere that does not create or consent to hostile symbols or discriminatory treatment.

Two novels used in the classrooms—*A Rose for Emily* and *The Adven-tures of Huckleberry Finn*—repeatedly used the word "nigger." Several

Black students claimed that they underwent emotional harm. A weak solution was proposed: the students were allowed to sit alone in the hall during the schoolroom discussion. The court used the slippery slope argument to dismiss the portion of the lawsuit dealing with the books.

Accordingly, this argument "holds that a new legal measure may inevitably lead to another, then another, then another, with the result that entire areas will be governed by excessive regulation" (Delgado, 2004b: 232). White students would sue to ban books by ethnic minority novelists and poets. Jews would try to get rid of books with anti-Semitism. Females would try to change or outlaw sexist writings.

Gilligan (1982), for example, has provided a sweeping critique of social psychology. She lambasted everyone from Freud to Erikson to Piaget to Kohlberg for using scales of individual development and theories that were based on male development and socialization and then rating women's development as inferior to men's. Women students would sue their professors for teaching sexist theories. Males would go after the feminists *ad nauseum*. There could be an endless and unpredictable stream of lawsuits, the court reasoned.

The circuit court, however, borrows the concepts—even some of the words—from critical race theory (see Chapter 1) to seemingly refute its own conclusion:

> Books can hurt, and . . . words can hurt—particularly racist epithets . . . the most lauded works of literature convey explicitly or in a more subtle manner messages of racism and sexism, or other ideas that if accepted blindly would serve to maintain or promote the invidious inequalities that exist in our world today . . . the younger a person is, the more likely it is that those messages will help form that person's thinking, and that the feelings of minority students, especially younger ones, are extremely vulnerable when it comes to books that are racist or have racist overtones. (*Montiero v. Tempe Union High School District*, 1998: 1031)

The circuit court added that it is important for students to learn about both the good and bad in our past history. In conclusion, the court dismissed the books part of the case because of the important need for young people to learn history and to avoid setting a bad precedent—the potential for the prohibition of countless books.

However, the circuit court, again using critical race theory, recognized the injury of hate speech and reversed the trial court's decision to throw out the part of the case alleging an explosion of racist hate speech and graffiti—including the word "nigger"—at school after their classmates read and discussed the provocative books. The court judged that this section of the suit met a cause of action for hostile racist environment under a federal statute (Title VI). The court ruled that the school was liable since school administrators knew about the speech, but did nothing to stop it. In short, books with racial epithets are constitutional, but hate speech by students is not—even if both use the same words.

Mass Media Effects on Children

> *If you don't speak English, get the fuck out!*
> —Bumper sticker (Panos, 2000: 27)

> *Kill all the niggers and you gas all the Jews*
> *Kill a gypsy and a colored too*
> *You just killed a kike*
> *Don't it feel right*
> *Goodness gracious, darn right*
> —RaHoWa, *Third Reich*, Resistance Records

The courts have given children special protection in some cases, even if doing so restricts the First Amendment rights of some adults. In *Federal Communications Commission v. Pacifica Foundation* (1978), infamously known as comedian George Carlin's "Seven Dirty Words," the Supreme Court was willing to block free speech for the sake of children and their development. The Court upheld an FCC policy that channeled offensive content to certain hours of the day. It was important to the Court in *Pacifica* that the FCC did not totally ban such speech on radio.

In the case, the high court ruled that the FCC could limit the times a radio disc jockey may broadcast a 12-minute segment of a comedy routine by Carlin using "the words you couldn't say on public, ah, airwaves, um the ones you definitely wouldn't say, ever" (1978: 729). The FCC decided the broadcast was obscene after an indignant listener processed a grievance against the station. The FCC could have taken administrative action against the station but chose not to. The Court heeded the potential injury of the "outlawed" words to children. In fact, the original complaint was filed by a father whose son was with him in the car when the broadcast came on the air at two in the afternoon (730).

The Court reasoned that radio and television are extremely accessible to children, even those too young to read. Pornographic magazines, for example, although legally restricted from children, are available to adults. Legal restriction, nevertheless, does not necessarily mean that children do not have access to pornographic materials. Such access is not difficult. The effortlessness with which children also have access to radio or television sufficiently rationalizes restrictions on the mass dissemination of obscene words, stories, songs, and so on.

Chapter 2 discussed the Web sites owned and operated by the Ku Klux Klan, racist skinheads, and neo-Nazis such as the National Alliance. Also, religious cults use increasingly stylish Web designs to snare the attention of children. The Internet has become the Disneyland of hate speech, targeting children. One neo-Nazi Web site used a crayon-like font linking children to Nazi misinformation. A second Web site displayed a cartoon of White children with guns shooting at a poster that read, "Kill the Jew pigs before it's too late" (Marriott, 1999: G1). Other Web sites offer variations of popular computer games modified so that the targets are members of minority groups. In *Ethnic Cleansing*, a video game produced by Resistance Records, players choose to take on skinhead or Klansman identities. The White supremacists then become hunters, pursuing Jews and "predatory sub-humans"—Latinos and Blacks. The game is used to entrap children into the Klan or skinhead gangs. A deluge of National Alliance symbolism and propaganda (see Chapter 2) is displayed throughout the game. Racist heavy metal music blasts on the soundtrack simultaneously.

Resistance Records is also aiming to advertise a video game based on William Pierce's racist novel, *The Turner Diaries*. In the ominous fantasy, heroic White supremacists use space-age weapons to wipe out hordes of ethnic minorities who are striving to decimate civilization (Southern Poverty Law Center, 1999).

The music industry uses sticker warnings on the covers of CDs, called Parental Advisory Labels, to inform potential purchasers that the music contains hate speech and/or violent messages. Heavy metal and rap music appear to garner the most warnings. Radio stations typically broadcast edited versions of songs. Hate speech and obscene words are cut out. Some songs are edited up to 60 times to filter out insulting and violent material (Strauss, 2000). There is a major inconsistency in radio broadcasting that probably would not be accepted in other settings—at schools, for example. A radio station will censor ethnic slurs against African Americans, Latinos, Native Americans, and Asians. However, misogynist and homophobic lyrics blare on, ignored and unchallenged by broadcasting officials.

Clearly, there is a difference between crude and hateful words. However, there are also marginal cases that play on the tension between free speech and discriminatory treatment. Others cases are clear-cut. Resistance Records, founded in Canada in 1993, aims to perpetuate hateful speech (Delgado, 2004b). The company moved from Canada to the United States to get away from laws prohibiting hate speech.

Alarmingly, the National Alliance bought Resistance Records in order to lure young people to their White supremacist movement. Racist rock is crossing over into mainstream heavy metal music, broadening its pool of potential young members. Music is perhaps the most influential mode of communication because of its power to impact immediately and a canny ability to transcend language barriers. The National Alliance and the Klan, recognizing this, have taken advantage of racist music to recruit new blood to the camp.

No one has yet successfully sued the National Alliance or its subsidiary, Resistance Records, over the *Ethnic Cleansing* video. As of July 2005, the video game is downloadable at resistance.com/ethniccleansing. While public outcry about the very brief exposure of Janet Jackson's breast during the Super Bowl halftime show was enormous, it seems puzzling why society seems oblivious to or willing to ignore—because of claims to First Amendment hegemony—these potentially harmful images of deadly violence combined with the hate speech of racial hatred on youngsters.

One of my recent students was a member of a heavy metal band. The band accepted a well-paid invitation to perform at a concert with other heavy metal bands. Unbeknownst to the band members, the concert was being used to stage a skinhead rally, featuring both racist and mainstream live heavy metal music. The band performed without incident. My student indicated that the sponsors were extremely hospitable—perhaps looking to use this small group that could attract an endless supply of young heavy metal fans.

Online owners of these lucrative distributorships, anticipating lawsuits for inciting hatred and violence, provide a disclaimer. They insist that they are just providing a service and in no way condone illegal activities or the "acting out" of lyrics contained in their products.

BEYOND LEGALISM: OPPOSING HATE SPEECH

When government—in pursuit of good intentions—tries to rearrange the economy, legislate morality, or help special interests, the costs come in inefficiency, lack of innovation, and loss of freedom. Government should be a referee, not an active player. In the United States, government has gone far beyond the basics.

—Milton Friedman, economist

When our legal system examines First Amendment issues, it uses unthinking checks; reliance on abstract, mathematical notions of justice (e.g., the stale distinction between speech and action); clichés that are widely used (e.g., "the cure for bad speech is more speech"); and beliefs that are widely held (e.g., "it's easy to permit the speech we agree with; we must also permit the speech we hate," "speech content should not be regulated"), especially those that interfere with somebody's ability to speak or think without preconception. In short, free speech is typically regarded from a rather narrow, limited, and overly simplistic perspective. In opposing hate speech, we cannot afford to wait on a legal system with an absolutist view of the First Amendment and an obsessive paranoia about monitoring hate speech.

Instead of merely relying on legal precedent to judge speech, one must use common sense and experience. In particular, speech should be studied in its context, tradition, history, and nuance in order to extrapolate its incendiary harm (Delgado, 2000). Free speech must occur in an arena of social equality. Speech without equality is a raging sermon or reprimand. For meaningful dialogue, egalitarianism is necessary. Similarly, equality assumes dialogue. Speech makes it possible for victims of wrongdoings to caucus for political purposes, collective conflict, and social reform.

First Amendment absolutists, with their romanticized blinders, fail to recognize or admit that language and free speech can be used to lacerate, pummel, and injure. The First Amendment has been kidnapped, taken from the downtrodden, by the libertarian right, White supremacists, pornographers, anti-Muslim hate-mongers, and their unsavory friends such as the Reverend Fred Phelps. Is it necessary to defend "the speech we hate" to protect what we love and cherish?

We must go beyond worshipping the First Amendment. It is a false idol. It was meant to be a sign for and to complement freedom, equality, and the dignity of human life. Hate speech is a perversion of the principles intended by our country's founders. It is not democracy; free speech has become harassment, discrimination, hatred, and violence—even genocide. We must recognize the multidimensional nature of speech and its role in maintaining a democratic society. It is necessary to understand how speech often functions as a political system of dominance and oppression.

The search for a legal remedy to hate speech is a good start, but it falls short. To prove that a specific incidence of hate speech caused severe emotional damage in victims is nearly impossible, and has to be based on a mechanical application of a tedious list of necessary requirements (see Chapter 1). For these reasons, litigation in civil court is impractical. Of course, Stage 1 (Unintentional Discrimination) hate speech is beyond the purview of the tort of intentional infliction of emotional distress.

Many victims of hate speech do not have the financial resources to hire an attorney and take their case to court. There is also the emotional drain of a legal suit. There are too many civil trials. We have become a society that sues at the drop of a pin, fueling the demand for even more lawyers. Our courts are oversaturated. What are the implications for a society that requires an official settlement to a problem that is better alleviated through prevention rather than intervention?

Instead of focusing on suing people for hate speech, perhaps moral education, an appreciation for diversity, and the development of high self-esteem may be useful in preventing young children from learning and internalizing hate and using hate speech. The media have sometimes used their pervasive influence in public service announcements (PSAs) to propose that parents provide anti-hate messages to their children. Since 1989, NBC's *The More You Know* public service campaign has been widely recognized in the community (nbc.com, 2004). This long-standing and respected endeavor has produced Emmy and Peabody Award–winning PSAs that educate the public and raise awareness about important social issues. The campaign has also provided valuable referral and resource information through on-air public service announcements, print materials, local community outreach efforts, and programming.

The More You Know's powerful and innovative public service announcements have effectively communicated messages ranging from hate and prejudice to domestic abuse to designated driver. Affiliate stations also implement numerous community outreach activities such as adopt-a-school initiatives and health and education fairs.

NBC's *The More You Know* public service announcements reach approximately 63 million viewers each week during NBC's lineup in prime-time, late-night, and Saturday morning programming—the latter targeting children. Hundreds of NBC celebrities have appeared in *The More You Know* spots. For example, in a recent one, *Will & Grace* star Eric McCormack urges parents not to use hateful words, since their children are likely to unknowingly repeat them. Perhaps the most important function of *The More You Know* is that it provides viewers with critical links to organizations that offer information and assistance. For example: "For more information on talking to children about prejudice and discrimination, visit the links below."

Speaking directly to young children or teens, these messages focus on bullying, diversity, anti-smoking, and other relevant issues.

Children are not born prejudiced. However, they often learn to hate before they are old enough to understand why, for example, the 3-year-old Carla mentioned above. Name-calling, bullying, harassment, and other bias-related behaviors are prevalent in the hallways of schools. Youth under age 21 committed 50 percent of all reported hate crimes in 2003 (FBI in nbc.com, 2004). But the transformation of prejudice into acts of hate can be fought with moral education and appreciation for cultural diversity.

Teachers, parents, and caregivers can educate children to celebrate the richness and beauty of our multicultural society by creating climates of respect at home and in the classroom. We all can profit from opportunities to learn about and interact with individuals who have diverse cultures, histories, and experiences. Through the education of our youth and the development of forums where dialogue on these topics can occur, we can transform our communities into respectful and caring places free from hate. Tackling the sources of both conscious and unconscious prejudice in our neighborhoods, communities, workplaces, and religious centers sets an example of courage and hope for the future of our society—a future that our children will take over.

On April 27, 2004, *The More You Know* launched new V-chip public service announcements, featuring *Today*'s Katie Couric. Targeting parents and caregivers, these PSAs reinforce the power of the V-chip, providing a toll-free number as well as guides for more information such as parental guideline ratings for specific programs and links to V-chip instructions by manufacturers. Downloadable versions of the PSAs on NBC.com/nbc/The_More_You_Know/ are now available.

NBC remains committed to raising awareness about the importance of the V-chip. In 1997, NBC began broadcasting *The More You Know* public service announcements on the interrelated issue of parents monitoring children's viewing habits, and then in 1999, specifically aired PSAs encouraging parents to use the V-chip.

In an added effort to help parents and caregivers monitor what children are watching, NBC is planning to feature an age-based rating, not only at the opening of each of its programs, but also near the half-hour of shows one hour or longer.

Because the need to protect our children has never been greater, the latest slate of *The More You Know* PSAs reinforce the importance of providing safe, loving, and nurturing environments for children. Campaign topics include how to deflect peer pressure to smoke or use drugs; Internet safety; parental involvement in education; reading; the importance of mentoring; and talking with children about critical issues such as prejudice, violence, and substance abuse.

Besides Eric McCormack (*Will & Grace*), other NBC stars participating in 2004's *The More You Know* campaign included: David Schwimmer (*Friends*), Alex Kingston, Goran Visnjic, and Ming-Na and Sharif Atkins (*ER*), Mariska Hargitay and Christopher Meloni (*Law & Order: SVU*), Joshua Malina (*The West Wing*), Sarah Chalke (*Scrubs*), Gail O'Grady and Brittany Snow (*American Dreams*), and Brian Williams (*NBC News*).

Television or film celebrities are able to use the power of their charismatic image to oppose hate speech, promote Internet safety, or raise awareness about critical issues such as child abuse and sexual assault. They send a message of hope that can empower parent viewers to take action in order to protect their children. Education such as this can be used in many venues to teach people how to treat others and also what speech or behavior is not acceptable.

The PSAs function to make children a priority in America. It is essential that mass media continue to provide valuable information to parents, caregivers, and youth about hate speech, First Amendment issues, and other topics that affect everyday life.

NBC partners with many other organizations to sponsor educational PSAs, including the U.S. Department of Education, U.S. Department of Health and Human Services, U.S. Department of Transportation/National Highway Traffic Safety Administration, Centers for Disease Control and Prevention/Office on Smoking and Health, Anti-Defamation League, Kaiser Family Foundation/Children Now, National Center for Missing and Exploited Children, Rape, Abuse and Incest National Network, National Mentoring Partnership, Childhelp USA, and Mothers Against Drunk Driving.

Directly targeting teens, these messages focus on ethnic, gender, religious, and sexual orientation tolerance, staying in school, domestic abuse, designated driver, and other relevant issues. *The More You Know* is the longest-running, most comprehensive, and powerful public service campaign in the media landscape. As such, it provides an efficacious model for preventing and opposing hate speech.

OPPOSING HATE SPEECH AT THE INDIVIDUAL LEVEL: A PRACTICAL GUIDE TO WHAT YOU CAN DO

The victims of hate speech cannot do it alone. They need others to speak out with them before it's too late. You can take any of the following actions to challenge hate messages. Some of these are adapted from Cortese (2004):

1. Speak out and confront hate speech against women, gays, and lesbians, and religious, racial, and ethnic minorities when you witness it. Condemn it as discriminatory and unacceptable. Speak loudly. Silence is acceptance. No hate.

2. Respect the diverse orientations of others. This means you should be more open-minded when interacting with others.

3. Challenge unjust laws and rules. Contact the congressional representative or state senator in your district.

4. Donate your time and resources to fight bigotry, sexism, racism, xenophobia, and homophobia.

5. Work to develop critical media literacy in order to offset the way that hate messages try to dim our awareness of social reality.

6. Boycott products and services that use hateful, demeaning, or stereotypical messages or images.

7. Boycott establishments whose policies or actual treatment of people is stereotypical, exclusive, discriminatory, or otherwise unjust.

8. Post signs on your property calling for tolerance and unity or opposing the blaming and hating of Muslims and other victims of hate speech.

9. Be alert to the prevailing power of hateful messages, especially their inauthenticity, intolerance of diversity, repetitive message, and their impetus to incite violence.

10. When traveling, adapt to local custom, culture, and cuisine.

11. Respect the law, and especially the principle of equitable treatment and the individual rights it is meant to protect.

12. Learn about and celebrate your own religion, race, and ethnic background.

13. Learn about and celebrate someone else's religion, race, and ethnic background.

14. Teach others, those both within and outside of your own religion and ethnic group, about your culture.

15. Learn to recognize and accept multiethnic and cross-gender identities.

16. Volunteer and donate your time and resources to fight sexism, misogyny, homophobia, zenophobia, ethnocentrism, racism, hunger, disease, poverty, or abuse.

17. Work to develop a balance between tradition and modernity in your life (Ritzer, 2000).

18. If you witness ethnic intolerance or racist stereotyping, talk back and condemn it.

CONCLUSION

The problem with traditional and current hegemonic constitutional and legal analysis is that hate speech is not really a First Amendment issue; it is a problem of equality—a Fourteenth Amendment issue. Using an absolutist perspective on the First Amendment unconsciously puts on blinders to issues of social inequality, ethnic stratification, and institutional discrimination. Implementation of individual and group equality must be the focus of the democratic process.

Hegemonic constitutional theory holds a sentimental, glamorized, or romanticized view of the First Amendment. Moreover, the most enthusiastic advocates of free speech are tobacco conglomerates—ever anxious to have cigarette smoking and advertising considered constitutional rights—and pornographers, including film producers, Web site sponsors, and magazine publishers. Pornographers and tobacco firms are also the biggest contributors to the ACLU and other civil liberties nonprofit organizations (Delgado, 2000).

Free speech, as it is now interpreted by the courts, has resulted in problems ranging from false advertising to hate speech that incites hatred and violence to way too much junk mail. The majority of e-mail messages are spam. Hate radio denigrates and provokes violence. Much of scripted television is pathetic; reality television, although drawing more viewers, is exploitive, intrusive, sadistic, and contentious. It should monitor itself better.

First Amendment absolutism is the prevailing structure of consciousness and authority that is used to uphold established social order. Law supported by the First Amendment, under the veil of neutrality and objectivity, actually determines how people submit to the authority of others. In the area of hate speech, we need a paradigmatic shift. *Legitimation crisis* refers to how commonly shared justifications for preserving the status quo become more questionable in the wake of exploding contradictions (Habermas, 1975).

If First Amendment absolutism is the status quo, exploding contradictions include burning crosses, murder instruction manuals, hate radio, pornography, racial profiling, and discriminatory treatment and genocide instigated by hate speech. The First Amendment demands confident loyalty to its legal hegemony. Yet First Amendment legitimating has resulted in crises and contradictions found in the often clashing laws protecting free speech and equal protection. The law "must simultaneously support both individual rights and societal welfare . . . The state should . . . be responsible for the collective welfare of the general population" (Cortese, 1990: 150). Habermas (1975) believes that the legitimation crisis results from contradictions inherent in capitalism.

The system of beliefs of postindustrial capitalism produces an ideology of *privatism* in individuals. The appeal to private interests is exemplified in virtually absolute free-speech protection, family consumption and leisure activities, and civic concern with little regard for the public good. Such egocentric ideologies have started to lose their legitimized authority; people are more cautious about affirming private over public concerns. In conclusion, I support a greater cosmopolitan image of people and the nature of human rights. Such a morality creates allegiances that surpass private and national interests and support the idea of a world community.

No longer should we trust in a rigid legal system or mathematical formulae to solve issues of inequality. Our notions of equality and freedom should be based on social responsibility; an open marketplace with which to communicate and express ideas, not abstract concepts of justice based on algebraic formulae. An equal treatment versus free-speech conflict should be resolved through role-taking, by examining the contextual infrastructure of the message; the relative social status of the messenger and the receiver; and possible violations of equal treatment, social responsibility, and respect for the dignity of all persons.

Listening to the victims of hate speech teaches us to understand their emotional range of responses—how prevalent hate speech is, as well as the severity of the harm done. Examining how some other Western postindustrial countries handle hate speech results in the knowledge that free speech and democracy, instead of being diminished, are actually as strong as ever.

If hate speech is learned, it can be unlearned, or better yet, never learned in the first place. Moral education offers a preventative approach to opposing hate speech that is potentially much more promising than legally restricting it and then litigating it in the already overcrowded civil and criminal courts. If our social relations become more equitable, inclusive, and fair, the incidence and need to litigate hate speech substantially lessens.

The face and color of America's cities have greatly changed in the past 50 or so years. This has been due to the vast movement of Blacks from the South to the North after World War II, a sharp increase in immigrants from Mexico and Latin America, and a constant flow of Asian newcomers, especially South Koreans and Filipinos (Cortese, 2003). By 2000, Latinos became this country's most numerous ethnic minority (35.4 million, U.S.

Census Bureau, 2001). This represents 12.5 percent of the total U.S. population. Data on Latinos are conservative since they do not include "undocumented" immigrants who cross the border illegally. There are estimates that 46.2 percent of all Latinos who immigrate to the United States do so without legal documentation.

African Americans (34.7 million) are the second-largest ethnic minority category in the United States, with 12.3 percent of the total population. Both the Black and Latino populations are younger than the White population. Latinos and Asians are the fastest-growing minorities. Half of all elementary school children in the United States are now ethnic minorities; nearly half (44 percent) of all residents in the United States under the age of 20 are non-White (U.S. Census Bureau, 2001).

The United States has been undergoing ethnic and racial change throughout its history, but never at the rate and of the type happening now. Within the next 50 years, Whites as a share of the total population will decline from 75 percent to just over 50 percent. The Black population will increase in size but remain at about 12 percent of the total population. Asians may increase from their present 3.6 percent (U.S. Census Bureau, 2001) to 8 percent. By 2050, Latinos will be about a quarter of the U.S. population and Blacks, less than a sixth.

With strong leadership, this culturally diverse and pluralistic society can reject hate speech as self-destructive; view stereotypes for what they are—prejudice; throw out demonized images of minority groups; and end marginalization through greater social inclusion. The issues raised by hate speech deserve significant attention, given their implications for our democracy and higher education's centrality to a more desirable American future.

Appendix: Gay, Lesbian, and Bisexual Television Characters

This is a list of television programs that have included gay, lesbian, and bisexual characters as a part of their regular (or recurring) casts. This does not include the many shows that have dealt with sexual orientation in a single episode or story line. The list is limited to network and widely syndicated entertainment shows in the English language.

To be listed, a character should have appeared in at least three episodes and be explicitly gay, lesbian, bisexual, or transgendered (Wyatt, 2002). Effeminate (but not gay) male characters, mannish (but not lesbian) female characters, and gender-shifting science fiction characters are not listed. For the purposes of this list, a character is described as "recurring" if he or she has appeared in at least three episodes.

THE TV NETWORKS

- ABC (American Broadcasting Companies, United States)
- ABCTV (Australian Broadcasting Corporation, Australia)
- BBC (British Broadcasting Corporation, United Kingdom)
- C4 (Channel 4, United Kingdom)
- C5 (Channel 5, United Kingdom)
- CBC (Canadian Broadcasting Corporation, Canada)
- CBS (Columbia Broadcasting System, United States)
- CC (Comedy Central, United States)
- CGS (CanWest Global System, Canada)
- CTV (Canadian Television, Canada)
- FOX (Fox Broadcasting Company, United States)
- Granada (United Kingdom)
- HBO (Home Box Office, United States)
- ITV (Independent Television, United Kingdom)
- Life (Life Network, Canada)
- LWT (London Weekend Television, United Kingdom)
- MTV (Music Television, United States)

- NBC (National Broadcasting Company, United States)
- 9NA (Nine Network Australia, Australia)
- PBS (Public Broadcasting System, United States)
- PrideVision (Canada)
- RTÉ (Radio Telefís Éireann, Ireland)
- 7N (Seven Network, Australia)
- Showcase (Canada)
- Showtime (United States)
- Teletoon (Canada)
- TEN (Network Ten, Australia)
- TVNZ (Television New Zealand, New Zealand)
- UPN (Universal Paramount Network, United States)
- USA (USA Cable Network, United States)
- WB (Warner Brothers, United States)

Table 1 shows the number of gay or lesbian characters that have been documented in English-language television series by decade, and Table 2 shows the number of gay or lesbian regular characters by TV network from 1961 through 2002.

Table 1
Number of Documented Gay or Lesbian Characters, English-Language Television Series, by Decade

1961–1970	1
1971–1980	58
1981–1990	89
1991–2000	306
2001–2002	47

Table 2
Number of Gay Regular Characters by Television Network, 1961–2002

United States	**118**
ABC (American Broadcasting Companies)	27
CBS (Columbia Broadcasting System)	22
CC (Comedy Central)	1
Fox (Fox Broadcasting Company)	15
HBO (Home Box Office)	7
MTV (Music Television)	4
NBC (National Broadcasting Company)	20
PBS (Public Broadcasting System)	3
Showtime	9
UPN (Universal Paramount Network)	2
USA (USA Cable Network)	1
WB (Warner Brothers)	7

Table 2 (continued)

Australia	12
ABCTV (Australian Broadcasting Corporation)	2
9NA (Nine Network Australia)	1
7N (Seven Network)	1
TEN (Network Ten)	8
United Kingdom	58
BBC (British Broadcasting Corporation)	30
C4 (Channel 4)	14
C5 (Channel 5)	1
Granada	2
ITV (Independent Television)	10
LWT (London Weekend Television)	1
Canada	20
CBC (Canadian Broadcasting Corporation)	5
CGS (CanWest Global System)	1
CTV (Canadian Television)	3
Life (Life Network)	1
PrideVision	7
Showcase	2
Teletoon	1
Ireland	1
RTÉ (Radio Telefís Éireann)	1
New Zealand	2
TVNZ (Television New Zealand)	2

PROGRAMS AND THEIR CHARACTERS

Absolutely Fabulous (sitcom), BBC, 1992–1994

- Justin (Christopher Malcolm), ex-husband
- Oliver (Gary Beadle), ex-husband's lover

The show featured Edina (Jennifer Saunders) and Patsy (Joanna Lumley), a some-what neurotic woman fashion designer and a somewhat bitter lush, respectively. Justin was Edina's second ex-husband and her daughter Saffron's father. Patsy claimed on more than one occasion (including in a 1996 *Roseanne* appearance) that she had been a female-to-male transsexual for a time, until it "fell off."

Action (sitcom), FOX, 1999 (episodes unaired on FOX syndicated, 2000)

- Stuart Glazer (Jack Plotnick)
- Robert "Bobby G." Gianopolis (Lee Arenberg), studio president

This sitcom centered on a hotshot Hollywood movie producer. Stuart was the lead character's right-hand man and Bobby G. was his boss, as well as Stuart's ex-wife's husband. Action-movie actor Cole Riccardi (Richard Burgi) appeared in two episodes.

After Henry (sitcom), ITV, 1988–1992 (radio, 1985–1988)

• Russell (Benjamin Whitrow, 1985–1988; Jonathan Newth, 1988–1992)

Russell, a friend and employer of the central character, operated a bookstore. His sexual orientation was "toned down," and practically undetectable, for television.

After the Beep (sitcom), ABCTV, 1996

• Mae (Genevieve Mooy)

The series was based on thirtyish Jo, who hated her life, her job, her mother, and her slutty sister. Her best friend, Mae, was a guppie lesbian who ran a bridal boutique.

Agony (serial sitcom), LWT for ITV, 1979–1981

• Rob Illingworth (Jeremy Bulloch)
• Michael (Peter Denyer), teacher

Rob and Michael were a gay couple who lived next door to Jane Lucas (Maureen Lipman), an Agony Aunt (advice columnist). There were several episodes dealing with gay issues directly, and Rob and Michael were in almost all of the episodes. Michael eventually commited suicide after being outed on a live phone-in radio show, fired from his job, and unable to find other work. See also the sequel, *Agony Again*.

Agony Again (sitcom), BBC, 1995

• Michael Lucas (Sacha Grunpeter), college student
• Will Brewer (Robert Whitson), actor

Maureen Lipman reprised the role of Jane Lucas from *Agony*, this time with a gay son, Michael. Michael met Will Brewer, the hunky star of an Australian soap opera called *Surfin' Around*.

All in the Family (sitcom), CBS, 1971–1979

• Beverly La Salle (Lori Shannon [Don McLean]), female impersonator, 1976–1977

Archie Bunker (Carroll O'Connor) performed mouth-to-mouth resuscitation on a woman, Beverly, who passed out in the back of his cab. Beverly turned out to be a man, and made two other visits to the Bunker household.

All My Children (daytime serial drama), ABC, 1970–present

1980s

• Dr. Lynn Carson (Donna Pescow), 1983

After Devon McFadden (Tricia Pursley Hawkins, 1977–1981 and 1983–1984) discovered that Lynn was a lesbian, she convinced herself that a relationship with a woman was the answer to her problems. Lynn wisely told her that a woman doesn't choose to become a lesbian because her affairs with men don't work out. After about two or three months, Lynn decided to get on with her life and moved away from Pine Valley.

1990s

• Michael Delaney (Chris Bruno), high school history teacher, 1995–1997 (occasional 1997–1998)
• Rudy (Lance Baldwin), TV station stage manager, 1995–1998
• Kevin Sheffield (Ben Jorgensen, briefly billed as Ben Monk), high school/college student and waiter, 1995–1998
• Dr. Bradford "Brad" Phillips (Daniel McDonald), orthopedic specialist, 1996–1997
• Rick (Kohl Sudduth), waiter, 1997
• Bianca Montgomery (Lacey Chabert, 1990; Eden Riegel, 2000–present)
• Rain Wilkins (Kelly Overton), 2000–2001
• Sarah Livingston (Elizabeth Harnois), 2000–2001

In 1995 producers introduced a full-time (as opposed to short-term) gay character. Michael's sexual orientation was revealed several months after his addition to the cast. In the ensuing controversy about a gay teacher in the classroom, "Mr. D." developed a platonic friendship with an employee of the local TV station. Kevin, one of Mike's students and the leading homophobe's younger brother, came out. By September 1996 Mike and Brad had started dating, and moved in together in January 1997. Actor Chris Bruno was contracted for only occasional appearances (a few times per year) after April 1997. During the summer of 1997 Kevin endured "reparative therapy" by a conversion therapist sponsored by his homophobic parents.

   In the fall of 2000 Bianca, the daughter of no less a central character than Erica Kane (Susan Lucci), began to cautiously admit to close friends that she knew she was gay. The story line involved lesbian occasional characters Rain, Bianca's homeless friend and guide, and Sarah, Bianca's anorexic former first love.

'Allo, 'Allo (sitcom), BBC, 1982, 1984–1992

• Lt. Hubert Gruber (Guy Siner)

Nazi Lieutenant Gruber had a crush on Rene, the cafe owner and central character, in this lowbrow comedy about the French Resistance.

All That Glitters (sitcom), syndicated, 1977

• Linda Murkland (Linda Gray), fashion model

This sitcom was set in the world of high-fashion modeling. Linda was a model and a male-to-female transsexual (Capsuto, 2000: 303).

American High (teen angst video verity documentary), FOX, 2000; PBS, 2001

• Brad Krefman

Fourteen teens at a high school near Chicago were given video cameras and followed by two professional camera crews during the 1999–2000 school year. The footage was then edited into episodes. One of the teens, Brad, was gay and out. The series was cancelled after four episodes aired (two nights); it resurfaced in its entirety on PBS in 2001.

American Journal (news magazine), syndicated, 1993–1998

• Charles Perez, co-anchor (1997–1998)

American Journal was a somewhat sensationalistic, tabloid-style news magazine.

And the Beat Goes On (drama), C4, 1996

• Kenneth Fairbrother (Dominic Jephcott)

This drama was set in 1960s Liverpool. Kenneth was a married but gay bar owner who was blackmailed over his sexual encounters with strangers in public toilets. The blackmailer turned out to be one of his employees, who was also gay and blackmailed Kenneth apparently from bitterness that Kenneth didn't fancy him and also from a loathing for his own sexual feelings.

Angels (hospital drama), BBC, 1976–1982

• Ken Hastings (Michael Howarth), nurse tutor, 1979–1980
• Paul (Michael Troughton), 1980

In this series about nurses, Ken campaigned to save the National Health Service from Margaret Thatcher (who proposed withdrawal of federal funds), and the hospital from closing. Paul was Ken's lover in a couple of episodes.

Anything But Love (sitcom), ABC, 1989–1992

• Jules "Julie" Kramer/Bennett (Richard Frank)

Jules was a gay editor's assistant on a magazine staff. The character's surname was changed.

As the World Turns (daytime serial drama), CBS, 1956–present

• Hank Elliot (Brian Starcher), 1988–1989

Hank was a dress designer who had come to town to find work away from his HIV-positive lover Charles (never seen). Various characters reacted differently to Hank's coming out to them.

At Home with the Braithwaites (drama miniseries), ITV, 2000

• Virginia Braithwaite (Sarah Smart)

A six-part series in which Alison Braithwaite, a middle-class wife and mother of three daughters, won £38 million and decided to keep it a secret from her dysfunctional family and set up a charity. Her college dropout daughter Virginia was secretly a lesbian until an emotional coming-out scene with her mother in episode three. Her mother Alison then revealed she was the big lottery winner. Virginia's lover is Tamsin (Lucy Whelan).

Attachments (drama), BBC, 2000–2001

• Sophie (Amanda Ryan)

This drama featured a group of twentysomethings launching a Web site. Sophie was the site's content manager. Luce (Claudia Harrison) considers a relationship with Sophie after a falling out with her husband and business partner Mike.

Bad Girls (prison drama), ITV, 1999

• Denny Blood (Alicia Eyo), prisoner
• Michelle "Shell" Doeckly (Debra Stephenson), prisoner
• Nikki Wade (Mandana Jones), prisoner
• Helen Stewart (Simone Lahbib), prison administrator

This drama was set in a women's prison. Shell was bisexual and Denny's girlfriend. Helen and Nikki became increasingly attracted to each other during the course of the series after Nikki split from her girlfriend, and in the penultimate episode shared a kiss in Nikki's cell.

Ball Four (baseball sitcom), CBS, 1976

• Bill Westlake (David-James Carroll), rookie baseball player

Baseball turned from national pastime to fun time on this comedy series, with former major league star Jim Bouton in the lead as a flaky relief pitcher on a team of highly individualistic players. Based loosely on Bouton's best-seller, *Ball Four* focused on the exploits of the mythical Washington Americans, who found fun and games in such diverse places as locker rooms, hotel lobbies, airplanes, and apartments. The Americans had a great deal of time on their hands between games—time to fret about the problems of money and fame (especially lack of both), marriage, and striking out—both on the field and off. In the pressure cooker of big-league play, the players found release in intense "jock" humor rife with pranks and elaborate practical jokes.

Bare Essence (drama), CBS, 1982; NBC, 1983

• Robert Spencer (Ted LePlat), friend of central character
• Larry DeVito (Morgan Stevens), professional football player

Robert, the best friend of a perfume company executive (Genie Francis), was a gay man whose lover, Larry, was a professional football player. The characters were featured in the 1983 miniseries but weren't visible in the series until the last few episodes.

Barney Miller (police sitcom), ABC, 1975–1982

- Marty (Jack DeLeon)
- Darryl Driscoll (Ray Stewart)
- Officer Zitelli (Dino Natali)

This sitcom was set in New York City's Greenwich Village and included a variety of recurring bit parts for victims and perpetrators. Among these roles were one male couple, Marty and Darryl. Officer Zitelli also came out at one point, late in the series run.

Bedtime (drama), Showtime, 1996

- Liz (Susan Gibney), banker
- Donna (Felicity Huffman), stage designer

A drama about relationships featuring a lesbian couple, told through their bedtime conversations.

Beggars & Choosers (drama), Showtime, 1999–2000

- Malcolm Laffley (Tuc Watkins), Vice President of Talent
- Wayne (Alex Zahara)
- Larry, aka Lola (Alexis Arquette)

A drama set behind the scenes at a struggling television network. Malcolm saw his sexual orientation as a potential glass ceiling for his career ambitions. Wayne was Malcolm's lover. Larry was a drag queen friend of Malcolm's.

Bette (sitcom), CBS, 2000–2001

- Oscar (James Dreyfus), Bette's accompanist

Oscar was one of several characters charged with taking care of high-maintenance diva Bette (Bette Midler).

Between the Lines (police drama), BBC, ca. 1993–1995

- Maureen "Mo" (Siobhan Redmond), police officer

Maureen was a lesbian police officer who in the third season acquired a lover named Kate. She was out to her partner Tony (Neil Pearson) on the series, but not out to her supervisors. She split up with her girlfriend later in the series.

Beverly Hills 90210 (high school/college drama), FOX, 1990–2000

- Mike Ryan (Brandon Douglas, 1993–1994; Jack Armstrong, 1994), 1993–1994
- Alison Lash (Sara Melson), 1994–1995
- Jimmy Gold (Michael Stoyanov), 1996
- Samantha Sanders (Christine Belford), 1991–1999

After appearing in a couple of episodes involving fraternity-related plots, Kappa Epsilon Gamma fraternity president Mike Ryan (recast) was accidentally outed by one of the regular characters. A couple of seasons earlier, the apparently gay (but not yet declared or decided) high school athlete Kyle Conner (David Lascher) appeared twice. Alison first appeared in a burning building with Kelly. In the fall of 1996, Kelly began volunteering at an AIDS hospice, where she met Jimmy. Late in the series run Steve's mother Samantha came out.

Big Brother ("reality" contest), CBS, 2000–present

- Bunky Miller, 2001
- Marcellus, 2002

An American copy of the British program of the same name. Contestants ("houseguests") are locked in a house with cameras, and voted out one by one until a winner is determined. No gay contestants appeared in the first season (2000).

Big Brother ("reality" contest), C4, 2000–present

- Anna Nolan, 2000
- Brian Dowling, 2001
- Josh Rafter, 2001

A group of contestants are isolated together in a house under 24-hour video and audio surveillance for a few months. They are voted out one by one, the last resident winning a cash prize. Anna was voted runner-up in 2000; Brian was voted the winner in 2001.

Big Brother ("reality" contest), TEN, 2001–present

- "Rotten" Johnny, 2001

An Australian copy of the British program of the same name. Contestants ("houseguests") are locked in a house with cameras, and voted out one by one until a winner is determined.

The Bob Newhart Show (sitcom), CBS, 1972–1978

- Craig Plager (Howard Hesseman)

Craig, an occasional character, was a patient of psychiatrist Bob Hartley (Bob Newhart) seeking help with his writer's block. His sexual orientation was mentioned only once, in the episode "Some of My Best Friends Are . . .".

Boston Public (high school drama), FOX, 2000–2004

- Jeremy Peters (Kaj-Erik Eriksen), high school student, 2001–2002

Vice-principal Scott Guber's (Anthony Heald) developing relationship with teacher's aide Meredith Peters (Kathy Baker) was complicated by his accidental discovery of her son Jeremy kissing his boyfriend Brandon. Jeremy eventually acquired a girlfriend.

The Box (serial drama), TEN, 1974–1977

- Viki Stafford (Judy Nunn), television producer
- Lee Whiteman (Paul Karo)
- Wayne Hopkins (Ian Gilmour), Lee's love interest
- Felicity (Helen Hemingway), Viki's love interest

This series was set among the behind-the-scenes bed-hopping and general goings-on at a TV station. It was another program of the *Number 96* genre. Lee was a TV station employee and quite stereotypically gay. Both Viki and Felicity were bisexual.

Brass (sitcom), Granada for ITV, 1982–1984; C4, 1990

- Morris Hardacre (James Saxon), 1982–1984, 1990

Morris was based on Sebastian in *Brideshead Revisited* (always carrying around a teddy bear).

Breakers (serial drama), TEN, 1998–1999

- Vince Donnelly (Simon Munro), waiter
- Lucy Hill (Louise Crawford), journalist
- Kelly (Gabriella Maselli), tutor
- Peter Hirsch (Vincent Atkinson), 1999

This serial drama centered on the lives and loves of the residents and employees of a building in Bondi, Australia, called Breakers. Lucy was bisexual, and Kelly was her romantic interest. Peter was Vince's boyfriend.

The Brian Benben Show (sitcom), CBS, 1998

- Billy Hernandez (Luis Antonio Ramos), weatherman

Billy was a supporting regular on this TV news station sitcom.

Brideshead Revisited (drama miniseries), Granada, 1981

- Lord Sebastian Flyte (Anthony Andrews)
- Charles Ryder (Jeremy Irons)
- Anthony Blanche (Nicholas Grace)
- Kurt (Jonathan Coy), Sebastian's German lover later in the book.

This miniseries was based on the Evelyn Waugh novel of the same name.

The Brittas Empire (sitcom), BBC, 1991–1997

- Gavin Featherleigh (Tim Marriott)
- Tim Whistler (Russell Porter)

The Brittas Empire centered around the disaster-prone Gordon Brittas (Chris Barrie). As manager of Whitbury Leisure Centre, Brittas had a natural talent for total chaos. Far from implementing his ideals, the staff and members of the Leisure Centre found themselves faced with a series of riotous mishaps. Brittas was the only person who didn't realize that Gavin and Tim were gay.

Brookside (serial drama), C4, 1982–2003

1980s

- Gordon Collins (Nigel Crowly, 1985; Mark Burgess, 1986–1990), 1985–1990
- Christopher Duncan (Stifyn Parri), 1986–1990

A twice-weekly serial in which one of the characters, Gordon, is gay. Gordon's homosexuality was key to an early plot line where he was "got at" at school by others who found out. He eventually acquired a lover, Chris.

1990s

- Lindsey Corkhill (Claire Sweeney), 1991, 1995–2003
- Beth Jordache (Anna Friel), ca. 1993–1995
- Shelley Bowers (Alexandra Westcourt), 1999–2003
- Paula, 1999–2003

Beth had relationships with a confused female neighbor and a lesbian college lecturer. Beth later died in prison. Later a second lesbian couple, Lindsey and Shelley, was introduced, the latter of whom sought to bed her lover's mother. Paula was Shelley's jealous ex-girlfriend, determined to win her back.

Brothers (sitcom), Showtime, 1984–1989

- Cliff Waters (Paul Regina)
- Donald Maltby (Philip Charles MacKenzie)

Cliff was one of the three "brothers" of the title and was much less comfortable with his gayness than Donald, his best friend.

Buffy the Vampire Slayer (supernatural teen angst drama), WB, 1997–2003

- Larry Blaisdell (Larry Bagby III), high school bully, 1997–1999
- Willow Rosenberg (Alyson Hannigan), student
- Tara (Amber Benson), student, 1999–2003

Buffy and her friends endured dating problems, school problems, and parent problems while slaying vampires. Larry, a fellow high school student, appeared in three episodes before being more prominently featured, revealing the secret his mean demeanor was meant to shield. Larry was likely killed in the graduation episode at the end of the 1998–1999 season. During the 1999–2000 season, previously heterosexual regular character Willow developed a intense friendship with fellow witch Tara, culminating in a declaration of love as the season ended.

Bump! (travel), PrideVision, 2001–2002

- JR Anderson, host
- Shannon McDonough, host

This travel show visited cities in North America and Britain. Each program highlighted general and GLBT-interest sights in a particular city.

Burnside (police drama), ITV, 2000

- Dave (Justin Pierce)

Burnside was based on the character detective Frank Burnside from *The Bill*. Burnside was an investigative member of the National Crime Squad. The show was gritty and dramatic with violence and strong language. Dave was a sidekick to the central detective.

Cagney and Lacey (police drama), CBS, 1982–1988
Later in the run of this series, one of the lead policewomen acquired a gay male neighbor, appearing on an occasional basis.

Casualty (hospital drama), BBC1, 1989–present

- Sam Colloby (Jonathan Kerrigan), nurse, 1996–1999

This medical drama is set in the emergency department of Holby General Hospital.

Check It Out (sitcom), CTV and USA, 1985–1988

- Leslie Rappaport (Aaron Schwartz)

This sitcom was set in a supermarket. Leslie was overtly homosexual and worked at the checkout registers.

Chicago Hope (medical drama), CBS, 1994–2000

- Robert Lawrence (Mark Benninghofen), doctor, 1996–1997
- Dennis Hancock (Vondie Curtis-Hall), doctor, 1994–1999

Occasional character Dr. Lawrence collaborated with principal character Dr. Shutt (Adam Arkin) on a research project and asked him out on a date (three episodes). Dr. Hancock came out in 1998.

The City (daytime serial drama), ABC, 1995–1997

- Azure C. (Carlotta Chang), supermodel, 1995–1996

This serial was a continuation of the 1983–1995 serial *Loving*, with the setting shifted to Manhattan. Supermodel Azure C. was revealed to be a male-to-female transsexual in 1996, much to the shock of her Latino fiancé Bernardo.

The City (drama), CTV, 1999–2000

- Lance (actor unknown)

A drama centered on City Hall employees.

City Life (serial drama), TVNZ, 1996–1998

- Ryan Waters (Charles Mesure), barman, 1996
- Michael Lee (Kenneth Moraleda), 1996

This serial followed the lives of several yuppies who were bequeathed a small apartment block in Auckland city. Ryan was a permanent member of the cast and a large part of episode five was devoted to meeting a new boyfriend, Michael.

CodCo (sketch comedy), CBC, 1990–1993

- Duncan (Tommy Sexton)
- Jerome (Greg Malone)

The program featured a recurring "Queen's Counselors" sketch about two queeny Newfoundland lawyers, Duncan and Jerome.

The Corner Bar (sitcom), ABC, 1972–1973

- Peter Panama (Vincent Schiavelli), 1972

This series was set in a New York City neighborhood bar called Grant's Tomb. The regular customers included Peter, a gay set designer. The show was reworked for the 1973 season in several elements, including dropping Peter, but the show was cancelled anyway.

Coronation Street (serial drama), BBC, 1960–present

- Hayley Patterson/Cropper (Julie Hesmondhalgh), 1998–present

After thirty-eight years on the air, and a dozen years after *EastEnders* introduced its first gay character, *Coronation Street*, Britain's longest-running soap opera, took the plunge, not with a gay or lesbian character but with Hayley, a male-to-female transsexual.

Courthouse (drama), CBS, 1995

- Rosetta Reide (Jenifer Lewis), judge
- Danny Gates (Cree Summer)

This ensemble drama was set among several judges and other courthouse workers, including a lesbian judge and her lover.

Crapston Villas, SE69 (puppet sitcom), C4, 1995–?

- Robbie and Larry

The series involves a cast of characters in a fictitious forgotten London slum, Slumington. Robbie and Larry are upstairs residents. "If Larry is all depth (opera, art and rampaging insecurity), then Robbie is all surface (Boyzone, gossip and the perfect peroxide)" (Wyatt, 2002).

The Crew (sitcom), FOX, 1995–1996

- Paul Steadman (David Burke), flight attendant

This sitcom featured four flight attendants, two men and two women. One of the men, Paul, was gay and out. Although a lead character, his principal role seemed to be as a foil for the man-hungry middle-aged woman supervisor.

Crossroads (daytime serial drama), Central Independent Television, 1964–1988; ITV, 2001–present

- Tom Curtis (Toby Sawyer), Internet cafe owner, 2001–present
- Bradley Clarke (Luke Walker), handyman, 2001–present

This daytime serial was set in a west Midlands hotel. Tom and Bradley were a couple.

Cutters (sitcom), CBS, 1993

- Troy King (Julius Carry), hairstylist

In this sitcom, a stodgy men's barbershop merged with the neighboring trendy women's beauty parlor. Troy, a supporting character, was a two-time Olympic track and field medal winner turned hair stylist (Capsuto, 2000: 293).

Cybill (sitcom), CBS, 1995–1998

- Waiter (Tim Maculan), actor-waiter

This sitcom centered on Cybill (Cybill Shepherd), a mature but struggling actress, and her best friend Maryann (Christine Baranski), a divorcee lush. At their favorite restaurant, they were served by their regular waiter. The waiter is nameless and rarely has more than a couple of lines.

Daddy's Girls (sitcom), CBS, 1994

- Dennis Dumont (Harvey Fierstein)

This sitcom was set in a clothing company. The action centered on a newly single father, Dennis, and his three daughters. Dennis was a fashion designer.

Dalziel & Pascoe (mystery), BBC, 1996–present

- Sgt. Edgar Wield (David Royle), detective

A series of 10 two-hour movies in a murder mystery/police format.

Dark Angel (science fiction), FOX, 2000–2002

- Original Cindy (Valarie Rae Miller) bicycle courier

In a series set in a post-apocalyptic America, Original Cindy is one of the central character's friends and co-workers.

Dawson's Creek (teen angst drama), WB, 1998–2004

- Mr. Benjamin Gold (Mitchell Laurance), teacher, 1998
- Jack McPhee (Kerr Smith), student
- Ethan Brody (Adam Kauffman), student, 1999–2000
- Tobey (David Monahan), 2000–2001
- David (Greg Rikaart), 2002–2004

Angst-ridden teens from dysfunctional families formed the core of the cast of this high school drama. Jack fit right in—his mother was mentally unstable, his dad was missing, his sister was on psychological medication, and after dating Joey [a girl] he could explain why he was such a non-pressuring gentleman. During the 1999–2000 season Jack met and became friends with Ethan but a romance was not to be. Tobey was Jack's 2000–2001 potential love interest. Jack met David in 2002.

Doctor, Doctor (medical sitcom), CBS, 1989–1991

- Richard "Dick" Stratford (Tony Carreiro)
- Hugh Persons (Brian George)

Richard was an English professor and the brother of one of the four doctors in the show. Hugh hosted the morning TV show where Dick's brother Mike did a medical segment.

Don't Wait Up (sitcom), BBC, 1983–1990

- ——— (Joe Dunlop)
- ——— (Timothy Carleton)

Two doctors (a father and son), estranged from their spouses, become roommates. They drive each other crazy as they share an apartment. An unnamed gay couple are their neighbors.

Dream On (sitcom), HBO, 1990–1996

- Mickey Tupper (Paul Dooley), 1992–1994
- Roger (actor unknown), 1993

This sitcom featured Martin, a divorced New York City book editor. Mickey is Martin's father, and Roger is Mickey's lover. Roger and Mickey were occasional characters.

Drop the Dead Donkey (sitcom), C4, 1991–1994

- Helen Cooper (Ingrid Lacey), 1993

Helen was the deputy editor of the news program in this newsroom sitcom.

Dynasty (serial drama), ABC, 1981–1989, 1991

- Steven Carrington (Al Corley, 1981–1982 and 1991; Jack Coleman, 1982–1986)
- Ted Dinard (Mark Withers), 1981
- Chris Deegan (Grant Goodeve), 1983
- Luke Fuller (William Campbell), 1984–1985
- Bart Falmont, 1985, 1991 (Kevin Conroy, 1985; Cameron Watson, 1991)

Ted was Steven's ex-lover, who followed him back to Denver and was killed by Steven's father Blake. For a few episodes Steven roomed platonically with his gay custody lawyer, Chris Deegan. For one whole season Steven and Luke courted one another and became lovers, until Moldavian terrorists killed Luke. Bart was a closeted son of Blake's political rival, until he was outed by Adam. In the four-hour 1991 reunion show, Steven had followed Bart to Washington, D.C., and they had become lovers.

EastEnders (serial drama), BBC, 1985–present

1980s

- Colin Russell (Michael Cashman), 1986–1989
- Barry Clark (Gary Hailes), 1986–1989
- Guido Smith (Nicholas Donovan), 1988–1989
- Queenie (John Labanowski), 1988

Colin was a guppie graphics designer who had moved into the gentrifying east end of London. There he met Barry and the two moved in together. After Barry left to join the merchant marine, Colin met Guido, who eventually moved in with him. Queenie belonged to another plotline. He was a jail enforcer working with "the Firm" (the mob).

1990s

- Joe Wallace (Jason Rush), 1991
- Della Alexander (Michelle Joseph), 1994–1995
- Binnie Roberts (Sophie Langham), 1994–1995
- Tony Hills (Mark Homer), 1995–1999
- Simon Raymond (Andrew Linford), 1996–1999
- Chris Clarke (Matthew Jay Lewis), 1998–1999

A straight regular character learned he was HIV-positive and became friends with Joe at an HIV counseling center. George (Colin Kerrigan), an AIDS hospice caregiver, appeared in two episodes in 1992. Lesbian couple Della and Binnie lived in the square for a time before moving to Spain. Tony broke off his relationship with his pregnant girlfriend Tiffany in order to take up with her brother Simon.

Eldorado (serial drama), BBC, 1992–1993

- Freddie Martin (Roland Curram), retired nurse
- Javier Fernandez (Iker Ibanez), local in the Spanish town

This serial followed a community of expatriate Britons in Spain. Javier was eventually discovered to be having an affair with Freddie.

Ellen (first season title: *These Friends of Mine*) (sitcom), ABC, 1994–1998

- Ellen Morgan (Ellen DeGeneres)
- Peter (Patrick Bristow), 1995–1998
- Barrett (Jack Plotnick), 1995–1998
- Laurie Manning (Lisa Darr), 1997–1998

Ellen's friends included gay couple Peter and Barrett (occasional characters). Ellen Morgan's self-acceptance as a lesbian at the end of the 1996–1997 season occasioned more real-world press attention than any other gay or lesbian character before as the first openly gay or lesbian lead/title character in U.S. commercial prime-time programming. ABC/Disney cancelled *Ellen* a year later, apparently displeased by the show's content.

Emmerdale (also known as *Emmerdale Farm*) (serial drama), ITV, 1972–present

- Zoe Tate (Leah Bracknell), 1989–present
- Richard (actor unknown), university student, 1993
- Jude Clayton (actor unknown), university professor, 1993
- Emma Nightengale (Rachel Ambler), interior designer, 1994–1996
- Susie Wilde (Louise Heaney), 1996
- Sophie Wright (Jane Cameron), nanny, 1996–1997
- Becky Cairns (Sarah Neville), receptionist, 1997–1998
- Frankie Smith (Gina Aris, 1999; Madeleine Bowyer, 2000), truck driver, 1999–present
- Maggie (actor unknown), Frankie's girlfriend, 1999
- Gavin Ferris (Robert Beck), oil rigger, 1999–2000
- Jason Kirk (James Carlton), roofer, 1999–2000

"Twice-weekly [now thrice-weekly] serial from Yorkshire TV set in the Dales. One of its regular characters, Zoe Tate, daughter of Frank, came out as a lesbian in June 1993" (Howes, 1993: 224). Richard appeared in several episodes as Zoe's first gay friend. Two of Zoe's lovers appeared in many episodes. Suzie took Zoe away from Emma just as the two were about to get "married." Zoe later dated two previously straight women, Sophie and Becky, and Frankie. Gavin lost his fiancée Bernice when she caught him kissing Jason.

E.N.G. (TV newsroom drama), CTV, 1991–1994

- Eric "Mac" MacFarlane (Jonathan Welsh)

Mac, a regular character in this series, came out to his co-workers and his brother when he was faced with blackmail by threat of outing.

ER (medical drama), NBC, 1994–present

- Dr. Maggie Doyle (Jorja Fox), 1996–1999
- Yosh Takata (Gedde Watanabe), nurse, 1997
- Dr. Kim Legaspi (Elizabeth Mitchell), psychiatrist, 2000

Dr. Maggie Doyle came out as a lesbian in 1997. In the fall of 1995 the cast included paramedics Shep and (until his death in a fire) Raoul (Carlos Gomez). Another character once remarked that Raoul was gay. Nurse Takata [a male] began appearing in 1997. In the fall of 2000 Dr. Kerry Weaver (Laura Innes) became closer to out lesbian psychiatrist Kim Legaspi.

Fair City (drama), RTÉ, 1988–present

- Eoin (actor unknown), 1998–present

Fair City is a gritty, controversial drama set in a fictional northside suburb of Dublin named Carrigstown. The program addresses real-life and controversial issues in its diverse story lines.

Fame (drama/musical), NBC, 1982–1983; syndicated, 1983–1986

• Montgomery MacNeil (P. R. Paul), 1982

The movie *Fame* had one gay character, Montgomery, and he was quickly written out at the start of the television series.

Family Affairs (serial drama), C5, 1996–present

• Susie Ross (Tina Landini)
• Holly Hart (Sandra Huggett)
• Clive Starr (Huw Bevan)

Bisexual Susie went out with Duncan Hart, then later dated his sister Holly. Holly announced that she was gay but the pair later split and Holly went back to dating men. A year later the pair got back together before splitting once more. Student Clive Starr (Huw Bevan) suffered gay-bashing and homophobia from his older brother, and had a crush on his straight roommate.

Felicity (teen angst drama), WB, 1998–2002

• Javier Clemente Quintata (Ian Gomez), coffee house manager

Javier managed the coffee house where lead character Felicity and one of her romantic interests worked. Javier and his boyfriend were married in the 1999–2000 season finale.

Fired Up (sitcom), NBC, 1997–1998

• Ashley Mann (Mark Davis), female impersonator

Ashley, an occasional character, was the son of Guy Mann, the owner of the bar where the principal characters congregated. Guy was very accepting of his son.

First Years (lawyer drama), NBC, 2001

• Warren Harrison (Mackenzie Astin)

This drama centered on a group of five young lawyers fresh out of law school.

413 Hope St. (drama), FOX, 1997–1998

• Melvin (Karim Prince), 1997

This drama was set in a New York teen crisis center. Characters included Melvin, a young, gay, HIV-positive African American. Although Karim Prince continued to be credited, Melvin disappeared after the first few episodes.

Friends (sitcom), NBC, 1994–2004

• Carol Willig (Anita Barone, 1994; Jane Sibbett, 1995–2004)
• Susan Bunch (Jessica Hecht)

This generation X sitcom centered on a group of six friends, one of which was divorced from his pregnant ex-wife, Carol. Participating in the pregnancy and the child's life meant accommodating Carol's new lifestyle, and Susan, her lover.

Gems (daytime serial drama), U.K., 1984–1987

• Paul Currie (William Armstrong)

This series was set in a Covent Garden fashion house. Paul held hands with his boyfriend in a 1985 episode, prompting a letter-writing protest from scandalized viewers.

General Hospital (daytime serial drama), ABC, 1963–present

• John Hanley (Lee Mathis), 1994–1995
• Ted Murty (Patrick Fabian), schoolteacher, 1997–1998

Beginning in 1994 the character of John Hanley was a recurring character, each year co-chairing the annual AIDS Ball charity fundraiser. The character and the actor were both HIV-positive, and when actor Lee Mathis died in early 1996, John Hanley's [offscreen] death was mourned on the show. Ted Murty [occasional from 1997] was erroneously suspected in the sexual assault of a female student.

Gimmie, Gimmie, Gimmie (sitcom), BBC, 1999

• Linda La Hughs (Kathy Burke)
• Tom Farrell (James Dreyfus), actor

In this apartment-sharing comedy, the heterosexual Linda (always going on about sex but rarely getting any) lived with Tom, a gay actor (always dreaming about starring roles but rarely getting any).

G.P. (medical drama), ABCTV, 1988–1996

• Martin Dempsey (Damian Rice), doctor, 1994–1995

Short for "General Practitioner," *G.P.* gained a positive reputation for its presentation of AIDS, gay/lesbian, and other social/medical issues. In 1992 a gay doctor joined the practice, but was graphically shown being gay-bashed (twice) and murdered in the second attack. In 1994 the show added another gay doctor, Martin, to the practice.

Grace and Favour (sitcom), BBC, 1991–1993

• Mr. [Wilburforce Clayborn] Humphries (John Inman)

Clayborn was gay, despite of the fact that he was seen in bed with a woman throughout the series. This sequel to *Are You Being Served* airs on some PBS stations under the title *Are You Being Served Again!*

Grange Hill (children's serial drama), BBC, 1978–present

• Mr. Tom Brisley (Adam Ray), art teacher, 1992–1998

This youth-audience serial drama covers the lives of kids and teachers in an inner city school. "Mr. B" was introduced into the popular children's drama as a gay man with no hangups about being gay. His sexuality wasn't discussed for the first year so that the audience would get to know him. Eventually students, parents, and other teachers [and the audience] discovered and came to terms with his homosexuality, after which his boyfriend Don and home life were referred to regularly (Ray, 2001).

Grosse Pointe (sitcom), WB, 2000–2001

• Richard Towers (Michael Hitchcock), actor

In this behind-the-scenes view of the production of a soap opera, actor Richard Towers is interested in a younger actor, who plays his son.

Hail to the Chief (sitcom), ABC, 1985

• Randy (Joel Brooks)

In this sitcom about the first U.S. woman president, Randy, the White House chief Secret Service agent, is gay.

Head Over Heels (sitcom), UPN, 1997

• Ian (Patrick Bristow)

A situation comedy set in a video dating service. The characters include Ian, a celibate bisexual romance counselor.

HeartBeat (medical drama), ABC, 1988

• Marilyn McGrath (Gail Strickland)
• Patti (Gina Hecht)

This short-lived drama included among its cast of characters Marilyn, a lesbian nurse-practitioner. Her lover Patti, a caterer, appeared occasionally.

Heartbreak High (teen angst drama), TEN, 1994–1999

• Graham Brown (Hugh Baldwin), music teacher, 1994

This drama focused on the lives and loves of the disadvantaged students at Hartley High. During a story about another teacher on the verge of an affair with a student, Graham wondered what the parents would think if they knew he was gay. In the next episode Graham was falsely accused of fondling a male student, and his question was answered.

Hearts Afire (sitcom), CBS, 1992–1995

• Diandra (Julie Cobb)
• Ruth (Conchata Ferrell)

In this political comedy, conservative John (John Ritter) met and fell in love with liberal Georgie (Markie Post). John's ex-wife Diandra and her lover Ruth made three guest appearances over the run of the show (Capsuto, 2000: 348).

He Shoots He Scores (hockey drama), CBC, 1986–1989

• Tom Snyder (Mark McManus), hockey coach, 1988

In this series, it was revealed that the Team U.S.A. coach had been blackmailed using pictures of him kissing his male lover. (Produced simultaneously in French as *Lance et Compte* for Quebec, France, and Switzerland.)

High Society (sitcom), CBS, 1995–1996

• Stephano (Luigi Amodeo), secretary

This sitcom featured Dott (Mary McDonnell), a woman in the publishing business, and her best friend Ellie (Jean Smart), an author/lush. Dott's personal assistant, Stephano, is gay.

Hill Street Blues (police drama), NBC, 1981–1987

• Eddie (Charles Levin)
• Officer Kate McBride (Lindsay Crouse), police detective, 1986–1987

Hill Street Blues was one of the most innovative and critically acclaimed series in recent television history. Although never highly rated, NBC continued to revitalize *Hill Street Blues* for its "prestige value" as well as the demographic profile of its ardently loyal audience. *Hill Street Blues* is perhaps the perfect example of the complex equation in U.S. network television between "quality programming" and "quality demographics." *Hill Street Blues* transformed the TV "cop show," combining action, drama, and mystery with elements from sitcom, soap opera, and cinema verite–style documentary. Moreover, it established the model for the hour-long ensemble drama: intense, fast-paced, and hyper-realistic, set in a densely populated urban workplace, and distinctly "Dickensian" in terms of twists and remarkable coincidences in character and plot development. In one episode, Detective Buntz reassured Officer McBride about her shooting of an armed robber. In another, McBride relived her father's death at an awards ceremony. Eddie was an informer working for Belker, the precinct's SWAT team leader, and snitched on his own lover.

Hollyoaks (teen serial drama), C4, 1995–present

• Bazz (Toby Sawyer), disk jockey
• Jasmine "Jas" Bates (Elly Fairman)

This teenage serial is set in a fictional suburb of Chester, England. Bazz is a disk jockey who came out as bisexual to his girlfriend but later realized he was gay after sleeping with another man. More recently, bisexual character Jas was introduced. She had previously been involved with another woman and slept with another previously heterosexual character, Ruth Benson (Terri Dwyer), who bitterly regretted their night of passion.

Hollywood Beat (police drama), ABC, 1985

• George Grinsky (John Matuszak)

This show was an attempted *Miami Vice* clone, and George ran the coffee shop where the two principal cops hung out.

Hollywood Squares (game show), NBC, 1966–1980; syndicated, 1972–1980, 1986–1989, 1998–2004

• Bruce Vilanch, 1998–2004

With regulars or guest celebrities like Paul Lynde and Richard Simmons there were often opportunities for oblique gay or fey humor, but it was not until the 1998 version that an openly gay celebrity occupied a square. Vilanch is also a head writer for the show.

Homicide: Life on the Street (police drama), NBC, 1993–1999

• Tim Bayliss (Kyle Secor), detective

As the 1997–1998 season went on, always sexually unconventional detective Bayliss began exploring a new tangent, eventually accepting the self-description "bi-curious."

Hooperman (police sitcom/drama), ABC, 1987–1989

• Rick Silardi (Joseph Gian), police officer
• Rudy (Rod Gist), 1988–1989

Silardi and his female partner DeMont were series regulars. Sometimes a story would revolve around them, but usually it didn't. Rudy was one of Hooperman's tenants. The series was set in San Francisco.

Hot l Baltimore (sitcom), ABC, 1975

• George (Lee Bergere)
• Gordon (Henry Calvert)

This sitcom was set in the dilapidated Hotel Baltimore (where the "E" in the sign was burned out). All of the characters were in some way eccentric. George and Gordon's eccentricity was that they were a homosexual couple.

Howard's Way (serial drama), BBC, 1985–1990

• Gerald Urquhart (Ivor Danvers)

"Upmarket, fearfully smug boating and bonking serial" (Howes, 1993: 365). In episode seven Polly revealed, that her marriage to Gerald was a sham; he was gay and needed the marriage to maintain respectability in business.

In Sickness and Health (sitcom), BBC, 1985–1992

• Winston Churchill (Eamonn Walker), 1985–1987

The *Til Death Us Do Part* character Alf Garnet (Archie Bunker in the U.S. version) received help from a social services worker assigned to him after his wife died. This character was black and gay, infuriating Alf.

It Ain't Half Hot, Mum (sitcom), BBC, 1974–1982

• "Gloria" Beaumont (Melvyn Hayes)

In this comedy, the character "Gloria" is considered to be a poof by the other members of the concert party (in World War II Burma) because he plays all the female parts.

It Takes a Worried Man (sitcom), C4, 1981–1984

• Simon (Nicholas Le Prevost), psychiatrist

Philip Roath (Peter Tilbury) is an insurance salesman in his mid-thirties. He can never make his mind up about anything. Even when his wife walks out on him, he can't decide how he really feels about the situation. Philip goes to see his gay analyst, Simon (Nicholas Le Prevost), regularly and tells him about all of the things that he sees as being wrong with his life.

Jawbreaker (talk), PrideVision, 2002–present

• Brad Fraser, host

This talk show features guests and topics of interest to the GLBT community.

The Jewel in the Crown (drama miniseries), Granada, 1984

• Ronald Merrick (Tim Pigott-Smith)
• "Sophie" Dixon (Warren Clarke)
• Count Dimitri Bronowsky (Eric Porter)

The Jewel in the Crown, adapted from Paul Scott's *Raj Quartet* novels, depicts the story of the final years before India gained independence in 1947 (Leake, 2005). It successfully preserved the richness and complexity of a great novel and triumphed both as personal drama and historical panorama. In 1942 Daphne Manners, a inexperienced young woman newly arrived in the town of Mayapore, make friends with Hari Kumar, and Indian-born journalist who has spent most of his life in England. With his dark skin and educated English accent, Hari is a marginal wherever he goes, but Daphne understands his plight and they become romantically involved. Their developing relationship is resentfully observed by local police chief Ronald Merrick, a gay man deep in the closet and haunted by his own demons. When the lovers are assaulted in the gardens of the ruined Bibighar palace and Daphne is raped, Merrick blames the crime on Hari and has the young man jailed. Hysterical, Daphne escapes to her aunt's home in Kashmir, where she dies giving birth to a half-caste child. The plot then shifts to Sarah Layton, a young Englishwoman who becomes fascinated by the story of Daphne and Hari, and who will have her own encounter with Ronald Merrick. With a huge cast and breathtaking location photography, *The Jewel in the Crown* was an enormous undertaking when it was made in the early 1980s.

The John Laroquette Show (sitcom), NBC, 1993–1996

- Teddi (David Shawn Michaels), 1993–1994
- Patrick (Jazzmun), 1995

In this sitcom set in a bus station, Teddi and Pat had recurring minor roles as gay transvestites.

The Kids in the Hall (sketch comedy), CBC, 1989–1995

- "Buddy Cole": Buddy (Scott Thompson)
- "Steps": Butch (Scott Thompson)
- "Steps": Riley (David Foley)
- "Steps": Smitty (Kevin McDonald)
- "Humanoids for Humanism": Shona (Bruce McCullough)

Among a wide range of comedy sketches on this show was the recurring role of Buddy, who pontificated from his bar stool on the differences or the parallels between gay and straight society, or about the ignorance of straights, or the tribulations of gay life. Another recurring sketch took place on the steps of a coffee house. Shona, a lesbian, appeared in the "Humanoids for Humanism" sketches, as well as others.

Kink (documentary), Showcase, 2001

- David
- Pat
- Stephen
- Sharia
- Ms. X
- Velvet

This unusual documentary series examined the lives and sexual kinks of several individuals. David spanked his submissive lovers 6,000 times; Pat, a woman with a Ph.D., admired the voices of whips; Stephen dressed in drag; Sharia and Ms. X maintained a dominant-submissive relationship; and Velvet was a transsexual.

L.A. Law (drama), NBC, 1986–1994

- Cara Jean "C. J." Lamb (Amanda Donohoe), 1990–1992
- Mark Gilliam (Stanley Kamel), 1986–1987

Lawyers C. J. Lamb and Abby Perkins (Michele Greene) shared a kiss in the parking lot that many interpreted as a lesbian advance. NBC seemed determined to explain that it wasn't. Later C. J. represented her ex-lover Maggie (Elizabeth Kemp) in a child custody case. Mark Gilliam was an occasional character, another lawyer.

The Larry Sanders Show (sitcom), HBO, 1992–1998

• Brian (Scott Thompson), 1995–1998

In 1995 Larry's sidekick Hank Kingsley (Jeffrey Tambor) hired Brian, his temporary personal assistant, full time.

Liberty Street (drama), CBC, 1995–1996

• Nathan Jones (Billy Merasty)
• James Wilder (Keith Knight), banker

This Generation X drama focused on the inhabitants of a warehouse converted into apartments. Nathan was one of the tenants, a gay native ex-bicycle courier. At the start of the second season Nathan introduced James, his new boyfriend.

Linc's (drama-sitcom), Showtime, 1998–2000

• Rosalee Lincoln (Tisha Campbell), army lieutenant

The show was set in a Washington, D.C. bar (Frutkin, 1998). Rosalee was the bar owner's niece.

Live Shot (TV newsroom drama), UPN, 1995–1996

• Lou Waller (Tom Byrd), sportscaster

Live Shot was a short-lived ensemble drama focusing on the people and personalities inside the frenzied, dog-eat-dog work environment of a local television newsroom. Sports anchor Lou was very closeted, even maintaining a separate apartment from his lover.

Living in Captivity (sitcom), FOX, 1998

• Gordon (Terry Rhodes), security guard

This sitcom centered on a group of upwardly mobile people living in a suburban gated community. Gordon manned the gate and leered at the residents.

Locker Room (sports magazine/variety), PrideVision, 2001–present

• Paul DeBoy, host/reporter
• Nina Arsenault, reporter
• Coach Jeff Fluff (Paul Bellini), 2001–2002
• Pete the Scalper (Paul DeBoy)

Reportage and sketch comedy on sports themes, from a gay perspective. A variable company of actors play sketch rolles, with closeted Coach Fluff and Pete the Scalper probably the most frequently recurring gay characters.

Love, Sidney (sitcom), NBC, 1981–1982

• Sidney Shorr (Tony Randall)

In the made-for-TV movie of the same name, Sidney was definitely gay. By the time the series reached the air, however, NBC had forbidden the mention of the character's sexual orientation.

Lush Life (sitcom), FOX, 1996

• Nelson Margarita Marquez (John Ortiz), bartender

Nelson was the gay bartender friend of the principal characters. The series was cancelled after three episodes.

Mad About You (sitcom), NBC, 1992–1999

• Debbie Buchman (Robin Bartlett), 1994–1999
• Dr. Joan Golfinos (Suzie Plakson), gynecologist, 1996–1999

Paul Buchman's sister Debbie, an occasional character, came out in 1996. Debbie's lover Joan became gynecologist to Paul's wife Jamie.

Madison (high school drama), CGS/Global, 1995–1996

• Beth (Shaira Holman), band member, 1995–1996

Beth, an occasional character, is a member of a band in which one of the regulars plays.

Mapp & Lucia (comedy), C4, 1985–1986

• "Quaint" Irene Coles (Cecily Hobbs)
• Georgie Pillson (Nigel Hawthorne)

While Emmeline "Lucia" Lucas and Elizabeth Mapp contested the social leadership of their town, Quaint Irene quietly carried a torch for Lucia. Georgie was a nervous, fussy man who spent his evenings with his embroidery. It is not clear if the orientation of either character was explicitly stated.

Mary Hartman, Mary Hartman (sitcom), syndication, 1976–1977

• Annie "Tippytoes" Wylie (Gloria DeHaven)
• Ed (Larry Haddon)
• Howard (Beeson Carroll)

This soap opera parody included Annie, a bisexual occasional character. Minor characters Ed and Howard were not just roommates.

Melrose Place (serial drama), FOX, 1992–1999

• Matt Fielding (Doug Savant), social worker, then medical student, 1992–1997
• Jeffrey Linley (Jason Beghe), sailor, 1994

- John Rawlings (Tom Schanley), police detective, 1995
- Paul Graham (David Beecroft), doctor, 1995
- Alan (Lonnie Schuyler), actor, 1995–1996
- David (Rob Youngblood), hospital social worker, 1996
- Valerie (Jeri Lynn Ryan), actress, 1996
- Dan Hathaway (Greg Evigan), rehab doctor, 1996–1997

Matt was a social worker who ran a shelter for runaways. The character's sexual orientation was mentioned repeatedly in pre-premiere publicity, but was hardly visible on the show for years. Jeffrey, a navy lieutenant, dated Matt briefly, then returned after leaving the navy, revealing his HIV-positive status. Detective Rawlings investigated Matt's second gay bashing and became violent when Matt refused to date him. Paul dated Matt behind his wife's back, and then framed Matt for her murder. In 1995 gay rights advocate Tom Riley (Lewis Smith) helped Matt with his wrongful dismissal suit (two episodes) and as year-end approached Matt began dating Alan, a struggling actor. Alan moved in with Matt in January 1996. David got Matt's old job at the hospital, and seemed to come between Matt and Alan while Alan entered a sham marriage with lesbian actress co-worker Valerie. While in rehabilitation for a drug dependency in the fall of 1996, Matt met Dan, whom he dated until Dan became physically abusive.

Metrosexuality (drama-comedy), C4, 2001

- Max (Rikki Beadle-Blair)
- Bambi (Davey Fairbanks)
- Dean (Paul Keating)
- Cindy (Carleen Beadle)

This six-week series centered on Kwame (Noel Clarke), a straight youth whose two dads have split up. Characters included Kwame's dad Max, Max's sister Cindy, and Kwame's friends Bambi and Dean.

Mission Hill (animated sitcom), WB, 1999–2000

- Gus
- Wally

Gus and Wally are the older gay couple living in the apartment next door to the French brothers (the main characters). Gus and Wally met in Hollywood in the 1950s (Wally was an Ed Wood–like director and Gus was a zombie). Wally quit his job to be with Gus.

Muscle (serial sitcom), WB, 1995

- Bronwyn Jones (Amy Pietz), anchorwoman

This soap opera parody was set in a gym. Bronwyn was a gym member and anchor of the local news.

My So-Called Life (teen angst drama), ABC, 1994–1995

- Enrique "Rickie" Vasquez (Wilson Cruz), student
- Richard Katimski (Jeff Perry), English teacher

This high school drama centered on a girl and her two best friends, one of whom, Rickie, is gay. When Rickie was kicked out of his home, Mr. Katimski struggled with whether or not to open his home to Rickie.

The Nancy Walker Show (sitcom), ABC, 1976

- Terry Folson (Ken Olfson), unemployed actor

Nancy Walker played talent agent Nancy Kitterage, operating out of the home she shared with her navy husband and Terry, a unemployed gay actor who earned his room and board by working as Nancy's secretary.

Nash Bridges (police drama), CBS, 1996–2001

- Stacy Bridges (Angela Dorhmann), assistant district attorney
- Pepe (Patrick Fischler), 1996–1998

In this series, set in San Francisco, Stacy was Nash Bridges' sister. Pepe, who thought partners Nash and Joe were lovers, had a talent for office organization. In addition, straight cop Joe Dominguez (Cheech Marin) owned a gay bar.

Neighbours (serial drama), TEN, 1985–present

- "Macca" MacKenzie (John Morris), builder, 1994
- Andrew Watson (Christopher Uhlmann), teacher, 1995–1996
- Sky Mangel (Stephanie McIntosh), student, 2003–present
- Lana Crawford (Bridget Neval), student, 2004–2005

Neighbours is a weekday soap opera exploring the lives and relationships of the residents of Ramsay Street in Erinsborough. Now in its twentieth year of production, *Neighbours* is Australia's most successful television program and a hit worldwide. None of the gay/lesbian characters so far has lasted long. Andrew became the subject of school student rumors, and then faced a campaign by parents for his removal from the classroom.

Normal, Ohio (sitcom), FOX, 2000

- Rex or Butch Gamble (John Goodman)

In this sitcom, Rex returned to his small town after coming out. The show's originally announced title was *Don't Ask*.

Northern Exposure (ensemble comedy/drama), CBS, 1990–1995

- Ron Bantz (Doug Ballard), 1991–1995
- Erick Hillman (Don R. McManus), 1991–1995

Occasional characters Ron and Erick operated a bed-and-breakfast serving primarily Japanese tourists. The show had another interesting gay angle: the fictitious town of Cicely was founded by lesbian lovers Roslyn and Cicely after their car broke down in the Alaska wilderness. The final episode of 1992 told the story of Roslyn (Jo Anderson) and Cicely (Yvonne Suhor). Ron and Erick's wedding made real-world headlines in 1994.

Number 96 (serial drama), TEN, 1972–1977

- Don Finlayson (Joe Hasham), lawyer [and 1974 feature film]
- Simon Carr (John Orcsik), public relations businessman, 1972 [and 1974 feature film]
- Bruce Taylor (Paul Weingott), photographer, 1972, 1973–1974
- Karen Winters (Toni Lamond), receptionist, 1972
- Dudley Butterfield (Chard Hayward), chef, 1973–1977 [and 1974 feature film]
- Marie Crowther (Hazel Phillips), volunteer counselor, 1973
- Paul Mathews (David Whitford), journalist, 1973
- Dr. Alistair Pascal (Raymond Duparc), psychiatrist, 1973
- Robyn Ross ("Carolle Lea," aka Carlotta of Les Girls), 1973
- Brad Hilton (Terry Bader), flight attendant, 1974–1975
- Grant Chandler (Michael Howard), chauffeur, 1976–1977
- Phillip Chambers (Henri Szeps), high school teacher, 1976
- Rob Forsyth (John McTernan), American architect on holiday, 1977
- Joshua (Shane Porteous), religious cult leader, 1977

This serial focused on life in and around a block of flats in Sydney, Australia. Don and Dudley were residents and lovers. "*Number 96* created a sensation when it went on the air in 1972, dealing graphically with homosexuality, drug and alcohol addictions, ambitious and promiscuous people, insanity, rape, and sex—mostly sex" (Brooks and Marsh, 1992: 616). Through the long run of the show, Don had affairs or relationships with Dudley, Simon, Grant, Rob, Joshua, Paul, and Bruce. Don was also the object of the affections of Brad, Dr. Pascal, and Phillip. Dudley, Simon, Grant, and Bruce were bisexuals, Karen was a lesbian (and a witch), and Robyn turned out to be a transsexual, much to her boyfriend's surprise.

An same-titled American version of the show (NBC, 1980–1981 and more of a sitcom) was much tamer and did not include any gay characters.

NYPD Blue (police drama), ABC, 1993–2005

- John Irvin (Bill Brochtrup), 1995–1996 and 1998–2005
- Abby Sullivan (Paige Turco), officer, 1997
- Kathy (Lisa Darr), Abby's partner, 1997

In 1995 detective Adrienne Lesniak (Justine Miceli) deflected an unwanted suitor by claiming to be gay, but then began to wonder whether or not she might be. In 1996 desk clerk John Irvin transferred from the 15th Precinct to the *Public Morals* division (and from drama to comedy, and from ABC to CBS). The 1996–1997 season saw the addition of officer Abby Sullivan and her lover Kathy.

Oh Grow Up (sitcom), ABC, 1999

- Ford Lowell (John Ducey), lawyer
- Sal (Ed Marinaro), construction boss

In this sitcom, three college roommates, now in their early thirties, are once again roommates. Ford has just moved in after coming out to his wife. Sal is the boss of one of the other roommates.

One Life to Live (daytime serial drama), ABC, 1968–present

- Billy Douglas (Ryan Phillippe), high school student, 1992–1993
- Jonathan Michaelson (Bruce McCarty), 1992, 1993
- Rick Mitchell (Joe Fiske), waiter, 1992–1993

Billy Douglas, a 17-year-old high school senior, moved into Llanview in the summer of 1992. Billy's struggle to come out to himself and his homophobic parents, in the midst of a town bitterly divided over a rumor that the local minister might be gay, occupied a substantial share of air time that summer. Jonathan, lover of the minister's late brother, showed up to ask for help making a quilt panel. Billy met Rick Mitchell caroling on Christmas eve 1992 and left for Yale the next summer.

Our Hero (teen-oriented sitcom), CBC, 2000–2002

- Ross Korolus (Justin Peroff)

This sitcom's central character is a high school student who writes and publishes a magazine. Ross is one of her circle of friends.

Oz (prison drama), HBO, 1997–2003

- Tobias Beecher (Lee Tergesen), prisoner
- Billie Keane (Derrick Simmons), prisoner, 1997
- Richie Hanlon (Jordan Lage), prisoner, 1998–1999
- Chris Keller (Christopher Meloni), prisoner, 1998–2002
- Jason Cramer (Rob Bogue), prisoner, 1999–2000
- Nat "Natalie" Ginsberg (Charles Busch), prisoner, 1999–2000

This gritty, critically praised prison drama series contained a lot of situational, often predatory homosexual behavior, and a prisoner or two described their sexuality as (more or less) "whatever I need to do to survive." Billie Keane, a minor character, was one of the few speaking roles self-identifying as gay [three episodes]. Richie represented gay inmates on the Em City council and took the fall for a jailhouse murder. After an appeal got him off death row he returned to the Em City unit where he was promptly killed. Beecher and Keller, both straight on the outside, passed through a brutal, vengeful, deceitful "courtship" to eventually admit to being lovers by the 2000 season. Cramer was imprisoned for murdering his lover. "Natalie" was another member of the prison's gay faction.

Pacific Drive (serial drama), 9NA, 1995–1997

- Zoe Marshall (Libby Tanner)
- Margeaux Hayes (Virginia Hey), Zoe's first girlfriend
- Dior Shelby (Clodagh Crowe), Zoe's second girlfriend
- Kay West (Brigid Kelly), Zoe's third girlfriend
- Sondra Westwood (Helen Dallimore), Zoe's fourth girlfriend
- Gemma Patterson (Katherine Lee), Zoe's fifth girlfriend
- Jo (Jason Langley), Tim's transsexual friend

The series focused on the lives of hungry young professionals who worked, lived, and played on the playground of Pacific Drive. Zoe was the bubbly young office administrator for Kingsley Inc., a conglomerate with real estate and media interests as well as a swimwear design company on Pacific Drive.

Paradise Falls (drama), Showcase, 2001–2002

- Nick Braga (Cameron Graham), aspiring writer
- Simon (Kristen Holden-Reid), personal trainer
- Bea Sutton (Dixie Seatle), restaurant owner
- Clive Hausenberg (Kent Staines), movie writer

This series, about the residents of a small town in Ontario cottage country, was shaded with more than a little *Twin Peaks*–like strangeness. The mayor's grandson, Nick, was a budding author and a closet homosexual, much to the horror of his Barbie-doll fiancée Jessica and the mayor (Art Hindle). Jessica tried to reconcile Nick with his estranged college buddy Simon, but was dumped herself. The mayor eventually discovered that his girlfriend Bea was a transsexual. When a movie production came to town Nick asked the film's writer, Clive, to mentor him, but Clive wasn't interested in Nick's writing talent.

Party Girl (sitcom), FOX, 1996

- Derrick (John Cameron Mitchell)

In this sitcom set among librarians, Derrick was a friend of the lead character.

Party of Five (drama), FOX, 1994–2000

- Ross (Mitchell Anderson), violinist, 1994–2000
- Perry Marks (Olivia D'Abo), writer, 1999
- Victor (Wilson Cruz), nanny, 1999–2000

Occasional character Ross was violin teacher to Claudia, the second youngest of the five Salinger orphans of the show's title. Older sister Julia (Neve Campbell) became enamored of a lesbian guest writer lecturing to her college writing class (three-episode guest appearance). Openly gay Puerto Rican actor and activist Wilson Cruz played Victor, the nanny of Owen (Jacob Smith), one of the five orphans. In separate episodes, Victor rejected Claudia's matchmaking, was disparaged by Owen's friend's father, and transformed the Salinger home into a haunted house with Gothic décor when Owen was not allowed to go trick-or-treating.

Penmarric (serial drama), BBC, 1979

• Phillip Castallack (Rupert Frazer)
• Alun Trevose (John Patrick)

This multigenerational serial drama was set in the British mining industry. Phillip, about to be married, fell in love with mining engineer Alun. Alun was killed in a mining accident and Phillip eventually commited suicide.

Playing the Field (sports drama), BBC1, 1997, 1999

• Angie (Tracey Whitwell)
• Gabi (Saira Todd)

This drama focused on a women's football [soccer] team in Northern England. Angie was a lesbian in a relationship with Gabi, a previously straight woman. The pair split at the end of the first season but by the end of the second were back together.

Porridge (prison sitcom), BBC, 1974–1978

• Lukewarm (Christopher Biggins)
• "Gay" Gordon (Felix Bowness)

Porridge is hailed as one of the best British comedy series of all time. The show followed the lives of criminal Norman "Fletch" Fletcher (Ronny Barker), a recidivist thief on his way to a five-year prison term, and his fellow inmates at H. M. Slade Prison. It spawned a spinoff series and a theatrical feature film. "Gay" Gordon was a semi-regular character. He worked in the kitchens but very little use was made of the character.

A Portrait of Marriage (drama miniseries), BBC, ca. 1990–1991

• Vita Sackville-West (Janet McTeer)
• Violet Trefusis (Cathyrn Harrison)

A biographical series about British author Vita Sackville-West.

The Practice (lawyer drama), ABC, 1997–2004

• Joey Heric (John Laroquette), 1997–1999

In a three-episode guest appearance, Joey was cleared of the knife murder of his lover, only to be charged with the knife murder of his new lover several months later.

Prisoner: Cellblock H (serial prison drama), TEN, 1979–1986

• Freida "Franky" Doyle (Carol Burns), prisoner, 1979
• Doreen Anderson/Burns (Colette Mann), prisoner
• Judy Bryant (Betty Bobbitt), prisoner, 1979–ca. 1984
• Sharon Gilmour (Margot Knight), Judy's partner, 1979
• Angela Jeffries (Jeanie Drynan), lawyer, 1979

- Joan "The Freak" Ferguson (Maggie Kirkpatrick), guard, ca. 1982–1986
- Ray "Gay Ray" Proctor (Alex Menglet), prison cook, 1984
- Terri Malone (Margot Knight), a guard, Joan's love interest, 1985

This serial drama was set in a women's detention center in Australia. Among the cast of prisoners was a lesbian named Franky. As the series developed, various characters came and went, including Judy, who committed a crime so that she could be jailed with Sharon, and bisexual prisoner Doreen.

Profiler (crime drama), NBC, 1996–2000

- George Fraley (Peter Frechette), computer specialist

George was a civilian member of the Violent Crimes Task Force, an elite law enforcement agency pursuing primarily psychopath serial killers.

Public Morals (police sitcom), CBS, 1996

- John Irvin (Bill Brochtrup)

John Irvin went from being a minor recurring character on the police drama *NYPD Blue* to a full-time member of the cast in this sitcom based in the NYPD public morals division. The show was cancelled after a single episode.

The Pursuit of Happiness (sitcom), NBC, 1995

- Alex Chosek (Brad Garrett), lawyer

This home-and-office sitcom centered on lawyer Steve Rutledge (Tom Amandes). His best friend and fellow lawyer, Alex, has a revelation to tell.

Push (sports drama), ABC, 1998

- Scott Trysfan (Eddie Mills)

This serial involved a group of young athletes training for the 2000 Olympics. Only two episodes aired, and it's not clear if Scott's sexual orientation made it to broadcast.

Quads (animated sitcom), Teletoon, 2001

- Spalding (Matthew King [voice])

In this irreverent comedy, four physically handicapped people shared a mansion. Spalding was the central character's "overtly homosexual Australian physical therapist." An alternate for the series was *John Callahan's Quads*.

Queer as Folk (serial drama), C4, 1999; *Queer as Folk 2* (serial drama), C4, 2000

- Stuart Jones (Aidan Gillen), public relations executive
- Vince Tyler (Craig Kelly), supermarket manager
- Nathan Maloney (Charlie Hunnam), student
- Romey Sullivan (Esther Hall)

- Lisa Levene (Saira Todd), solicitor, 1999
- Siobhan Potter (Juley McCann), 1999
- Dane McAteer (Adam Zane), 1999
- Bernard Thomas (Andy Devine)
- Alexander Perry (Anthony Cotton)
- Cameron Roberts (Peter O'Brien), accountant, 1999
- Phil Delaney (Jason Merrells), 1999
- Daniel "Dazz" Collinson (Jonathon Natynczyk)

This British drama was set in and among a group of gay friends and acquaintances. Stuart and Vince were friends since childhood. Nathan, Vince said, was "the one night stand that never went away." Bernard described Stuart as "Manchester's champion shagger." Lesbian couple Romey and Lisa were parents of a newborn son. Another lesbian couple, Siobhan and Susie (Sarah Jones), were their friends. An American version was produced for the Showtime cable channel in 2000.

Queer as Folk (serial drama), Showtime, 2000–2005

- Michael Charles Novotny (Hal Sparks), supermarket assistant manager [the "Vince" character]
- Brian Kinney (Gale Harold), advertising executive [the "Stuart" character]
- Justin Taylor (Randy Harrison), high school student [the "Nathan" character]
- Emmett Honeycutt (Peter Paige), boutique manager [the "Alexander" character]
- Theodore "Ted" Schmidt (Scott Lowell), accountant [the "Phil" character]
- Dr. Dave Cameron (Chris Potter), chiropractor, 2000–2001 [the "Cameron" character]
- Lindsay Peterson (Thea Gill), art professor [the "Romy" character]
- Melanie Marcus (Michelle Clunie), lawyer [the "Lisa" character]
- Vic Grassi (Jack Wetherall) [the "Berniard" character]
- Blake (Dean Armstrong), 2000–2001
- Kip Johnson (Barna Moricz), 2001
- Ben Bruckner (Robert Gant), professor, 2002–2005
- Ethan Gold (Fab Filippo), violinist, 2002–2005
- George Schickel (Bruce Gray), pickle magnate, 2002
- Leda (Nancy Anne Sakovich), 2002

This American adaptation of the British production *Queer as Folk* transferred from Manchester, England, to Pittsburgh, Pennsylvania. Michael's boyfriends: Dave and Ben. Brian's boyfriend: Justin. Justin's boyfriends: Brian and Ethan. Emmett's boyfriend: George. Ted's boyfriends: Blake and Kip.

Raw FM (drama), ABCTV, 1997–1998

- Mark "Marco" Mulholland (Dan Spielman), disk jockey
- Sam (Sophie Heathcote), dancer and singer

This series was set in a GenX radio station.

The Real World (video-verity documentary), MTV, 1992–present

- Norman Korpi, 1992
- Beth Anthony, 1993

- Pedro Zamora, 1994
- Sean Sasser, 1994
- Dan Renzi, 1996
- Arnie, 1996
- Johnny, 1996
- Genesis Moss, 1997
- Ruthie Alcaide, 1999
- Justin Deabler, 1999
- Jason Daniel "Danny" Roberts, 2000
- Paul, 2000

Each season, MTV gathers together seven young people to live in an apartment, under the watchful eye of the television camera. Each year has involved a different location and residents. In 1992 (New York) one of the roommates was Norman, a bisexual. He dated Charles Perez (one episode). The 1993 (Los Angeles) cast included a lesbian named Beth. The 1994 (San Francisco) edition included Pedro, an AIDS educator. Pedro and Sean's wedding was the principal content of one episode. The 1996 (Miami) cast included Dan, who dated Arnie and then Johnny. The 1997 (Boston) edition included Genesis, a lesbian. The 1999 (Hawaii) edition included bisexual rapper-poet Ruthie and Harvard law student Justin. The 2000 (New Orleans) edition included Danny, and occasionally the digitally obscured image of Paul, Danny's military boyfriend. The 1995 (London) and 1998 (Seattle) editions included no explicitly gay, lesbian, or bisexual cast members.

Relativity (drama), ABC, 1996–1997

- Rhonda Roth (Lisa Edelstein)

First there was the *L.A. Law* kiss in 1992 between bisexual attorney C. J. Lamb and her bi-curious colleague, and then the Roseanne–Mariel Hemingway kiss on *Roseanne* in 1994 (which was shown from the back to block the actual kiss). However, the first *real* lesbian kiss (i.e., a kiss between two lesbian or bisexual women) on television occurred in this short-lived drama on January 11, 1997. The series also featured the first recurring lesbian character who was a central part of the cast (Warn, 2002). The show followed a twentysomething heterosexual couple, Isabelle (Kimberlkey Williams) and Leo (David Conrad), and the lives and loves of their assorted friends and adult siblings. Although Leo's lesbian sister Rhonda (Lisa Edelstein) was introduced at the beginning of the series, her sexuality was not featured in any of the early episodes except one, in which Isabelle and Rhonda commiserate over their recent respective breakups. Rhomda's love interest was Suzanne (Kristin Dattilo).

Revelations (drama), ITV, 1994, 1996

- Gabriel

This drama focused on a family living near Manchester, England. Bisexual drug addict Gabriel had an affair with another man before marrying Rachel, and when Rachel disappeared he had a one-night stand with another man. The show also featured possibly TV's first lesbian vicar.

Rhona (sitcom), BBC2, 2000–2001

• Rhona (Rhona Cameron)

In this sitcom, Rhona was a freelance video reviewer.

Riverdale (serial drama), CBC, 1997–2000

• George Patillo (Hugo Dann), newspaperman

This serial drama of the *Coronation Street/EastEnders* variety was set in a diverse Toronto neighborhood. George was the owner/operator of the *Riverdale Community News*, a shoppers' weekly he wanted to turn into a "real" newspaper or a scandal sheet.

The Roads to Freedom (drama), BBC, 1970; seen on PBS, 1971

• Daniel Sereno (Daniel Massey)

Paris on the eve of World War II, based on the novel trilogy of the same name by Jean-Paul Sartre. Mathieu, the main character of the series, was a philosophy professor who defined himself and tried to give his life meaning by trying to be completely "free." Marcelle was Mathieu's mistress of seven years and had recently become pregnant by him. Daniel was an extremely handsome man who was able to hide his corruption behind his alluring appearance. Daniel loathed himself, partly due to his inability to accept his homosexuality. He tried in vain to muster up the courage to kill himself and projected his self-hate on others. Marcelle nicknamed him Archangel. Mathieu astutely realized that this was an ironic name for Daniel, as his dashing appearance and corrupt soul were reminiscent of Lucifer. Because of Daniel's hatred for Mathieu he refused to lend him the money for an abortion and tried to convince him that in order to remain free, he would have to marry Marcelle, against his wishes. Daniel later changed his plan to devestate Mathieu by seducing Marcelle, convincing her that she would not be happy with Mathieu because he did not love her, and eventually proposing to her.

Rude Awakenings (sitcom), Showtime, 1998–2000

• Jackie (Rain Prior), recovering drug addict
• Rosalee (Tisha Campbell), 1998

Rude Awakenings detailed the trials and tribulations of Billie Frank (Sherilyn Fenn), an aspiring writer and has-been actor who was forced to attend Addiction Anonymous meetings after a DUI accident. At the meetings she interacted with a cast of eccentric characters including Jackie, a lesbian recovering drug addict, and Trudie (Lynn Redgrave), Billie's alcoholic, abrasive mother.

St. Elsewhere (hospital drama), NBC, 1982–1986

• Kevin O'Casey (John Scott Clough), 1985–1986
• Brett Johnson (Kyle Secor), 1986

St. Elsewhere often featured guest roles that spanned several episodes or that recurred periodically over longer time frames. Kevin was the latest generation of a family of hereditary patients at St. Eligius. His lover Brett had AIDS. In another, two-episode story arc, Dr. Anne Cavanaro (Cynthia Sikes) rebuffed the advances of visiting specialist Dr. Christine Holt (Caroline McWilliams).

Santa Barbara (daytime serial drama), NBC, 1984–1993

- Channing Capwell Jr. (Robert Wilson), 1985
- Lindsay Smith (Joel Bailey), 1985

This serial opened its first episode with the release from prison of the wrongly convicted murderer of Channing Capwell Jr. In the course of finding the real killer, it was discovered that Channing's past included affairs with his father's mistress and someone named Lindsay Smith. Further investigation identified Lindsay as another man. Some of this story was played out in flashback wherein Channing and Lindsay appeared.

Sara (sitcom), NBC, 1985

- Dennis Kemper (Bronson Pinchot)

Dennis was one of four young lawyers in this office sitcom. The show didn't last long and star Geena Davis left TV for the movies.

The Secret Life of Us (drama), TEN, 2001–2005

- Simon Trader (David Tredinnick), bartender
- Richie Blake (Spencer McLaren), actor

This ensemble drama centered on a group of twentysomethings, most of whom lived in three flats in the same Melbourne apartment building. Richie shared one flat with his girlfriend Miranda and his best friend Will. Simon tended bar where the rest of the residents went to unwind.

Seinfeld (sitcom), NBC, 1990–1998

- Susan Biddle Ross (Heidi Swedberg), 1992–1993 and 1995–1996

George Costanza's on-and-off relationship with Susan was perhaps never more off than when Susan was dating women.

Sex and the City (sitcom), HBO, 1998–2004

- Stanford Blanche (Willie Garson)

Occasional character Stanford was lead character Carrie's friend.

Shortland Street (serial drama), TVNZ, 1992–present

- Jonathan McKenna (Kieran Hutchison), laboratory assistant/medical student, 1993–present
- Meredith Fleming (Stephanie Wilkin), doctor, ca. 1994–1995
- Annie
- Willow
- Jamie Forrest (Karl Urban), paramedic
- Mani
- Ewan, clinic pharmacist, 1999
- Blake Crombie (Gesse Peach), sailor, 1999–2001

- Dr. Laura Hall (Larissa Matheson), 1999–2000

This drama is set in a privately run emergency clinic. Jonathan is the twentysomething son of the clinic's original owner and has had relationships with a variety of characters, including his first boyfriend Jamie. Another story line involved him sleeping with Mani, a bisexual male who was also seriously dating one of the female nurses. Central character Nick Harrison's girlfriend Willow was bisexual. Ewan and Jordan's relationship was a surprise for Jordan's mother Moira.

Shout (magazine), PrideVision, 2001

- Michael Serapio, co-host/reporter
- Rachel Guise, co-host/reporter
- Guy Gagnier, co-host/reporter

This magazine-format program covers topics generally of interest to the GLBT community.

The Simpsons (animated sitcom), FOX, 1989–present

- Waylon Smithers (Harry Shearer [voice])

Smithers is the ultimate sycophant, positively doting on his boss, nuclear power plant mogul Monty Burns. But the interest is more than business, often extending into the romantic, and the erotic.

Sisters (drama), NBC, 1991–1996

- Norma Lear (Nora Dunn), 1993–1996

Occasional character Norma is the producer of one of the title sisters' local television talk show.

Six Feet Under (drama), HBO, 2001–2005

- David Fischer (Michael C. Hall), funeral director
- Keith Charles (Matthew St. Patrick), policeman

This series followed the lives of a family of undertakers, including middle child David. Keith was David's boyfriend.

Snips (sitcom), syndicated, ca. late 1970s

- Michael (Walter Wonderman), hairdresser

This comedy centered around a divorced hairdresser and his ex-wife. Their friend Michael was a series regular. This sitcom was developed for NBC for the fall 1976 season but cancelled before it aired. Episodes reportedly appeared in syndication in Australia in the late 1970s (Capsuto, 2000: 127–128).

Soap (serial sitcom), ABC, 1977–1981

- Jodie Dallas (Billy Crystal)
- Dennis Phillips (Bob Seagren), 1978

- Alice (Randee Heller), 1979

Jodie was a regular character throughout the run of the show, although he was eventually involved with women. Dennis was the very closeted pro football quarterback involved with Jodie the first season. Alice was a lesbian friend of Jodie's later in the show's run.

SoGayTV (talk), PrideVision, 2001–2002

- Mathieu Chantelois, 2001, host
- Jason Ruta, 2002, host

Using a talk show format, this program featured guests and gay themes, and was interrelated with *The Lofters*, from which the hosts were drawn. It originated as a Webcast in 2001 from the U8TV Web site, U8TV.com, and was simulcast on PrideVision from September 2001.

Some of My Best Friends (sitcom), CBS, 2001

- Warren Fairbanks (Jason Bateman)
- Vern Limoso (Alec Mapa)

This sitcom was based on the independent film *Kiss Me Guido* about a gay man and a straight Italian American sharing an apartment. Between the first publicity and eventual airing the show passed through at least three titles: *Kiss Me, Guido*, *Me and Frankie Z*, and *Some of My Best Friends*.

Sons and Daughters (serial drama), 7N, 1981–1987

- Colin Turner (Nicholas Ryan), ca. 1985

This serial drama focused on the lives and loves of two families and their children (and friends).

South Park (animated sitcom), CC, 1997–present

- Big Gay Al (Trey Parker [voice])

This popular cartoon for grown-ups centers on a group of fourth graders in South Park, Colorado. Occasional character "Big Gay Al" operates a boat ride and a gay animal refuge.

Spin City (sitcom), ABC, 1996–2002

- Carter Sebastian Heywood (Michael Boatman), gay activist

Michael J. Fox played the deputy mayor of New York in this sitcom about politics and media relations. The mayor's staff included Carter, a gay activist. Carter's love life included ex-lover Spence (Luke Perry), fashion designer Isaac Mizrahi (Isaac Mizrahi) and navy officer Nate (Lou Diamond Phillips) (one episode each), and boxer Bennett (Clayton Prince) (two episodes).

Spyder Games (serial drama), MTV, 2001

- Ivan Carlisle (Byron Field)
- Temple Simms (Craig Robert Young), hair stylist

Ivan was the second oldest son of the Carlisle family central to the series. He married Julie after a two-year-long engagement. Temple was Natalie Carlisle's stylist.

Suddenly Susan (sitcom), NBC, 1996–2000

- Pete (Bill Stevenson), 1996–1999

Brooke Shields starred as Susan Keane, a columnist with San Francisco's *The Gate* magazine. An occasional character, Pete worked in the mail room. His partner Hank (Fred Stoller) also appeared. The cast was revamped for the 1999–2000 season.

The Super Adventure Team (puppet sitcom), MTV, 1998

- Chief Engineer Head (Benjamin Venom [voice])

In this adult-audience satire of children's super hero programming, Head was closeted, revealing his orientation in the way he reacted to other male characters.

Survivor ("reality" contest), CBS, 2000–present

- Richard "Rich" Hatch, 2000 (Malaysia)
- Brandon Quinton, 2001 (Africa)

Part *The Real World*, part *Lord of the Flies*, part *Beat the Clock*, and just a little bit *Gilligan's Island*, sixteen individuals isolated as a group for more than a month compete and cooperate to survive. Richard, one of the contestants, turned out to be gay. He also turned out to be the sole survivor (contest winner) and a million dollars richer. No (out) gay contestants appeared in season two (2001, Australia), season four (2002, Marquesas), or season five (2002, Thailand).

Sweat (drama), TEN, 1996–1997

- Steve "Snowy" Bowles (Heath Ledger)

This series was based on the "Sports West Academy," a training academy for young elite athletes. The young athletes were thrown in together in a "live-in" situation at SWA. Snowy was a 17-year-old cyclist.

Taggart (detective drama), ITV1, 1983–present

- Constable Stuart Fraser (Colin McCredie), detective, 1996–2004

Long-running British detective/murder mystery series. Set in Glasgow, it focused on a group of detectives in the Maryhill Criminal Investigation Department.

Tales of the City (serial drama miniseries), C4, 1993; seen on PBS, 1994;
More Tales of the City (serial drama miniseries), C4 and Showtime, 1998;
Further Tales of the City (serial drama miniseries), Showtime, 2001

- Michael "Mouse" Tolliver (Marcus D'Amico, 1993; Paul Hopkins, 1998, 2001), waiter
- Mona Ramsay (Chloe Webb, 1993; Nina Siemaszko, 1998), advertising copy-writer
- Anna Madrigal (Olympia Dukakis), landlady
- Jon Fielden/Fielding (William Campbell), doctor
- Dorothy "D'orothea" Wilson (Cynda Williams, 1993; Francoise Robertson, 1998), model
- Beauchamp Day (Thomas Gibson), advertising executive, 1993, 1998
- Peter Cipriani (Kevin Sessums), A-gay, 1993
- Charles Hillary "Chuck" Lord (Paul Bartel), A-gay

Armistead Maupin's first and second "Tales" novels (of six) were brought to television by British financing. The miniseries focused on the residents of 28 Barbary Lane, and their friends and lovers. This was the first series with gays, lesbians, bisexuals, and others since *Number 96*. *Tales* cameo appearances included Arch Gidde (Ian McKellen), Bill Hill (Lance Loud), and Rick Hampton (Bob Mackie). *More Tales* "A Gays" cameos included Henry Callaway Kent (Brian Bedford), Edward Bass Matheson (Dan Butler), and Arlington Luce (Scott Thompson).

Tenko (prisoner-of-war drama), BBC, 1981–1984

- Nellie Keene (Jeananne Crowley), 1981–1982

This series centered on women interned by the Japanese in Singapore during World War II. Nellie, a nurse, came to care for another prisoner, Sally (Joanne Hole). When a third prisoner, Dorothy, outed them, Sally was disgusted by the suggestion and disassociated herself from Nellie.

These Arms of Mine (drama), CBC, 2000–2001

- Steven Armstrong (Conrad Coates), drama teacher
- Randy (Max Martini)
- Adam (actor unknown), florist, 2001

In this story of a diverse group of upscale friends in Vancouver, Randy was Steven's friend and neighbor. Adam and Steven later dated.

Thirtysomething (drama), ABC, 1987–1991

- Russell Weller (David Marshall Grant), 1989–1991
- Peter Montefiori (Peter Frechette), 1989–1991

In this drama, occasional character Peter was an art designer who worked at the advertising company central to the main characters. Peter had a brief affair with Russell, a painter. By New Year's of the last season of the show, it looked like Russell and Peter were reuniting.

This Life (serial drama), BBC2, 1994–1995

- Warren Jones (Jason Hughes), trainee lawyer
- Ferdy Garcia (Ramon Tikaram), motorcycle courier, 1995
- Lenny (Tony Curran), plumber, 1995
- Sarah Newly (Clare Clifford), lawyer, 1996–1997

Warren was a wry gay solicitor at the law firm of Moore Spencer Wright. He underwent therapy to deal with the repression of his small-town upbringing. Ferdy had separate encounters with Warren and Lenny.

Tinker, Tailor, Soldier, Spy (espionage miniseries), BBC, 1979

- Bill Haydon (Ian Richardson)

Tinker, Tailor, Soldier, Spy told the story of how protagonist George Smiley (Alec Guinness) was brought out of retirement from his job at the British Secret Intelligence Service to help find a mole that had infiltrated the deepest levels of the organization. The mole—his own wife's lover—was eventually killed by a male lover, Jim Prideaux (Ian Bannen), whom he betrayed during a mission to Prague (Howes, 1993: 847).

Tinsel Town (drama miniseries), BBC2, 2000–2001

- Ryan Taylor (David Paisley)
- Lewis (Stevie Allen), police officer
- Lex (Kate Dickie), disk jockey
- Stella (Jim Twaddale), club owner
- Robin (Chris McQuarry), bartender, 2000
- Ash (Marc Oliver), bartender, 2001

This drama was set in the Glasgow club scene. Ryan did not know that Lewis was a cop, and Lewis did not know that Ryan was under age. Lex was a bisexual woman and the target of a stalker. Stella, a transvestite, owned the club "Tinsel Town," the series main setting. Robin was a friend of Ryan's. Ash replaced Robin behind the bar as Ryan's work buddy in the 2001 season.

Together (serial drama), Southern Television for ITV, 1980–1981

- Trevor Wallace (Paul Hastings), rail steward
- Pete Hunt (Stephen Churchett), nursing assistant

Daytime serial about residents of Rutherford Court, set in a sheltered accommodation block.

To Play the King (drama miniseries), BBC, 1994; also seen on PBS

- David Mycroft (Nicholas Farrell), press secretary and chief of staff to the king

Mycroft, a closeted homosexual at the beginning of the series, seemed reluctant to admit even to himself that he might be gay. After meeting and falling in love with flight steward Ken Charterhouse (Jack Fortune), he was forced to admit his homosexuality to the press and resigned his position in the royal service.

Total Security (detective drama), ABC, 1997

• George LaSalle (Bill Brochtrup)

The characters in this private investigator drama included George, the office manager.

The Tracey Ullman Show (sketch comedy), FOX, 1987–1990

• David (Dan Castellenata)
• William (Sam McMurray)

Within the sketch format there were several recurring characters. One such "continuing saga" was that of 14-year-old Francesca (Tracy Ullman), who lived with her father David and his lover William. They were depicted as ordinary parents with an unordinary characteristic—they were gay.

U8TV: The Lofters ("reality" programming), Life, 2001–2002

• Mathieu Chantelois, 2001
• Marcello, 2001
• Valery Gagne, 2001
• Jason Ruta, 2002

This series used a format similar to *Big Brother* and *The Real World*: eight young adults lived in a house wired with 24-hours cameras in every space. In 2001 Mathieu was one of the residents, and his boyfriend Marcello was a regular visitor. About three months into the year fellow lofter Valery came out as bisexual. The 2002 cast included Jason.

UnderCovers (call-in advice), PrideVision, 2001–2002

• Elley-Ray, co-host
• Dr. Keith, co-host

This call-in program offered advice on sex, health, and relationship issues for the GLBT community.

Undressed (serial drama), MTV, 1999–2002

• Andy (Nicholas Gonzalez), 1999
• Joel (Eyal Podell), 1999
• Jonathan (Phillip Rhys), 1999
• Joan (Julie Anna Laffer), 1999
• Samantha (Francesca Ingrassia), 1999
• Kirk (Peter Paige), 1999
• Evan (Jon Huertas), 1999
• Chuck (Christopher Delisle), 2000
• Neil (Jason Lasater), 2000

This anthology drama series examined the diverse sexual relationships involving the different genders, races and ethnicities, and sexual orientations and fetishes of high school and college students and post-college roommates. Characters appeared generally for short runs of a half-dozen episodes or so.

Unhappily Ever After (sitcom), WB, 1995–1999

• Barry Wallenstein (Ant), 1995–1997

In this sitcom, a couple, Jack and Jennie Malloy, are having a hard go at marriage. Barry is the best friend of Ryan and Tiffany, the couple's children.

Veronica's Closet (sitcom), NBC, 1997–2000

• Joshua (Wallace Langham)

"Veronica's Closet" was a women's lingerie company. Josh, the company president's assistant, insisted that he was straight, but everyone else (including his own mother) told him he was gay. As the show wrapped up its last season Josh came to realize that he in fact was gay.

A Very Peculiar Practice (comedy/drama), BBC, 1986, 1988

• Dr. Rose Marie (Barbara Flyn)
• Greta Gretowska (Joanna Kanska), 1988
• Glenn Oates (James Noble), an athlete patient of Dr. Buzzard

In this lowbrow sitcom set in a university health service, Dr. Rose Marie ran a men's sexuality counseling service wherein she advised her clients to avoid orgasm no matter what. Rose was bisexual.

Wasteland (drama), ABC, 1999

• Russell Baskind (Dan Montgomery), actor

This short-lived series followed six post-college friends, including Russell, a deeply closeted soap opera actor.

Water Rats (police drama), 9NA, 1996–2001

• Sergeant Helen Blakemore (Toni Scanlan)

Helen Blakemore was the Sydney Harbor Patrol's alluring but fearsomely efficient intelligence officer. Although desk-bound, her job required great responsibility and put her in contact with all of the officers. Some of the younger officers were intimidated by her competence and sharp mind. She felt that her private life as a lesbian with a live-in lover was no one's business but her own.

Will & Grace (sitcom), NBC, 1998–present

• Will Truman (Eric McCormack)
• Jack McFarland (Sean P. Hayes)
• Matthew Moshea (Patrick Dempsey), 2000–2001
• Larry (Tim Bagley), 2000–present
• Joe (Jerry Levine), 2000–present

Grace is a straight woman, Will is her best friend. The shtick is that they are perfect for each other, except that she's a woman. Will was the first American post-*Ellen* lead gay character. Will finally dated someone during the 2000–2001 season, closeted sportscaster Matthew. Will and Grace's friends Larry and Joe appear occasionally.

Women in Prison (prison sitcom), FOX, 1987–1988

• Bonnie Harper (Antoinette Byron)

In this sitcom, set in a women's prison, prisoner Bonnie was a lesbian English hooker.

You Rang, M'Lord (sitcom), BBC, 1988–1993

• Cissy (Catherine Rabett), lesbian daughter

In this comedy version of *Upstairs Downstairs*, Cissy is the archetypal stereotype for a lesbian (dresses up as a male, etc.). The program uses nonflattering stereotypes.

SOME ALSO-RANS

Babylon 5 (science fiction), syndicated, 1994–1998. Susan Ivanova (Claudia Christian) and Talia Winters (Andrea Thompson) had an implied lesbian relationship. In an episode after Talia's character was written out, Susan confessed that she loved Talia.

Dallas (serial drama), CBS, 1978–1991. This serial drama was set among Texas oil barons. In 1978 J. R. Ewing (Larry Hagman) schemed to have his niece Lucy (Charlene Tilton) married to Kit Mainwaring (Mark Wheeler), the heir of the Mainwaring Oil Company. Lucy was smitten by the handsome young man, but it was not to be—Kit had just broken up with his boyfriend (two episodes).

Days of Our Lives (daytime serial drama), NBC, 1965–present. In 1977 the unhappily married Sharon Duval (Sally Stark) admitted to her dear friend Julie Williams that she was bisexual and was in love with her. The story line was quickly wrapped up when problems broke out backstage between head writer Pat Falken Smith and the NBC top brass.

F Troop (sitcom), ABC, 1965–1967. Before there were overt gay characters on television there were coded representations, such as mannish women and effeminate men. One such character was Roaring Chicken (Edward Everett Horton), the Hekawi medicine man on *F Troop*.

The Golden Girls (sitcom), NBC, 1985–1992. Blanche's gay brother Clayton Farnsworth (Monte Markham) appeared twice. In another episode Dorothy's lesbian friend Jean appeared. The pilot for *The Golden Girls* included a gay cook/houseboy as a regular cast member, but the character was eliminated when series production began.

Hope and Gloria (sitcom), NBC, 1995–1996. Hair stylist Isaac (Eric Allan Kramer) appeared in the first few episodes but was quickly written out.

In the Life (talk/variety), PBS, 1992–present. Monthly, then quarterly show focusing on gay and lesbian life in the United States. Some PBS stations elected not to broadcast it. No roles (therefore no gay characters).

Keeping Up Appearances (sitcom), [U.K.] 1990–1993, 1995. We never saw Mrs. Bucket's son Sheridan (or even heard his voice), but he called his mummy regularly from college, usually to ask for money or to talk about his very best friend Tarquin.

Murder One (legal drama), ABC, 1995–1997. Publicity for this show included the news that one of the minor recurring characters was gay. Most watchers assumed that character would be the lead lawyer's legal assistant, Louis Heinsbergen (John Fleck, 1995–1996), but the revelation seemed never to occur. One e-mail correspondent reported having seen the "coming out" episode in Germany, but that it was never broadcast in the United States.

Roc (sitcom), FOX, 1991–1994. An interracial gay couple appeared twice.

Saturday Night Live (sketch comedy/variety), NBC, 1975–present. After thirty years of supposedly pushing the envelope of television conventions, *Saturday Night Live* has yet to produce a regular or recurring gay, lesbian, or bisexual character, although there have been many close encounters: Franz (Kevin Nealon, 1986–1995) once experienced a moment of clarity about his affection for bodybuilding buddy Hans (Dana Carvey, 1986–1992); androgynous Pat (Julia Sweeney, 1990–1994) kept everyone guessing; and out actor Terry Sweeney (1985–1986) played several one-off gay characters but is probably best remembered for his Nancy Reagan. In the fall of 1996 an animated segment titled "The Ambiguously Gay Duo" began appearing irregularly, featuring Ace and Gary, two superheroes battling evil and patting each other on the behind.

Star Trek: Deep Space Nine (science fiction), syndicated, 1993–1999. The episode "Rejoined" also used the Trill host–symbiotic construct to portray love between two Trills, now both female.

Star Trek: The Next Generation (science fiction), syndicated, 1987–1994. In an unproduced first season script, Dr. Beverly Crusher's orderly, Ensign Freeman, was supposed to be gay. A 1991 promise by series creator Gene Roddenberry to introduce minor regular gay characters during the 1991–1992 season was reneged on by Paramount after Roddenberry's death. Two other episodes touched on orientation identity issues: In "The Host" (1991), Dr. Crusher fell in love with Odan, a Trill ambassador whose body was merely a host that lived in a symbiotic relationship with a parasite-like creature—the actual being that was Odan. In "The Outcast" (1992), Commander Riker fell in love with a member of the J'naii, an androgynous society where male–female relationships were prohibited.

Three's Company (sitcom), ABC, 1977–1984. The archetype of the airhead sitcom. The premise of the living arrangements was that the landlord would only allow Jack to live with Janet and Chrissy if he was gay. (I guess some things were morally acceptable and others weren't.) There were no "really" gay characters, though.

SOME THAT DON'T BELONG

It can be said with some certainty that the following were/are not gay or lesbian couples, urban legends to the contrary:

- The Lone Ranger and Tonto, *The Lone Ranger* (western), ABC, 1949–1957; radio, 1933–1955.

- Spin Evans (Tim Considine) and Marty Markham (David Stollery), *Spin and Marty* and *The Further Adventures of Spin and Marty* (children's adventure), broadcast within *The Mickey Mouse Club* (children's anthology), ABC, 1955–1959.

- Peppermint Patty and Marcie, various *Peanuts* specials since 1965, CBS.

- Bruce Wayne and Dick Grayson, *Batman* (comic-book drama), ABC, 1966–1968.

- Bert and Ernie, *Sesame Street* (children's education), PBS and worldwide syndication, 1969–present.

- Frank and Joe Hardy (Parker Stevenson and Shaun Cassidy), *The Hardy Boys Mysteries* (detective drama), ABC, 1977–1979.

- Xena (Lucy Lawless) and Gabrielle (Reneé O'Connor), *Xena: Warrior Princess* (adventure), syndication, 1995–2001.

References

Abramson, Jill, and Jane Mayer. 1994. *Strange Justice: The Selling of Clarence Thomas.* Boston: Houghton Mifflin.

ACLU. 1994. "Hate Speech on Campus." http://www.aclu.org/StudentRights/ StudentRights.cfm?ID=9004&c=159, December 31.

Advocate. 2003a. "Casper, Wyo., Rejects Anti–Matthew Shepard Monument." http://www.advocate.com/new_news.asp?id=10330&sd=10/31/03.

Advocate. 2003b. "Fall TV Listings." http://www.advocate.com/html/stories/899 /899_tvlistings.asp.

Advocate. 2003c. "Germany Will Build Monument to Nazi-Persecuted." http://www. advocate.com/new_news.asp?id=10489&sd=11/14/03.

Advocate. 2003d. "Greek Gay Activists Hold Kiss-in Protest." http://www.advocate. com/new_news.asp?id=10488&sd=11/14/03.

Advocate. 2003e. "Hatch Joins Kennedy on Hate-Crimes Legislation." http:// www.advocate.com/new_news.asp?id=10486&sd=11/14/03.

Advocate. 2003f. "Jeb Bush Says San Franciscans Are Endangered." http://www. advocate.com/new_news.asp?id=10484&sd=11/14/03.

Advocate. 2003g. "Phelps Hate Monument Stirs Protest in Boise." http://www. advocate.com/new_news.asp?id=10760&sd=12/16/03.

Advocate. 2003h. "Transgender Day of Remembrance Set for November." http:// www.advocate.com/new_news.asp?id=10302&sd=10/28/03.

Alexander, Charles C. 1962. *Crusade for Conformity: The Ku Klux Klan in Texas, 1920–1930.* Vol. 6, No. 1. Houston: Texas Gulf Coast Historical Association.

Allport, Gordon. 1958. *The Nature of Prejudice.* Garden City, NY: Doubleday.

American Association of University Women. 2001. *Hostile Hallways: Bullying, Teasing, and Sexual Harassment in School.* www.aauw.org/2000/hostilebd.html.

American Broadcasting System. 2001. ABCNews/*Washington Post* Poll. http://abc news.go.com, September 13.

American Journal of International Law. 2004. "RwandaTribunal." April.

American-Arab Anti-Discrimination Committee. 2002. "ADC Fact Sheet: The Condition of Arab Americans Post 9/11." http://www.adc.org, March 27.

Anderson, Elijah. 1999. *Code of the Streets: Decency, Violence, and the Moral Life of the Inner City*. New York: W. W. Norton.

Anson, Robert Sam. 1977. "Kiddie Porn." *San Francisco Chronicle*, October 25, p. 19.

Arab American Institute. 2003. *FBI Forms First Arab Advisory Committee*. http://aaiusa.org.

Associated Press. 2004. "Las Vegas Casino Boots Singer Linda Ronstadt for Praising 'Fahrenheit 9/11.'" http://www.commondreams.org/headlines04/0719-10.htm, July 19.

Associated Press. 2005. "High School Senior Challenges Rule Against Same-Sex Dance Dates." http://www.fox23news.com/news/national/story.aspx?content_id=AD6B218A-A461-4FF8-AAF7-5CB48D9287EB.

Attorney-General's Commission on Pornography. 1986. *Report to the Attorney General*. Washington, DC: U.S. Government Printing Office.

Azaloa, Elena. 2000. *Boy and Girl Victims of Sexual Exploitation in Mexico*. Mexico City: UNICEF-DIF (Mexico Office of the United Nations Children's Fund and the National System for Integral Family Development).

Bachman, Ronet, and Linda Saltzman. 1995. "Violence Against Women: Estimates from the Redesigned Survey." Bureau of Justice Statistics Special Report (August), Table 4, p. 3.

Barnes, Clive. 1970. "Introduction." In *The Report of the Commission on Obscenity and Pornography*. New York: Bantam Books.

Bauder, David. 2003. "MSNBC Fires Savage on Anti-Gay Remarks." Miami World Herald.com, http://www.miami.com/mld/miamiherald/entertainment/6251351.htm?1c, July 7.

Bauman, Zygmunt. 1989. *Modernity and the Holocaust*. Ithaca, NY: Cornell University Press.

Beck, Ulrich. 1992. *The Risk Society*. New York: Sage.

Becker, Katherine. 1996. "Culture and the Politics of Signification: The Case of Child Sexual Abuse." *Social Problems* 43: 57–76.

Berelson, Bernard, and Patricia J. Salter. 1946. "Majority and Minority Americans: An Analysis of Magazine Fiction." *Public Opinion Quarterly* 10 (Summer): 168–191.

Berrigan, Ginger. 2002. "'Speaking Out' about Hate Speech." *Loyola Law Review* 1: 5.

Biocco, Michael. March 1996–present. "Gay TV." A weekly compilation published online at http://www.jersey.net/~not2/gaytv.htm.

Bloom, Leonard. 1971. *The Social Psychology of Race Relations*. Cambridge, MA: Schenkman.

Boeckmann, Robert, and Carolyn Turpin-Petrosino. 2002. "Understanding the Harm of Hate Crime." *Journal of Social Issues* 58(2): 207–225.

Bogardus, Emory S. 1933. "A Social Distance Scale." *Sociology and Social Research* 17 (January–February): 265–271.

Boyle, Kevin. 2001. "Hate Speech—The United States versus the Rest of the World?" *Maine Law Review* 53: 488.

Brooks, Tim, and Earle Marsh. 1992. *The Complete Directory to Prime Time Network TV Shows: 1946–Present*. 5th ed. New York: Ballantine Books.

Brooks, Tim, and Earle Marsh. 1999. *The Complete Directory to Prime Time Net-*

work and Cable TV Shows: 1946–Present. 7th ed. New York: Ballantine Books.

Brownmiller, Susan. 1976. *Against Our Will: Men, Women, and Rape.* New York: Bantam Books.

Brown v. Board of Education. 1954. 247 U.S. 483.

Brugge, Doug. 2001. "Brandeis Students Rally after Asian and Women Hate Acts." http://www.aamovement.net/hatecrime/brandeishate.html, December 10.

Budd, Dave "DeaconBlu," ed. *The Definitive UK Sitcom List.* A compilation posted monthly to the USEnet newsgroups *alt.comedy.british* and *rec.arts.tv.uk* by zlsiida@fs1.mcc.ac.uk (DeaconBlu), and hosted at the Internet gopher site gopher://info.mcc.ac.uk:70/11/miscellany/sitcom.

Bureau of Justice Statistics. 2002. *Criminal Victimization in the United States.* Washington, DC: U.S. Department of Justice, Office of Justice Programs.

Burroughs, William. 1959. *Naked Lunch.* New York: Grove Press.

Cappella, Joseph N., Joseph Turow, and Kathleen Hall Jamieson. 1996. *Call-In Political Talk Radio: Background, Content, Audiences, Portrayal in Mainstream Media.* A report from the Annenberg Public Policy Center, University of Pennsylvania, August 7.

Capsuto, Steven. 2000. *Alternate Channels: The Uncensored Story of Gay and Lesbian Images on Radio and Television, 1930s to the Present.* New York: Ballantine Books.

Castillo, Marlon S. 2003. "Student Alleges Anti-Muslim Hate Speech." *Yale Daily News,* http://www.yaledailynews.com/article.asp?AID=22491, April 9.

Castleman, Harry, and Walter J. Podrazik. 1989. *Harry and Wally's Favorite TV Shows: A Fact-Filled Opinionated Guide to the Best and Worst on TV.* New York: Prentice Hall.

Castorina v. Madison County School Board. 2001. Sixth Circuit Court. 246 F.3d 536.

Chaplinsky v. State of New Hampshire. 1942. 315 U.S. 568.

Chicago Tribune. 2000. "Rally Strengthens Skokie Resolve." http://www.chicago tribune.com/, December 18.

Christian Gallery. 2001. christiangallery.com.

Chronicle of Higher Education. 2004. April 9.

Clare, Kenneth B., and Mamie P. Clark. 1947. "Racial Identification and Preferences in Negro Children." In Theodore M. Newcomb and Eugene L. Hartley, eds., *Readings in Social Psychology,* pp. 169–178. New York: Holt, Rinehart & Winston.

Cohen, Jeff. 1994. "The 'Hush Rush' Hoax: Limbaugh on the Fairness Doctrine." http://www.fair.org/extra/9411/Limbaugh-fcc.html, November/December.

Cohen, Jeff, and Norman Solomon. 1994. "Spotlight Finally Shines on White Hate Radio." http://www/fair.org/media-beat/941103.html, November 3.

Cohen, W., and D. Danelski. 1997. *Constitution Law: Civil Liberties and Individual Rights.* Westbury, NY: Foundation.

Collins, Scott, and Cynthia Littleton. 2003. "CBS Mulls Canceling Reagan Mini-Series." *The Hollywood Reporter,* http://www.hollywood-hero.us/the_ reagans.htm, November 3.

Collis, Rose. 1993. "Telling Tales." *Gay Times* (September): 10–12.

Cortese, Anthony. 1985. "The Sociology of Moral Judgment: Social and Ethnic Factors." *Mid-America Review of Sociology* 9: 109–124.

Cortese, Anthony. 1990. *Ethnic Ethics: The Restructuring of Moral Theory*. Albany, NY: SUNY Press.

Cortese, Anthony. 2003. *Walls and Bridges: Social Justice and Public Policy*. Albany, NY: SUNY Press.

Cortese, Anthony. 2004. *Provocateur: Images of Women and Minorities in Advertising*. 2nd ed. Lanham, MD: Rowman and Littlefield.

Cortese, Anthony, and Stjepan G. Mestrovic. 1990. "From Durkheim to Habermas: The Role of Language in Moral Theory." In J. Wilson, ed., *Current Perspectives in Social Theory*, pp. 63–91. Greenwich, CT: JAI Press.

Cowan, Gloria, Miriam Resendez, Elizabeth Marshall, and Ryan Quist. 2002. "Hate Speech and Constitutional Protection: Priming Values of Equality and Freedom." *Journal of Social Issues* 58(2): 247–263.

Davis v. Monroe County Board of Education. 1999. 526 U.S. 629.

Deaux, Ka, Anne Reid, Kim Mizrahi, and Kathleen A. Ethier. 1995. "Parameters of Social Identity." *Journal of Personality and Social Psychology* 68 (February): 280–290.

Delgado, Richard, ed. 1995a. *Critical Race Theory: The Cutting Edge*. Philadelphia: Temple University Press.

Delgado, Richard. 1995b. "Words That Wound: A Tort Action for Racial Insults, Epithets, and Name-Calling." In Richard Delgado, ed., *Critical Race Theory: The Cutting Edge*, pp. 159–168. Philadelphia: Temple University Press.

Delgado, Richard. 2000. "Toward a Legal Realist View of the First Amendment." *Harvard Law Review* 113: 778.

Delgado, Richard. 2004a. "Hate Cannot Be Tolerated." usatoday.com, March 3.

Delgado, Richard. 2004b. *Understanding Words That Wound*. Boulder, CO: Westview Press.

Delgado, Richard, and Jean Stefancic. 1992. "Images of the Outsider in American Law and Culture: Can Free Expression Remedy Systemic Social Ills?" *Cornell Law Review* 77: 1258–1262.

Delgado, Richard, and Jean Stefancic. 2001. *Critical Race Theory: An Introduction*. New York: New York University Press.

de Mause, Lloyd. 1974. *The History of Childhood*. New York: Harper Torchbooks.

Denno v. School Board of Volusia County, Florida. 2000. Eleventh Circuit Court. 218 F.3d 1267.

Dixon, Thomas, Jr. 1902. *The Leopard's Spots: A Romance of the White Man's Burden—1865–1900*. New York: Doubleday, Page & Company.

Dixon, Thomas, Jr. 1905. *The Clansman: An Historical Romance of the Ku Klux Klan*. New York: Doubleday, Page & Company.

Donahue, Hugh Carter. 1989. *The Battle to Control Broadcast News: Who Owns the First Amendment?* Cambridge, MA: MIT Press.

Dorais, Michel. 2002. *Don't Tell: The Sexual Abuse of Boys*. Montreal: McGill–Queen's University Press.

Dworkin, Andrea. 1991. "Against the Male Flood: Censorship, Pornography, and Equality." In Robert M. Baird and Stuart E. Rosenbaum, eds., *Pornography: Private Rights or Public Menace?*, pp. 56–61. Buffalo, NY: Prometheus Press.

Edgerton, Brooks, and Brendan Case. 2003. "Child Sex Industry Thriving in Mexico." *Dallas Morning News*, November 2, pp. A1, 24–25.

Ehrlich, Howard. 1973. *The Social Psychology of Prejudice*. New York: Wiley.

Eisner, Joel, and David Krinsky. 1984. *Television Comedy Series: An Episode Guide to 153 TV Sitcoms in Syndication*. Jefferson, NC: McFarland & Co.

Eliadis, Pearl. 2003. "Rwanda's Riverboat Excursion: A Recent Court Decision Threatens to Justify Genocide." *Maisonneuve*, http://www.keepmedia.com/pubs/Maisonneuve/2003/11/15/481165, November 15.

Elson, R. M. 1964. *Guardians of Tradition*. Lincoln: University of Nebraska Press.

Expatica. 2004. "Rights Group Sues Cardinal over Gay 'Pervert' Comments." http://www.expatica.com/source/site_article.asp?subchannel_id=48&story_id=4015, January 26.

Federal Bureau of Investigation. 1995. *Crime in the United States*. Washington, DC: U.S. Government Printing Office.

Federal Bureau of Investigation. 2002. *Crime in the United States, 2001*. Washington, DC: U.S. Government Printing Office.

Federal Bureau of Investigation, Counterterrorism Division. 1999. *Terrorism in the United States*. Washington, DC: U.S. Government Printing Office.

Federal Communications Commission v. Pacifica Foundation. 1978. 438 U.S. 726.

Finn, Ed. 2003. "Move Over, Mahathi: Malaysia's Firebrand PM Retires." http://slate.msn.com/id/2090598, October 31.

Franklin, John Hope, and Alfred A. Moss, Jr. 1988. *From Slavery to Freedom*. 6th ed. New York: Alfred A. Knopf.

Freuer, Jane, Paul Kerr, and Tise Vahimagi, eds. 1984. *MTM: "Quality Television."* London: British Film Institute.

Frutkin, Alan. 1997a. "The Best Fall Television." *The Advocate*, September 16, 1997, p. 55.

Frutkin, Alan. 1997b. "Television's 23 Gay Characters." *The Advocate*, February 18, pp. 30–31.

Frutkin, Alan. 1998. "TV's 26 Gay Characters." *The Advocate*, September 15, pp. 34–36.

Frutkin, Alan, and Gerry Kroll. 1996. "Gays on the Tube." *The Advocate*, August 20, pp. 11–22. Revised edition published online at http://www.advocate.com/html/issuelinks/gaytube1.html, January 31, 1997.

Gallacher, Michelle, and Graeme Murray. 2004. "Protests Set for Topless Hairdressers; Outrage at Launch of 'Sordid' Business." *Evening Times* (Glasgow, Scotland), April 14, p. 19.

Gallagher, Neil. 1977. *How to Stop the Porno Plague*. Minneapolis: Bethany Fellowship.

Gertz v. Robert Welch, Inc. 1974. No. 72-617. U.S. Supreme Court, 418 U.S. 323.

Gilligan, Carol. 1982. *In a Different Voice: Psychological Theory and Women's Development*. Cambridge, MA: Harvard University Press.

Giltz, Michael. 1996. "TV Gayed." *Out* (October): 70.

Giuffre, Patti, and Christine Williams. 1994. "Boundary Lines: Labeling Sexist Harassment in Restaurants." *Gender & Society* 8: 378–401.

GLAAD TV Scoreboard. 1997. http://www.glaad.org/glaad/scoreboard.html, April.

Goffman, Erving. 1976. *Gender Advertisements*. Cambridge, MA: Harvard University Press.

Gold, Taro. 2003. "America's Poisoning of Love." Advocate.com, November 25.

Goodstein, Laurie. 2003. "Seeing Islam as 'Evil' Faith, Evangelicals Seek Converts." *New York Times*, May 27, pp. A1, A22.

Gourevitch, Philip. 1998. *We Wish to Inform You That Tomorrow We Will Be Killed with Our Families: Stories from Rwanda.* New York: Farrar, Straus, and Giroux.

Graham v. Guiderland Central School District. 1998. New York Appellate Court. 256 A.D.2d 863.

Gray-Little, Bernadett, and Adam Hafdahl. 2000. "Factors Influencing Racial Comparisons of Self-Esteem: A Qualitative Review." *Psychological Bulletin* 126(1): 26–54.

Greene, J., C. Ringwalt, J. Kelly, R. Iachan, and Z. Cohen. 1995. *Youth with Runaway, Throwaway, and Homeless Experiences: Prevalence, Drug Use, and Other At-Risk Behaviors.* Vol. 1: *Final Report.* Research Triangle Park, NC: Research Triangle Institute.

Greenfeld, Lawrence. 1997. "Sex Offenses and Offenders." Bureau of Justice Statistics Executive Summary. Washington, DC: U.S. Printing Office, January.

Grossman, Lawrence K., and Newton N. Minow. 2003. "*The Reagans*: What CBS Should Have Done." *Columbia Journalism Review Monitor*, no. 6 (November/December), http://www.cjr.org/issues/2003/6/reagans-grossman.asp.

Habermas, Jurgen. 1975. *Legitimation Crisis.* Boston: Beacon Press.

Hamad, Imad. 2001. "Anti-Terrorism Law." Op-Ed, *Detroit Free Press*, http://www.bintjbeil.com/articles/en/011123_hamad.html, November 23.

Hamlin, David, 1980. *The Nazi/Skokie Conflict.* Boston: Beacon Press.

Harmon, Amy. 1997. "For Parents, a New and Vexing Problem." *New York Times*, June 27, p. A1.

Harrison, Stella Ann. 2001. "The Internet, Cyber-advocacy, and Citizen Communication." *Vital Speeches of the Day* 67 (August 1): 624.

Hatch, Orrin. 1999. "News Release—Statement of Senator Orrin Hatch." Chairman of the Senate Judiciary Committee, September 14.

Heritage Foundation. 2003. "The 'Fairness Doctrine': Pulling the Plug on Talk Radio." Heritage Foundation Panel Discussion, October 7.

Hess, Laura. 2003. "The Violent Loss of Free Expression." *Yale Daily News*, http://www.yaledailynews.com/article.asp?AID=22496, April 10.

Higginbotham, A. 1978. *In the Matter of Color: Race and the American Legal Process.* New York: Oxford University Press.

Hill, Anita, and Emma Jordan, eds. 1995. *Race, Gender, and Power in America: The Legacy of the Hill-Thomas Hearings.* New York: Oxford University Press.

Hippensteele, S., and T. C. Pearson. 1999. "Responding Effectively to Sexual Harassment." *Change* (January–February): 48–54.

Hitler, Adolf. 1939. *Mein Kampf.* New York: Stackpole Sons.

Hopper, Jim. 2003. *Child Abuse: Statistics, Research, and Resources.* Web-posted at www.jimhopper.com/abstats.

Howes, Keith. 1993. *Broadcasting It: An Encyclopedia of Homosexuality on Film, Radio and TV in the UK 1923–1993.* London: Cassell.

Ibish, Hussein. 2003. "Analysis: Experience of Arab Americans since 9/11." National Public Radio, http://www.npr.org/programs/totn/transcripts/2003/mar/030311/ibish.html, March 11.

Idupuganti, Anura. 2001. "Lists of Racist Attacks Across the Country Since 9/11."
    http://www.incite-national.org/issues/attacks.html, September 20.
Imperial Diner, Inc. v. State Human Rights Appeal Board. 1980. 52 N.Y. 2d 72,
    417 N.E. 2d 525, 436 N.Y. S2d 231.
Ingrassia, Michele. 1993. "Abused and Confused." *Newsweek*, October 25, p. 57.
The Internet Movie Database. http://us.imdb.com/.
Jacobs, A. J. 1996. "Out." *Entertainment Weekly*, October 4, pp. 18–25.
Jacobs, James B., and Kimberly A. Potter. 1998. "Hate Crimes: A Critical Per-
    spective." In M. Tonry, ed., *Crime and Justice: A Review of Research.* Chi-
    cago: University of Chicago Press.
Jennes, Valerie, and Kendall Broad. 1997. *Hate Crimes: New Social Movements
    and the Politics of Violence.* New York: Aldine de Gruyter.
Jones, Christopher. "The Point: On the Air." Weekly column in *The Washington
    Blade Online*, http://www.washblade.com/point/ontheair.htm.
Kant, Immanuel. 1949. *Immanuel Kant's Critique of Practical Reason and Other
    Writings in Moral Philosophy.* Trans. and ed. L. W. Beck. Chicago: Univer-
    sity of Chicago Press.
Katchadourian, Herant A., and Donald T. Lund. 1972. *Fundamentals of Human
    Sexuality.* New York: Holt, Rinehart & Winston.
Kling, Samuel G. 1965. *Sexual Behavior and the Law.* New York: Bernard Geis As-
    sociates.
Kohlberg, L. 1966. "Cognitive Stages and Preschool Education." *Human Devel-
    opment* 9: 5–17.
Kohlberg, L. 1971. "Stages of Moral Development as a Basis for Moral Educa-
    tion." In C. Beck, B. Crittenden, and E. Sullivan, eds., *Moral Education: In-
    terdisciplinary Approaches*, pp. 23–92. Toronto: University of Toronto.
Kohlberg, L. 1981. *Essays in Moral Development.* Vol. I, *The Philosophy of Moral
    Development.* New York: Harper & Row.
Kohlberg, L. 1984. *Essays in Moral Development.* Vol. II, *The Psychology of Moral
    Development.* New York: Harper & Row.
Koss, Mary P., C. J. Gidycz, and N. Wisniewski. 1987. "The Scope of Rape: Sex-
    ual Aggression and Victimization in a National Sample of Students in Higher
    Education." *Journal of Consulting and Clinical Psychology* 55: 162–170.
Kubler, Frederich. 1998. "How Much Freedom for Racist Speech? Transnational
    Aspects of a Conflict of Human Rights." *Hofstra Law Review* 27: 335.
The Larkhall Insider: ITV's Bad Girls. 1999. http://www.fortunecity.com/village/
    turner/381.
Lawrence, Charles, and Mari Matsuda. 2000. "We Won't Go Back." In Henry L.
    Tischler, ed., *Debating Points: Race and Ethnic Relations.* Upper Saddle
    River, NJ: Prentice Hall.
Lawrence, Charles R., III. 1993. "If He Hollers Let Him Go: Regulating Racist
    Speech on Campus." In Mari Matsuda, Charles R. Lawrence III, Richard
    Delgado, and Kimberle Williams Crenshaw, *Words That Wound: Critical
    Race Theory, Assaultive Speech, and the First Amendment*, pp. 53–88. Boul-
    der, CO: Westview Press.
Lawrence, Frederick M. 1999. *Punishing Hate: Bias Crimes under American Law.*
    Cambridge, MA: Harvard University Press.
Leake, Simon. 2005. Amazon.com. Editorial review of *The Jewel in the Crown.*

http://www.amazon.com/exec/obidos/tg/detail/-/B000053VA4/103-7616251-3635815?v=glance#product-details.

Lederer, L., ed. 1980. *Take Back the Night: Women on Pornography.* New York: William Morrow.

Leets, Laura. 2002. "Experiencing Hate Speech: Perceptions and Responses to Anti-Semitism and Antigay Speech." *Journal of Social Issues* 58(2): 341–361.

Leets, Laura, and Howard Giles. 1997. "Words as Weapons—When Do They Wound? Investigations of Harmful Speech." *Human Communication Research* 24(2): 260–301.

Levin, Brian. 2003. "Cyberhate: A Legal and Historical Analysis of Extremists' Use of Computer Networks in America." In Barbara Perry, ed., *Hate and Bias Crime: A Reader*, pp. 363–382. New York: Routledge.

Levin, Jack. 1992–1993. "Bias Crimes: A Theoretical and Practical Overview." *Stanford Law and Policy Review* (Winter): 165–171.

Levin, Jack. 2002. *The Violence of Hate: Confronting Racism, Anti-Semitism, and Other Forms of Bigotry.* New York: Allyn and Bacon.

Levin, Jack, and Jack McDevitt. 1993. *Hate Crimes: The Rising Tide of Bigotry and Bloodshed.* New York: Plenum.

Levin, Jack, and Monte Paulsen. 1999. *Encyclopedia of Human Emotions.* Vol. 1. New York: Macmillan Reference.

Lydersen, Kari. 2003. "The Ignoble Savage." AlterNet.com, June 9.

M., Jack. 2002. "Confessions of Date Rapist." http://www.campusoutreachservices.com/resources/confessions.htm. See also: http://www.survivingtothriving.org/confessions.

Macdonald, Andrew. 1978. *The Turner Diaries: A Novel.* Hillsboro, WV: National Vanguard.

Macdonald, Andrew. 1989. *Hunter: A Novel.* Hillsboro, WV: National Vanguard.

Macionis, John. 2002. *Social Problems.* Upper Saddle River, NJ: Prentice Hall.

MacKinnon, Catharine. 1993. *Only Words.* Cambridge, MA: Harvard University Press.

MacKinnon, Catharine. 1995. "Online Fantasies." *Time*, March 1, pp. 7–9.

MacKinnon, Catharine. 2001. "Pornography: Not a Moral Issue." In John Macionis and Nijole Benokraitis, eds., *Seeing Ourselves: Classic, Contemporary, and Cross-Cultural Readings in Sociology*, pp. 294–301. 5th ed. Upper Saddle River, NJ: Prentice Hall.

MacKinnon, Catharine A., and David D. Caron, eds. 2004. "International Decision: *Prosecutor v. Nahimana, Barayagwiza, & Ngeze.* Case No. ICTR 99-52-T. Judgment and Sentence." http://www.ictr.org, International Criminal Tribunal for Rwanda, December 3.

Maclean's. 1997. "Disturbing New Figures about Child Abuse." July 21, p. 15.

Magee, James. 2002. *Freedom of Expression.* Westport, CT: Greenwood Press.

Majority Staff of U.S. Senate Judiciary Committee. 1992. *Violence against Women: A Week in the Life of America.* Washington, DC: U.S. Government Printing Office.

Marcus, Laurence R. 1996. *Fighting Words: The Politics of Hateful Speech.* New York: Praeger.

Marriott, Michel. 1999. "Rising Tide: Sites Born of Hate." *New York Times*, March 18, p. G1.

Matsuda, Mari. 1993. "Public Response to Racist Speech: Considering the Victim's Story." In Mari Matsuda, Charles R. Lawrence III, Richard Delgado, and Kimberle Williams Crenshaw, *Words That Wound: Critical Race Theory, Assaultive Speech, and the First Amendment*, pp. 17–52. Boulder, CO: Westview Press.

Matsuda, Mari, Charles R. Lawrence III, Richard Delgado, and Kimberle Williams Crenshaw. 1993. *Words That Wound: Critical Race Theory, Assaultive Speech, and the First Amendment*. Boulder, CO: Westview Press.

Maynard, Kevin. 1999. "Culture: 'Real' Dirt." *Out* (May): 32.

McGonagle, Tarloch. 2001. "Wrestling (Racial) Equality from Tolerance of Hate Speech." *Dublin University Law Journal* 23: 20, 29.

McLean, Ian. 1997. "An Annotated Character List of Gay/Bi Characters in *Number 96*." Personal e-mail correspondence dated January 13 and 24.

McLemore, S., and H. Romo. 2005. *Racial and Ethnic Relations in America*. 7th ed. Boston: Allyn and Bacon.

Mead, George Herbert. 1934. *Mind, Self, and Society*. Chicago: University of Chicago Press.

Merton, Robert K. 1957. *Social Theory and Social Structure*. Rev. ed. Glencoe, IL: The Free Press.

Millet, Kate. 1983. In *Not a Love Story* (National Film Board of Canada).

Modeste, Petal Nevella. 2001. "Race Hate Speech: The Pervasive Badge of Slavery That Mocks the Thirteenth Amendment." *Howard Law Journal* 44: 311, 326, 328.

Montiero v. Tempe Union High School District. 1998. Ninth Circuit Court, 158 F.3d.

Mortimer, Carol. 1994–1996. "Gay TV." A weekly article posted (and reposted) to several Internet locations, including the USEnet forum *soc.motss*.

National Victim Center. 1992. *Rape in America*. April.

Naureckas, Jim. 1995. "50,000 Watts of Hate: Bigotry Is Broadcast on ABC Radio's Flagship." http://www.fair.orgextra/9601/bob-grant.html, January/February.

NBC.com. 2004. http://www.nbc.com/nbc/footer/tmyk/pgv_tmyk_overview.shtml.

New York Times. 2003. "A Decision on Cross-Burning." Editorial, April 8, p. A30.

New York Times v. Sullivan. 1964. No. 39. U.S. Supreme Court, 376 U.S. 254.

Nielsen, Laura Beth. 2002. "Subtle, Pervasive, Harmful: Racist and Sexist Remarks in Public as Hate Speech." *Journal of Social Issues* 58(2): 265–280.

NORC. 1999. *General Social Surveys, 1972–1998: Cumulative Codebook*. Chicago: National Opinion Research Center.

Nordheimer, Jon. 1993. "Divided by Diatribe, College Speech Ignites Furor over Race." *New York Times*, December 29, pp. B1, B6.

Owen, Diana. 1996. "Who's Talking? Who's Listening? The New Politics of Radio Talk Shows." In Stephen C. Craig, ed., *Broken Contract? Changing Relationships Between Americans and Their Government*, pp. 127–146. Boulder, CO: Westview Press.

Panos, Jim. 2000. "Stretching Limits of Free Speech." *New York Times*, May 7, p. 27.

Parrillo, Vincent, John Stimson, and Ardyth Stimson. 1999. *Contemporary Social Problems*. 2nd ed. Boston: Allyn and Bacon.

Pearlstein, Steven. 1999. "In Canada, Free Speech Has Its Restrictions." *Washington Post*, December 12, p. A41.

Pela, Robert L. 1997. "The Days of *Whose* Lives." *Genre* (May): 46–49, 95.

Peter, Jennifer. 2003. "Massachusetts Court Strikes Down Gay-Marriage Ban." Advocate.com, November 18.

Peters, Rich. 2003. "Gay Kiss-in Disrupts Politician's Speech." The Lesbian & Gay Equality Project, Johannesburg, South Africa. http://www.equality.org.za/news/2003/07/23kissin.htm. 365Gay.com Newscenter, Western Canada Bureau Chief, July 23.

Phillips, Susan, and Margaret Schneider. 1993. "Sexual Harassment of Female Doctors by Patients." *New England Journal of Medicine* 329 (December 23): 1936–1939.

Piaget, Jean. 1926. *The Language and Thought of the Child*. Trans. M. Gabain and R. Gabain. London: Routledge and Kegan Paul.

Piaget, Jean. [1932] 1965. *The Moral Judgment of the Child*. 2nd ed. New York: The Free Press.

Piaget, Jean. 1952. *The Origins of Intelligence in Children*. London: Routledge and Kegan Paul.

Piaget, Jean. 1954. *The Construction of Reality*. New York: Basic Books.

Piaget, Jean. 1960. "The General Problems of the Psychobiological Development of the Child." In J. M. Tanner and B. Inhelder, eds., *Discussion on Child Development: Proceedings of the World Health Organization Study Group on the Psychobiological Development of the Child*, vol. 4, pp. 3–27. New York: International Universities Press.

Planned Parenthood v. American Coalition of Life Activists. 2001. 224 F.3d. 1007 (9th Cir. March 28), vacated, en banc rehearing ordered, 268 F.3d 908 (October 3).

Pierce, William. 1994. "Reorienting Ourselves for Success." *National Alliance Bulletin* (January): 5.

Pitchal, Erik. 1996. "Just a Little Kiss?" http://www.zmag.org/ZMag/articles/dec96pitchal.htm, December.

Poniewozik, James. 1999. "TV's Coming-Out Party." *Time*, October 25, pp. 54–56.

Powell-Hopson, Darlene, and Derek Hopson. 1988. "Implications of Doll Color Preferences among Black Preschool Children and White Preschool Children." *Journal of Black Psychology* 14 (February): 57–63.

Public Broadcasting System. 2003. "Caught in the Crossfire." http://www.pbs.org/itvs/caughtinthecrossfire.

Quinn v. National Railroad Passenger Corporation. 1999. WL 637170 (N.D. Ill).

R.A.V. v. St. Paul. 1992. 112 S. Ct. 2538.

Religion & Ethics Newsweekly. 2004. "Muslim Populations in Europe." PBS. WNET-TV. Anchor: Bob Abernethy; reporter: Saul Gonzalez.

Reno et al. v. American Civil Liberties Union et al. 1997. 521 U.S. 844.

Richmond-Abbott, Marie. 1992. *Masculine and Feminine: Gender Roles over the Life Cycle*. New York: McGraw-Hill.

Ritzer, George. 2000. *The McDonaldization of Society*. Thousand Oaks, CA: Sage.

Roddy, D. 2001a. "Abortion Clinic Stalker Arrested." *Pittsburgh Post-Gazette*, December 6, p. A1.

Roddy, D. 2001b. "Fugitive Abortion Foe: I Sent Anthrax: Waagner Makes Visit to Web Site Operator." *Pittsburgh Post-Gazette*, November 25, p. A7.

Rogers v. Elliot. 2001. 135 F. Supp. 2d 1312 (N.D. Ga).

Romano, Elisa, and Rayleen DeLuca. 1997. "Exploring the Relationship Between Childhood Sexual Abuse and Adult Sexual Perpetration." *Journal of Family Violence* (March 12): 85–98.

Rosenberg, Richard S. 1993. "Free Speech, Pornography, Sexual Harassment, and Electronic Networks: An Update and Extension." *The Information Society* 9(4): 285–331.

Rosenberg, Richard S. 2003. "Free Speech, Pornography, Sexual Harassment, and Electronic Networks: An Update and Extension." http://www.lexum. umontreal.ca/conf/ae/en/rosenberg.html.

Rosenthal, R., and L. Jacobson. 1968. *Pygmalion in the Classroom: Teacher Expectation and Intellectual Development*. New York: Holt, Rinehart and Winston.

Ross, Bobby, Jr. 2004. "Gay Hispanic Woman Elected Dallas Sheriff." HoustonChronicle.com, http://www.chron.com/cs/CDA/ssistory.mpl/metropolitan /2883619, November 4.

Rothstein, Edward. 2002. "Connections: Hateful Name-Calling vs. Calling for Hateful Action." *New York Times*, November 23, Arts & Ideas/Cultural Desk, p. 9.

Rowe, Michael. 2003. "The Incredible Hunk: Daniel Petronijevic Stars as a Pro Football Player Coming Out of the Closet on ESPN's *Playmakers*." Advocate.com, http://www.advocate.com/html/stories/900/900_petronijevic.asp, October 14.

Rush, Florence. 1980. "Child Pornography." In Laura Lederer, ed., *Take Back the Night: Women on Pornography*, pp. 71–81. New York: William Morrow.

Russell, Diana E. H. 1982. *Rape in Marriage*. New York: Macmillan.

Russell, Diana E. H. 1986. *The Secret Trauma: Incest in the Lives of Girls and Women*. New York: Basic Books.

Sadowitz, Steve. 2003. Personal correspondence from Brooks Egerton, November 4.

Salter, Anna. 1988. *Treating Child Sex Offenders and Victims*. Newbury Park, CA: Sage.

Saunders, Kevin W. 2003. *Saving Our Children from the First Amendment*. New York: New York University Press.

Saxe v. State College Area School District. 2001. Third Circuit Court. 240 F.3d 200.

Schmalleger, Frank. 2004. *Criminology Today: An Integrative Introduction*. 3rd ed. Upper Saddle River, NJ: Pearson–Prentice Hall.

Schmitt, Richard. 2000. "Radical Philosophy: 'Philosophers Combating Racism' Conference." *American Philosophy Association Newsletter* 99(2) (Spring).

Sedler, R. 1992. "The Unconstitutionality of Campus Bans on 'Racist Speech': The View from Without and Within." *University of Pittsburg Law Review* 53: 632–683.

Sheffield, Carol J. 2004. "Sexual Terrorism." In Michael S. Kimmel and Rebecca F. Plante, eds., *Sexualities: Identities, Behaviors, and Society*, pp. 409–423. New York: Oxford University Press.

Showbizdata. 2003. *"The Reagans* Draws only 1.2 Million Viewers." http://www.admin.showbizdata.com/contacts/picknews.cfm/34100/,1.THE_REAGANS</1>_DRAWS_ONLY_1.2_MILLION_VIEWERS, December 4.

Smolla, Rodney. 1992. *Free Speech in an Open Society.* New York: Alfred A. Knopf.

Southern Poverty Law Center. 1999. "The Alliance and Its Allies: Pierce Builds Bridges at Home, Abroad." *Intelligence Report* 93 (Winter). http://www.splcenter.org/intel/intelreport/article.jsp?aid=358.

Southern Poverty Law Center. 2005. "Active U.S. Hate Groups in 2004." http://www.splcenter.org/intel/map/hate.jsp.

Sproat, Ron. 1974. "The Working Day in a Porno Factory." *New York Magazine,* March 11, pp. 37–40.

Steele, Edgar J. 2001. "Lonny Mae Meets the Thought Police." http://www.freerepublic.com/forum/a3b64d65cOea4.htm.

Stephan, Walter G. 1985. "Intergroup Relations." In Gardner Lindzey and Elliot Aronson, eds., *Handbook of Social Psychology.* 3rd ed. New York: Random House.

Strauss, Neil. 2000. "Policing Pop: A Special Report." *New York Times,* August 1, p. A1.

Sumner, William Graham. [1906] 1960. *Folkways.* New York: American Library.

Talk Radio Research Project. 2002. Talkers Magazine Online, http://www.talkers.com/talkaud.html, Fall.

Taslitz, Andrew. 2000. "Hate Crimes, Free Speech, and the Contract of Mutual Indifference." *Boston University Law Review* 80: 1283.

Texas v. Johnson. 1989. 491 U.S. 397.

Tinker v. Des Moines Independent School District. 1969. 393 U.S. 503.

Tjaden, Patricia, and Nancy Thoennes. 1991. *Prevalence, Incidence, and Consequences of Violence Against Women: Finding from the National Violence Against Women Survey.* Washington, DC: National Institute of Justice and Centers for Disease Control and Prevention.

Tribe, Laurence H. 1991. "The Constitution in Cyberspace: Law and Liberty beyond the Electronic Frontier." http://www.epic.org/free-speech/tribe.html.

Trustee Subcommittee. 1994. *Report of the Subcommittee.* Union, NJ: Kean College Board of Trustees, June (Patricia Weston Rivera, Chair).

"TV Comes Out of the Closet." 1999. *Globe,* March 16, pp. 24–25, 32.

Uk.gay.com. 2003. "Gay Tourists' Arrival Marked by Demo in Tanzania." http://uk.gay.com/headlines/3967.

United Methodist Women. 2003. "Post 9/11 Hate Crimes." http://gbgm-umc.org.

United Nations. 1995. "Risk of Rape in U.S. Higher than in Europe." *The Record,* December 13, p. A15.

United States Merit Protection Board. 1981. *Sexual Harassment of Federal Workers: Is It a Problem?* Washington, DC: U.S. Merit Systems Protection Board.

United States Merit Protection Board. 1988. *Sexual Harassment of Federal Workers: An Update.* Washington, DC: U.S. Merit Systems Protection Board.

Upmeyer, Nick. 2003. "Texas Family Wins Cross-Burning Trial." *National Law Journal,* March 10, p. B1.

U.S. Census Bureau. 2001. "Resident Population Estimates of the United States by Sex, Race, and Hispanic Origin: April 1, 1999, to July 1, 1999, with Short-

Term Projections to November 4, 2000." http://www.census.gon//population/estimaes/naton/intile3-1.txt.

U.S. Department of Health and Human Services. 1995. National Center on Child Sexual Abuse and Neglect, National Child Abuse and Neglect Data System. *Child Maltreatment*. Washington, DC: U.S. Government Printing Office.

Van Ausdale, Debra, and Joe R. Feagin. 2002. *The First R: How Children Learn Race and Racism*. Lanham, MD: Rowman and Littlefield.

Walker, Samuel. 1990. *In Defense of American Liberties*. New York: Oxford University Press.

Walker, Samuel. 1994. *Hate Speech: The History of an American Controversy*. Lincoln: University of Nebraska Press.

Warn, Sarah. 2002. "*Relativity* and the First Lesbian Kiss on Primetime Television." http://www.afterellen.com/TV/relativity.html, November.

Washington Law Review. 1991. "Antimask Laws: Exploring the Outer Bounds of Protected Speech Under the First Amendment—*State v. Miller*, 260 Ga. 669, 33 S.E. 2d 547 (1990)," pp. 1139–1158.

Washington Times. 2004. "Discrimination Against White Male Found; Accused of Using 'Hate Speech.' " September 24, p. A01.

Weisman, Robyn. 2001. "AOL Stung by Hate Speech Lawsuit." *CIO Today*, News Factor Network. http://www.cio-today.com/, August 31.

West, John, and Donald J. Templer. 1994. "Child Molestation, Rape, and Ethnicity." *Psychological Reports* 75 (December): 1326.

West v. Derby Unified School District No. 260. 2000. Tenth Circuit Court. 206 F.3d 1358.

Williams, Robin. 1964. *Strangers Next Door*. Englewood Cliffs, NJ: Prentice Hall.

Williams v. Saxbe. 1976. 413 F. 654 (D.D.C.).

Wyatt, David. 2002. "Gay/Lesbian/Bisexual Television Characters." http://home.cc.umanitoba.ca/~wyatt/tv-characters.html.

Zogby International. 2001. "Arab Americans Are Strong Advocates of War Against Terrorism." Arab American Institute Poll, http://www.aaiusa.org, October.

Index

About the Author

ANTHONY CORTESE is Professor of Sociology at Southern Methodist University in Dallas, Texas. His major areas of research and teaching are social problems, ethnic and race relations, social policy, social ethics, media and gender, and sociological theory. He is the author of four other books, including *Provocateur: Images of Women and Minorities in Advertising, Second Edition* (2004).